GRASS ROOTS

Also by Albert Goldman

The Mine and the Mint:
    Sources for the Writings of Thomas De Quincey

Wagner on Music and Drama
    (co-editor with Everett Sprinchorn)

Freakshow: The Rocksoulbluesjazzsickjewblackhumorsexpoppsych
    Gig and Other Scenes from the Counter-Culture

Ladies and Gentlemen—LENNY BRUCE!!!

Carnival in Rio

Disco

GRASS
ROOTS

Marijuana
in America
Today

by
Albert Goldman

HARPER & ROW, PUBLISHERS
NEW YORK
HAGERSTOWN
SAN FRANCISCO
LONDON

Grateful acknowledgment is made for permission to reprint:

"If You're a Viper," words and music by Rozetta Howard, Horace Malcolm, and Herbert Moren, copyright 1938 by MCA Music, Inc., New York, NY, used by permission. All rights reserved.

Excerpt from *El Dorado Trail* by Ferrol Eagin. Copyright © 1970 by Ferrol Eagin. Used with permission of McGraw-Hill Book Company.

Excerpts from *Really the Blues* by Milton Mezzrow and Bernard Wolfe. Copyright 1946 by Random House, Inc. Copyright renewed 1974 by Bernard Wolfe and Milton Mezzrow. Reprinted by permission of Harold Matson Co., Inc.

The following articles originally appeared in *New York* magazine: "The Rites of Fall: Driving the Demon Out, Letting the Good Times In," September 13, 1971; "Picking Away at the Past," November 15, 1971; "Witnessing Obscenity for Fun and Profit," April 10, 1972; "I Have Seen the Future—And It's Fire Island," July 24, 1972; "How to Redeem Next Year's Jazz Festival and, Thereby, the Whole City," August 28, 1972; "Blue Is Beautiful," May 15, 1972; "Jazz Come Home," July 3, 1972; "The Real Lenny Bruce Is Alive and Well in Brooklyn," August 6, 1973; "Why Is This City Laughing," August 27, 1973; "Funny, I Never Noticed That Bump on the Side of My Nose Before," December 3, 1973; "Entering the New Age of Pot," August 25, 1975; "Two Yanks on the Marijuana Trail," October 18, 1976.

FIRST EDITION

Designed by Sidney Feinberg

Library of Congress Cataloging in Publication Data

Goldman, Albert Harry
  Grass roots.
  1. Marijuana. 2. Drug abuse—United States.
1. Title.
HV5822.M3G58 1979   301.2′2   77-11806
ISBN 0-06-011554-8

---

79 80 81 82 83 10 9 8 7 6 5 4 3 2 1

For Tommy—who led the way

Contents

GRASS ROOTS

1 *The Age of Pot*

Marijuana? Where *don't* you find it today? From the outhouse to the White House the weed has spread until it has become the national habit. Go to a discotheque, the pungent smoke assails your nostrils almost as powerfully as the winky-blinky lights your eyes or the loud music your ears. Go to a suburban cocktail party, all the nice respectable home owners are passing around reefers just as coolly as if they were hors d'oeuvres. Stand in line at the movies, some black dude comes jouncing by chanting: *"Loose joints? Loose joints?"*

If the film is *Star Wars*, the most colorful and engaging character is a space-age dope smuggler. He gets a big laugh when he explains why he had to dump his last load of "spice." If the picture is a rock event, like *The Last Waltz*, you could get bombed just by inhaling the atmosphere of the theater.

Walking home after the show, you stop to stare in the window of a head shop. Bent plastic tubing, precision scales, machine-tooled stash boxes, futuristic electric dope stills—the store could be a drug laboratory. Even at the deli, where you pause to buy a pack of cigarettes, the cash register is flanked by foot-high stacks of rolling papers.

When you open the door to your home, the air reeks of grass. The aroma means your thirteen-year-old son is turning on again. When you ask the kid where he gets the stuff, he replies matter-of-factly that he "scores" on the school playground. You

1

flash a spivey-looking pusher with a pencil-line mustache and a slouch-brim hat. Then the kid tells you that his "connection" is just another kid in his class. As he describes this prepubescent dope dealer, you realize suddenly that peddling weed in a junior high today is regarded not much differently than were the paper routes and soda-jerking jobs of your youth. At an earlier age than you started smoking cigarettes, these kids are into dope. "What do your teachers say about this stuff?" you ask the boy. He tells you that they lecture on the dangers of drugs but the greatest danger is getting caught.

Many young people today never do anything without first getting stoned. Whether it be going to the dentist or going out on a date, their first thought is getting their heads tight. You've seen them do it so many times that it's patterned itself into a ritual. First comes that Ziploc bag bottomed with stuff that looks like barnyard scrapings. Then, around go their eyes searching for a slick magazine or album sleeve on which to clean the crud. Back and forth scratches the curled-up matchbook cover as the seeds and twigs are curried out. Finally, the ritual reaches its climax as the roller sprinkles the crumbled weed into the trough-shaped paper, gives it a couple of practiced turns with his fingertips and then seals the joint with a long satisfied cat lick, holding the finished product upright for a moment as if to say: "It is finished." When future ages look back on our day—as we do on the Thirties—what they will see as its most characteristic social act is this classic modern tea ceremony.

The Age of Pot is upon us. The Day of the Reefer has dawned. Should you still have any doubts about the matter, consider these statistics. According to a survey made in 1977 by the National Institute on Drug Abuse, 53 percent of Americans in the eighteen-to-twenty-five age group had smoked marijuana. In a parallel study conducted by Gallup, 55 percent of all college students had tried pot. A New York State school survey estimated that marijuana use had doubled in grades seven to twelve from 1971 to 1978. The numbers are less significant than the trend. Just ten years ago only one in twenty college students admitted to having smoked weed. In ten years more, who can doubt the percentage will be much higher? "In seven years," concludes the NIDA report, "what was once clearly statistically deviant behavior has become the norm for more than half the population in this age group."

There are lots of other dope statistics that are even more startling. With 16 to 20 million regular marijuana users in this country, the consumption of weed has soared to colossal proportions. The figures on government seizures suggest that in the current year something like 50 *million pounds* of pot will be smuggled into the United States. Assuming a wholesale price of $250 a pound, the annual volume of this illicit trade is nearly $12.5 billion. The street value of the merchandise is impossible to calculate— but it cannot be less than double the wholesale value. Even deducting 10 percent for government seizures, you come out with a figure of $22.5 billion annually. This makes dope dealing and smuggling not only the biggest illegal business in history but one of the biggest businesses of any description. If you compare the earnings of America's favorite "recreational" drug with the money made by our huge entertainment industry, you get the real measure of dope as business. Twenty-two and a half billion dollars is nearly four times the combined revenues of the two largest entertainment industries: movies and records. Even the giant cigarette industry, averaging $16 billion annually, is far surpassed by dope.

Marijuana smoking is by no means confined to the younger generation. The habit has made enormous inroads among the older and more responsible portions of the population, including many successful middle-aged business and professional people, who once viewed grass as a potentially harmful or distasteful drug. These same people are now embracing dope for a great variety of reasons, ranging from reduction of drinking (pot as martini) to the need to cool out and relax after the hectic business day (pot as tranquilizer) to the effort to think creatively (pot as inspiration) to the rejuvenation of their sex lives (pot as aphrodisiac) to the desire to share in their children's experiences (pot as family therapy) or to appear themselves as young, with it and hip to what's going down (pot as monkey glands).

Saying that lots of people smoke doesn't tell us anything about what they actually experience when they get high. Though marijuana has become a familiar feature of American life, nearly as common as the can of beer or the filter-tip cigarette, you will seek in vain in contemporary literature for detailed accounts of people smoking or living under the influence of dope. The generation that introduced marijuana into American life on a grand scale was notoriously semiliterate. Though the hippies mooted many insights into drugs through pop songs or verses, though they elaborated an immense underground mythology of marijuana that every young person masters to a greater or lesser degree, though they created a whole new social etiquette of drug use, the life effects of marijuana usage remain largely unremarked in American literature. What is more to the point: there has not been a single major motion picture about dope.*

Actually, it is very difficult to assess the impact of such a remarkable cultural innovation. How often in the history of any civilization does some alien substance come along that subtly modifies millions of people's consciousness? The adoption of a new drug by a culture is a revolutionary event that can have far-reaching consequences. We know how Chinese civilization was nearly destroyed by the introduction of opium. (One of the first consequences was an all-out war between the Chinese government and the Western capitalist nations, who wished to continue the immensely lucrative opium trade and who succeeded in doing so after administering to the Chinese a severe and humiliating military defeat.) We know how the introduction of alcohol corroded the traditional civilization of the American Indian. What we do not know is what marijuana will do to America.

At the same time that we are scanning anxiously the behavior patterns of our youth for signs of moral and mental decay, we are also being bombarded by a great deal of propaganda, some of it emanating from reputable scientists and cultural authorities, that suggests that far from being the assassin of youth, marijuana may actually be a panacea for many of the ills of modern civilization. In an age when everyone is being exhorted constantly to relax, cool out and lay back, when half the ailments in the medical textbooks are being attributed to tension, stress and anxiety, it is beguiling to think that a few puffs of a relatively harmless narcotic may make us as serene as Buddhists. Marijuana has even been credited recently with some genuine medical benefits in cases of nausea produced by chemotherapy for cancer or as relief for suf-

---

* As this book was going to press, Cheech y Chong's *Up in Smoke* completed its first run. The hottest movie of the season, it grossed $45 million in six months of exhibition.

ferers from glaucoma or asthma. Had Marcel Proust switched from opiates to cannabis, he might have lived to round off his masterpiece instead of strangling to death.

While the layman puzzles over these contradictory claims, following the billowy fortunes of grass in the popular press, the modern world zooms right along its jet-powered paths. Perhaps the most striking sign of marijuana's growing social acceptability is the inescapable fact that the drug is gradually being legalized through a tactful process called "decriminalization." New, lenient laws have won endorsement from an impressive list of prestigious organizations, including the American Bar Association, Consumers Union, National Council of Churches, American Medical Association, National Education Association and many state bar associations. As of this writing, eleven states—Oregon, Alabama, Maine, Colorado, California, Ohio, Minnesota, Mississippi, New York, North Carolina and Nebraska—have enacted decriminalization laws (which drastically reduce penalties for possession of small amounts of marijuana) and several others seem destined to follow suit. Though Jimmy Carter has retreated from his original recommendation that marijuana be federally decriminalized, the Congress and the bureaucracy continue to explore the topic. A Gallup survey in 1978 indicated that 60 percent of all Americans support decriminalization, with 28 percent favoring outright legalization.

What is decriminalization and how does it work? Basically, the idea is to draw a line between small-scale possession and large-scale dealing. The typical decriminalization law changes the charge for possession of up to an ounce of marijuana (about one month's supply for a once-a-day smoker) from a misdemeanor to a violation like a parking ticket, carrying a $100 fine. Under these new laws, hundreds of thousands of young smokers will be spared the trauma of being arrested, jailed and stigmatized with a criminal record for the rest of their lives. At the same time, felony charges remain in effect for growing, smuggling or selling marijuana. The meaning of the new law is plain. It says: "We're not going to ruin your life if we catch you smoking, but we're going to make it as hard as we can for you to get the stuff. Marijuana will be scarce, unreliable and expensive."

Meanwhile, marijuana remains an illicit drug, totally outlawed in four-fifths of the nation. Behind the smiling facade of growing social acceptance frowns the grim face of the criminal underworld that supplies this tolerated but unsanctioned substance. The marijuana underworld extends from kids pushing "nickel" bags on street corners, to smuggling rings that bring ton-loads into the country in four-engine transports or fishing trawlers, to the highest levels of officialdom in many South American countries, whose national economies are now deeply dependent on the American dope dollar. This vast criminal conspiracy has woven its webs of intrigue and corruption over the entire Western world, producing precisely the same symptoms of social pathology that were familiar during Prohibition.

If at this moment, you could switch on a magic TV set and dial it to DOPE, you would see an astonishing replay of the bad old days of bootlegging. You'd see the same tropical isles and banana ports. The same fast little contact boats and rusty old tramp steamers. The same old game of cat and mouse played between the smugglers and the Coast Guard.

Once again, you'd witness the monumental corruption of Chicago and Cicero: whole cities in thrall to criminal overlords, with crooked mayors and crooked police chiefs and crooked politicians in the nations' capitals. You'd see new Capones and new Mafias no less bloodthirsty than their infamous prototypes gunning down their enemies en masse, just as they did in the days of the Saint Valentine's Day Massacre. Given one good look at the spectacle of the Dope Game, you'd sicken with disgust and cry out with horror. For, make no mistake, the New Prohibition is just as violent and evil as the old. The sole difference is that instead of having Chicago in the heart of our country, we have learned in the Age of Vietnam to keep such horrors at a comfortable distance. The "Chicago" of marijuana prohibition is in Mexico or Colombia, a long way from home.

Considering the vast sums of money to be won in the Dope Game, it is not surprising that thousands of men, hundreds of gangs, even the highest officials of the exporting countries should have laid their lives on the line to make the big score. What is astounding is the way this dirty business has been kept so quiet. Instead of the papers and TV blaring forth the news of the latest criminal outrages or pondering editorially America's moral responsibility for encompassing the ruin of our nearest good neighbors, we hear only the faintest echoes of the machine guns, the crashing planes and the dying men who labor every day to bring you that little joint you accept with the word "Peace!"

This book will lift the seal of silence from the Dope Game. The American public will be given a long hard look at the crimes in which all Americans are implicated either as unthinking consumers of contraband drugs or as moralistic supporters of laws that serve no other purpose than the promotion of crime. Having seen in concrete detail precisely what Marijuana Prohibition entails, I doubt whether many people will still be willing to support it. The truth is that the current politically motivated compromise between allowing and forbidding, between right and wrong—the policy so slyly titled "decriminalization"—is based on nothing better than a mixture of ignorance, cowardice and opportunism. Once it is recognized that this shoddy expedient can be sustained only by paying an enormous price in life, health and public morality, it will be hard to argue that decriminalization is either a practical or a morally tolerable solution to the marijuana problem.

My own introduction into the world of marijuana took place back in 1975. At that time, I was working on a book titled *The Ghettoing of America*. The book was the outgrowth of years of studying the counter-culture, first as a jazz critic, then as a rock critic and finally as the biographer of the late Lenny Bruce. All of those years of research, reflection and writing had established two very profound convictions in my mind. One idea I summed up in the formula *the counter-culture is the criminal culture*. This meant two things, first, that the roots of the counter-culture as a defiant or even revolutionary way of life lay not so much in the sources that the kids were proud to avow—the political treatises of Marcuse, the racial theories of Fanon, the Eastern religious doctrines of Zen, the folk music of the blacks and hillbillies, much less the sophisticated parodies of these last by the famous rock bands—but rather in that culture that had always been the most antagonistic to conventional values and codes of behavior, the culture that had always acted out the most basic fantasies of the American psyche and created the whole underground world of drugs, violence, street argot and antisocial defiance: the criminal culture. The other meaning of the formula was the observation that the counter-culture had actually become the criminal culture. In the late Sixties and early Seventies one-time hippies and Yippies had turned into bomb-planting anarchists, into kidnapers and terrorists and into gangs of smugglers who lay back on their bales of dope in cargo planes or boats listening to the songs of the rock bands and fancying themselves the heirs of the rock stars because they were actually doing what the songs of the Sixties had merely suggested.

As one of America's few full-time students of the counter-culture, I felt at this moment that my calling was to follow this latest trend right over the line and down into the criminal underworld where the more adventurous kids were heading, later to be followed by thousands if not millions of other people. For that was my other conviction: that the counter-culture, far from being an antagonist to the conformist culture, was in fact merely a social avant-garde that was never more than a step in advance of the country as a whole.

Everybody had witnessed during the Sixties how the fads and fashions of the hippies had swept across the country and been adopted by the most conventional-minded middle-class people. Whatever the kids were into today—whether it were wearing blue jeans or smoking dope or contracting herpes simplex—lots of other people would be into tomorrow. That was the law of a restless and dissatisfied society. So if I was right about this drift toward criminality, then it would follow that what America was building up to was a generation of outlaws. Outlawry was, as Rap Brown said about violence, "as American as cherry pie." Outlaws were our most common and enduring national heroes. Outlaws were the subjects of our legends and songs. Outlaws were the most drastic embodiments of some of our most cherished American values and traits. Outlawry was deep in the American grain. All that was required to bring out this strain of defiantly antisocial behavior were certain inciting social conditions: a depression or an unpopular war or bad laws, like the amendment that saddled America with Prohibition. All of these conditions were developing simultaneously in the mid-Seventies. It seemed obvious to me that more and more people were dreaming the dream of criminal advantage and adventure.

Knowing where the culture is heading and being able to come to close quarters with it are very different things, as I had learned to my dismay on more than one occasion when I got myself into what promised to be an ideal observation post and then discovered that I was trapped inside a nightmare. As I contemplated the challenge which my latest work posed, I suffered many qualms and much self-doubt. I was a middle-aged college professor with the intellectual's typical preference for thought as opposed to action. I was not a rugged type physically nor a man who had ever evinced any remarkable degree of courage. I hated crime and had no firsthand experience of criminals. Though I could imagine virtually anything, the thought of actually getting down into the filth that fascinated me was profoundly repugnant to both my moral and esthetic sensibilities. It was natural, therefore, that I should have chosen almost instinctively to follow a track that seemed relatively safe and honorable: the study of marijuana.

My own knowledge of drugs was strictly secondhand. Though I had written about such famous addicts as Thomas De Quincey, Charlie Parker and Lenny Bruce, I had never shared their habits. Even grass, that mild and apparently harmless drug that every kid used, was something I knew virtually nothing about from actual experience. Naturally, I had puffed from time to time on a skinny little toothpick joint handed around at a party or a rock concert. I had even tried hashish a couple of times, once with disastrous results. Basically, however, my habit was alcohol. I knew a lot about Scotch liquor, German beer and French wines; I knew nothing about marijuana, cocaine and the endless array of ups and downs, reds and blues, hypnotics, narcotics and hallucinogens that are the staples of the drug culture. Nothing, that is, but what I had read, which was, perhaps, even worse than nothing, most writing about drugs being either medical gobbledygook or hippie folklore. Putting it all together, I would say that I was hardly the ideal man for the job. Only one thing was to my advantage: I began the study of the marijuana culture with a very blank if not a genuinely open mind.

For four years I followed the track that is traced out in this book. I started on the lowest rung of the dope ladder, with nickel bags purchased from street dealers, and worked my way up, step by step, from neighborhood dealers to weight wholesalers to small-time smugglers to the men who hyphenated the word "load" to "ton-load." Eventually, I reached the source of the Green Nile that is pouring millions of pounds of dope into this country every year. That source is our near Good Neighbor, Colombia. In the course of this long haul, I interviewed dozens of men in the Dope Game, including, on the one side, the dealers and smugglers, airplane pilots and ship captains, dope farmers and South American connections who move the weed and, on the other side, the uniformed and plainclothes cops, the Customs and DEA agents, the Coast Guard crewmen and officers and even the undercover narcs and secret informers who work just as hard to stem the dope tide. I got as close to the action on both sides of the line as a writer can get without compromising himself morally or getting killed. A couple of times, I missed death by very narrow margins.

Though the marijuana world is much too vast for any man to ever survey completely, I think I covered the ground as thoroughly as any Ph.D. candidate has ever covered his field of specialization. A lifetime of professional scholarship prepares a man very well for the task of searching any subject to the bottom. Looking back on this once-impossible task, I find myself smiling at the thought of my first timid steps, tottering baby steps, attended by the same fears that infants must feel when they first stand upright and start to explore that mysterious and frightening world that lies before their astonished eyes.

NEW YORK'S MARIJUANA UNDERGROUND

Imagine a hot, funky summer night in Manhattan. The street lights have halos of smog. Lots of people are sitting out on front stoops. Lots of cops are cruising the streets. I'm on my way down to Hell's Kitchen, where I've heard dope is being sold in the streets to passing motorists. I make a right on 51st Street and drive past old tenements, churches, stores. Slowing down for the light on the corner of Tenth Avenue, I catch sight of the boys. At first, they look like any bunch of Puerto Rican street kids chasing each other around the block. Then two of them advance boldly toward the car with keen eyes, expectant glances. "Hey, man! Whatcha lookin' for? Wanna *nickel?*"

The foremost kid opens his hand and flashes a stack of little tan mailing envelopes, the kind in which you receive the keys to an apartment. They're five-dollar bags of marijuana—being peddled as openly as pretzels or Good Humors. I take the bag and squeeze it. There's something soft and crumbly inside. If I were less anxious and guilty about what I am doing, I would open it up and examine it carefully. Frankly, at this point in my career, I don't know whether I would be able to tell at a glance whether it was marijuana or oregano. Actually, all I'm thinking about is buying the stuff and getting away fast. I peel off a bill and pass it through the window. The swarthy little kid cracks a big grin. As I catch the green light and lurch forward, he yells after me: "If ya dig it, come back! Remember—the name is Flaco!"

As I pull away I glance in the rear-view mirror. With a shudder I realize that as the sale was being made, there was a car standing behind me. A police car.

As I learned soon afterward from interviews with agents of the Drug Enforcement Administration and the Narcotics Division of the New York City Police Department, the overworked cops of New York simply hadn't the time to run down every little violator of the marijuana law. The one time they did raid the kids on 51st Street—from the concealment offered by a construction site across the street—the kids outran the cops. The only person who was arrested was some poor schmuck who had bought a nickel bag. The judge threw out the case.

Generally speaking, most people who got busted for little amounts in New York at that time beat the rap. They received an "adjournment in contemplation of dismissal." If after one year the prosecutor did not move to restore the case to the calendar (because of a new arrest), the case was dismissed automatically and the record sealed. This practice undermined the zeal of the police in small-quantity possession cases. As District Attorney Robert Morgenthau remarked: "We have in effect already decriminalized marijuana in New York." (In 1977, marijuana was officially decriminalized in the state.)

The people who put the kids out on the streets are the local dealers, who operate on the assumption that if a kid gets busted, he'll get off, whereas if an adult is busted, he may have to serve time. This makes the local dealer sound like an evil Fagan, but the fact of the matter is that today there is a whole new breed of "good guy" dope dealers who have revolutionized the peddling of illegal drugs. Early in my search, I happened on one of these "ethical" dealers and struck up an acquaintance with him. One night I traveled out to the working-class neighborhood in Queens where the dealer lived. It was Friday night, payday, the time of week when people think about buying grass and have the money to score.

When I drive up to the door, Tony is standing out in the street with his shirt off, displaying his muscular, tattooed torso. A friendly, almost pretty-looking guy of Latin extraction, he gives me a warm but quiet greeting and takes me into his apartment, a warren of tiny cluttered rooms above an Italian grocery. The place is teeming with life. I meet Tony's pretty young wife, his wife's sister and his eighteen-month-old kid, sitting plop in the middle of the little living room playing with Fang, the patient but vicious-looking German shepherd. Tony points with pride to his zoo. The snakes in glass cases, the hamsters running up and down the walls in plastic tubes, the tropical fish flaring against the wall, the black cat, the white cat and finally the star of this menagerie, Bernie, a huge hairy Saint Bernard who looks completely out of scale in this cramped and crowded mouse house.

Though Tony's regular customers are arriving to make buys, the atmosphere is that of a party or an open house. The TV is blaring, the women gossiping, the animals chasing each other through the rooms. Tony is sitting in a favorite chair rolling joints with oversize papers called e-z widers. He's handing out a lot of good dope for free. "I don't charge for drinks," he says with a smile as he passes me a fuming bomber.

Tony's first customer is Angie, his oldest buddy. Both boys grew up in the neighborhood, both went off to the "Nam." Both are so well liked that once when they were "tossed" by the police and nailed with an ounce, the cops let them go after giving them a good lecture. "We're not all pricks, ya know," said one cop as they went down the stairs. Now Tony is a fixture in the neighborhood. A guy everybody likes and trusts. Without him the neighborhood wouldn't be as much fun.

When Tony and Angie have finished hugging each other and talking trash, they leave the women in the living room and go into a tiny bedroom that doubles as Tony's store. A white pharmaceutical scale is on the bureau. Next to it is a pile of neatly wrapped nickel bags. Putting his arm around Angie's shoulder, Tony says in his husky, intimate voice: "Listen, this shit cost me five-fifty. I gotta get forty bucks for it. From *you*. Anybody else, it's sixty." Angie nods. Nobody ever doubts Tony's word or weight. Angie pulls some bills from his jeans while Tony reaches in the closet for a fat plastic bag filled with grass. Pouring out the pot on the scale, he measures an ounce accurate to a tenth of a gram. Then he bags it, hands it to Angie, pockets the money without a glance and with the air of a man eager to return to his party, leads the way back to the living room.

At that moment the bell rings and in walk four neighborhood girls all dressed up for a dance. With a lot of laughing and giggling, they tell Tony that they've got thirty dollars between them. What can he give them for that money? Tony smiles and offers them a joint. As they take and pass it on, he settles in his chair and assumes his most charming manner. "Hey, you know what! I'm embarrassed to tell you what I gotta charge ya. Take my advice, don't spend your money. Buy a nickel." Then he leaves the girls smoking in the room while he goes back to the kitchen, where dinner is cooking.

When Tony returns, the girls all shout: "Tony, wow!" This is dynamite! You gotta give us some! We want to buy an ounce but we just don't have the money this week. Hey, com'on, Ton!" Tony throws his hands up in mock despair. Then he makes his pitch. "Look," he says, with thumbs and forefingers held up like he is about to go *bang! bang!*, "here's the deal. I gotta get fifty a lid to make my money. I wuz thinkin' maybe I'd give ya a couple grams over 'an—since you'ze my people—I'm gonna give ya all buds. O.K.?" (A lid was once as much weed as you could cram inside the lid of a Prince Albert tobacco can. Today, it's synonymous with an ounce.)

The bell rings again. Tony's sister-in-law goes to answer, giving a sharp look through the fish eye. Tony is starting to feel a little pressured. These girls have smoked a lot of his dope, and now they're taking up space that belongs to his other customers. Very politely, he hustles them: "Ladies, is there something else with which I can serve you?" "No, Ton, we're splittin'. Later, man, later . . . !"

Tony has many sources of supply because in the smoke trade people poop out all the time, owing to arrests, screw-ups or the failure to make a deal further up the pipeline. To facilitate the whole business of dealing and to provide the dealers with a comfortable and convenient setting in which to compare notes and wares, the practice has sprung up in recent years of establishing protected apartments or lofts called "smokeasies." One night I went to one of these secret establishments way the hell out in Brooklyn.

My passport was an engraved invitation on expensive parchment paper. Inside a border of fanciful Moroccan ornamentation was inscribed in elaborate script the name of the smokeasy: "Au Contraire." Then followed the date and at the bottom was the admonition: "Hold card in hand while waiting." Opening the flap, you read: "Pick-ups every 15 minutes between 9:00 P.M. and midnight. Location: Candy store/News stand, 1944 Avenue J (beneath the Avenue J Station of the IND elevated line)." More detailed instructions were printed on a yellow insert that offered directions by subway, bus and car from Queens, eastern Long Island and Manhattan. The refinement and elaboration of the invitation surprised me. Also, I thought, "Who the hell goes to a dope dealer's convention by bus?"

It is about ten when I take my stand at the candy store. I am trying not to be obvious in the way I hold the invitation—yet I *do* want to be noticed. Suddenly, someone taps me on the shoulder. Wheeling about, I confront a pretty blond girl dressed in jeans, with a halter top. She can't be more than sixteen years old, yet she's cool as a Snokone. "Won't you come with me, please?" she says, as if she were the hostess at the Playboy Club. Taking me to the corner, she opens the door of a waiting car. Inside I find a man and a woman and a long-haired driver who knows everybody's name and makes introductions by first names only. Though I don't know it at the time, as we drive down the nearby block of old-fashioned apartment houses, a sentinel on the roof of the building is watching our approach through binoculars and signaling our arrival to another lookout stationed in the kitchen of the smokeasy.

The building is old and tired, but when our guide raps on the door of the top-floor apartment, it swings open instantly to admit us to the coolest, hippest atmosphere in New York. The latest sounds from Philadelphia come prancing to my ears, the pungent smell of exotic grass distends my nostrils. Our host appears. He's a handsome sun-tanned Jewish boy with a curly Afro and a perfectly fitting white sailor suit topped with a black silk neckerchief. He hands me two neatly rolled joints and a huge Moroccan pillow; then he leads me into the living room, where an odd-looking crowd is standing about smoking and drinking or reclining on the heavily pillowed floor.

The pad is the last word in smoke-trade luxury. Erotic tapestries from India adorn the walls, a splendid collection of hookahs, narghiles, thuribles and bongs decorates the low tables, which have been made by laying Moroccan silver trays on squat wooden cradles. At one end of the room is a small conventional bar offering the usual drinks. At the other end is another bar whose surface is covered with a great assortment of shallow bowls filled with various kinds of grass: green, brown, gold, black and red. Before I can make a move, our host proffers the "menu" with an air of a maitre'd in a fashionable French restaurant.

Gazing at the heavy piece of pasteboard in my hand, I recognize the familiar iconography of the dope world. The exotic-looking mushrooms that are called in Mexico "the flesh of the gods." The hookah, with its cobralike drawing tube. The beautiful sevenfold spread of the marijuana leaf intertwined with the peace symbol, to suggest the pacific character of marijuana as opposed to alcohol and the "death drugs." Opening the menu, I find the list of dopes on sale this night and the suggested price by ounce, bag or gram. Thai sticks, the most popular grass in New York that year (the top 5 to 6 inches of a peculiarly potent and spicy plant wrapped around a slender strip of bamboo and bound by a deft oriental hand in white thread) are going for the astounding price of $25 apiece. At 13 sticks to the ounce, that comes to $325 an ounce, or $5,100 a pound! The next item on the menu is Colombian shake (the crumbled grass that sifts to the bottom of the bag beneath the buds) at $35 an ounce. Indian hash comes next at $10 a gram. Then, in a bold red block, comes the mainstay of the New York dope trade: Colombian Gold, which is offered at $5 a bag, $20 a large bag and $50 an ounce.

By this point I'm puffing on somebody's extraspecial supergreat Panama Red, I'm examining somebody else's special portable dope stash—a flat leather case containing eight plastic vials, each with a different sort of grass designated by a label pasted on the tube—and I'm struggling, with some difficulty, to figure out who these people are and what they're actually doing. As the night wears on, I gradually accustom myself to the surroundings and the crowd. Most of the men are dope dealers, all right, but they don't correspond with my image of the type. Instead of being super-sharp studs in white plantation suits with special tailoring around the shoulder holster, they look like the crowd at the Knicks' games. One beefy pale-faced man in his late thirties tells me that he works as a doorman in a building on Central Park West. He's got a wife, three kids and a salary that wouldn't pay for snuff much less Colombian Gold. Dealing has solved all his financial problems, however, and endeared him to the tenants in his building—who buy all the dope he can lay his hands on. With the thousands of tax-free dollars he makes every year standing in the lobby booking orders, he has bought himself a nice two-family house in Rego Park. Now he dreams of owning a parking lot.

Another dude, I'm told, is a cab driver. He works by radio phone. People who are hip know they can dial and ask for this driver and make a buy from the back seat of a cab. Like all dealers, this guy is a nut about his "cover." No matter how much dope you buy, you've got to take a ride. When a customer tries to score and run, he cries: "I've got to show something on this meter!"

Yet another dealer to whom I'm introduced is a cute little Jewish kid who runs the beach at Brighton and Coney Island. His gimmick is that he squats on everybody's blanket and strikes up a conversation about dope. "Hey, do you smoke? What do you smoke? Would you like to try mine? Sure I could get you some." His best customers are the lifeguards, who are condemned to sit all day staring out into the blank sea.

As the evening wears on, you begin to appreciate the skill and address of the host. He runs this joint like a jet-age Figaro. He seems to be in on every conversation, every deal, every vibe that is winging through the room. One minute he's separating the girls from the men so that the dealers can go off into the bedroom and get down to business. The next minute, he's giving orders for more refreshments or dispatching a car to pick up new arrivals. Then he ducks upstairs and across the roof to make sure that in case of a raid the escape path is clear. At a given signal, all the dope in the apartment can be scooped up in a garbage bag, run up to the roof and down the other side of the building, where it can be stashed in a safe apartment.

The host's payoff for all this hustling is a piece of every deal that goes down. He'll take it, he tells you, in either dope or cash.

It makes no difference because in his world the two are interchangeable. He even pays the building super in dope—which the guy bags and sells. After a while you begin to get the impression that instead of a little larceny lurking in everybody's heart, what lurks there today is an itch to deal.

Late at night I'm finally allowed to go into the bedroom where the business is really being conducted. Two guys are sitting face to face across a table. One guy wants to sell ten pounds. The other is ready to buy. They've hammered out the price. Now they just have to transfer the merchandise. Their problem is that the dope is in an apartment in Queens. They call in the host. Can he help? Sure, he'll put a driver and a car at their disposal immediately. Just one more service for the patrons of Au Contraire.

A half-hour later, the dealer is back with his ten pounds in a suitcase. Instantly, he's closeted with the other cats who have gotten wind of the deal. The back bedroom is blue now with smoke. Time has stopped, and the monotony of the conversations has begun to blunt my brain. Eventually, the individual phrases crisscross each other like verbal jackstraws. "Hey, man, the fucking price is getting outrageous! . . . I know things are tight! But I gotta have something to keep my customers . . . the way the bust went down . . . We could meet tomorrow. Do you like to work days or nights? . . . I'm gonna give you one deal, one time. . . . You got it for four seventy-five—now don't talk to me no more!"

The step above dealer in the dope trade is just what it is in any business: wholesaler. In fact, one of the most amusing features of the dope trade is the way its hustlers go out of their way to mimic the language and style of legitimate merchants. The further up the dope ladder you climb, the squarer the attitudes, the more abstract the numbers, the more Wall-Streetish and M.B.A.-ish the whole outlaw operation.

Thus, if you're being very professional you don't call marijuana "dope"; the correct term is "material." You don't speak about smuggling gangs; you call them "syndicates" or, even better, "machines." Smugglers will talk about the "Tampa Machine" or the "Gainesville Machine." The idea is that the operations are so slick and well planned, all the little gears are meshing so smoothly, that there's no danger, no sweat, no hassle. It's just a machine. What is the machine producing? "Flow." That's another magic word. Instead of a little score here, a little load there, an occasional tachycardic run, you have a steady flow. That's the big promise. "Man, we can get you *flow!*" That's the dream. The load arrives every month, like interest from the bank. Nor is it just a dream; the Dope Game is so well organized today that when grass is legalized finally, all the big dealers will have to do is change the signs on their doors and put their phone numbers in the directory.

Dope is not just big business: it's the only business in which a young adventurer can start out one day with a few thousand dollars in his kicks and end up a couple of years later a multimillionaire. No other business offers such an incredible profit margin on such a huge volume of trade. The pound of grass that sells for $60 in South America can be divided and subdivided until it is parceled out in tiny packages on the streets of New York for $1,500. In one big deal millions of dollars can change hands. As the number of users climbs year after year from 14 to 16 to 20 million, the airplanes get bigger, the boats longer and the scams for slipping the stuff into the country more and more audacious. With legalization glimmering on the horizon, most of the big boys figure that now is the last chance to make a killing. They're out there killing. And being killed.

Some guys want to live. That includes Goldfinger, one of Tony's suppliers, who got his name smuggling Colombian Gold. This man has been in the Game for so many years that he gets nostalgic when he thinks back upon the days of his youth, before they had gram scales and exotic grasses with unpronounceable names. He knew this business before it was dominated by rich kids trying to show up daddy by making as much bread in a couple of years as the Old Man made in a lifetime.

Goldy is a pretty tough *hombre,* a California version of Charles Bronson. His features are massive and craggy. His chin is cleft like a split rock. His chest is broad and bare. His arms are pile drivers embossed with crude tattooes. Tattooed on the knuckles of one big cruel hand are four purple letters: LOVE.

Goldy came to New York from southern California years ago intent on a stage career. His introduction to the city's criminal underworld was spectacular. Walking down Central Park West one afternoon, he sees a big black gangstermobile pulling up to the curb. The next second he turns his head around and spots a black dude lurking in a doorway, just a shadow poured into that slot. Suddenly, it flashes through Goldy's skull that the guy in the doorway is a hit man, that when the guys in the Cadillac open the door of the car and step out, the Shadow is going to gun them down. That's a pretty weird thought. Even more bizarre is what Goldy does about it.

The moment he flashes HIT MAN, he pivots like a ballet dancer, brings up LOVE and smashes it into the Shadow's face so hard that he drops the dude as if he'd put a bullet through his brain. Then he bops on down the avenue. But he can't stand the fact that he isn't seeing what happens next. So he takes a quick look over his shoulder. All the doors in the car have swung open. Guys are swarming out. They pick up the Shadow. They lay him up against the building. They beat him—virtually to death.

Goldy, meanwhile, is stepping briskly along. He's down to the Sixties when—*uh, oh!*—the big black limo slides up beside him. A window slips down and a black dude growls, "Hey, man, come'ere." "No," Goldy says, throwing up a hand nonchalantly. "That's all right, forget it, man!" But the guy says, "Hey, man, get in this car!"—and he means it. So Goldy gets in. Instantly, he starts rolling down his window, warning, "I don't know what you guys are gonna do, but it's gonna make a lotta noise!"

The black dudes are profoundly grateful. Goldy has saved their lives. The Shadow *was* a hit man. He would have blown them all away. They take Goldy to a bar and peel off twenty-five $100 bills. They put them in his hand. They give him a piece of paper with a phone number. The boss says, "If you're ever in trouble or you need bread, just dial this number." Then they send him about his business.

About two months later, Goldy finds himself down and out. He figures, "What the hell!" He rings the number. *Wham!* Aladdin's lamp. A big limo rolls up and there's the dude: "What do you need? A thousand? Here it is." Then the guy says, "Look, this is foolish. Let me put you on the payroll." Goldy doesn't want that. The guy says, "No, no, it won't be anything much. I'll give you $250 a week, walk-around money, and you'll run some errands for me." For the next two years Goldy works for this guy, who turns out to be the link between the Mafia and the black racketeers of Harlem.

Such were Goldy's humble origins. From there he went on

to robbing casinos in Vegas, trading porno films across state lines—for both crimes he served time in federal prisons—then dope smuggling. Today, he's a wholesale dealer who moves 100-pound lots of grass.

Now picture Goldy at age forty, leaning way back against the sofa cushions, spreading his arms wide apart, his shirt split down to his navel, a greasy old Mexican gold piece hanging from a chain around his neck, as he takes a long drag on his joint and in a voice of California nasality, a Cheech y Chong voice, he gives you the Game:

"At my level, wholesaling, I could make a couple hundred thousand dollars a year. But I do it the lazy way. I only work with people I know, mostly by telephone. Ninety percent of my work is with one supplier. I never have to go out of the country to get it. There's no trip involved with people bringing out scales or anything like that. If I say it's there, it's *there*. And if they give me an envelope stuffed with cash, I know it's O.K. No heavy-weights involved with guns or anything like that. All very clean and nice and comfortable.

"In this business, you net almost half. Fifty percent goes to getting the stuff; your staff comes out of the other half. You make a lot of money, tax free. But you're putting yourself in a position where any time you can lose a tremendous amount. Let's say you invest your own capital in a large move and it gets busted—or ripped off by hijackers. Then, you've got to go back to square one and start all over again with money borrowed from a shylock at ten percent *per week!*

"So I keep my business at a certain level. I can have a hundred pounds in my possession for the length of time I want it and sell it for the amount I want to make. If I go any higher, it means adding to my group; and it's going to involve cash, more cash, which means, if you're on the street, more danger. On my level it's more comfortable, I can handle it. It works well and there's no heat on me. The cash always turns itself over. It's like a play with a thousand actors, but the roles are always the same. The deal is made. The deal is consummated. The end.

"The only thing that changes is, maybe, drop-off locations, modes of transportation, that sort of thing. I sometimes get it into the city the same way four or five times in a row. Then I'll switch to something else. I had one deal that broke down into five twenties. I keep paying people to do these things, take all these risks. And if they end up getting me my hundred pounds up here via whatever means, then, great! If not, then I've lost my investment. Very rarely do I lose shipments.

"I know where I stand as far as New York as a port of entry goes: Kennedy and La Guardia or any of the boat places. And you kinda get a feeling about the Customs people—what level they function on. I even try to hang out in the same bars and psych these guys out. Then, you just work around that.

"The enforcement agencies claim they get ten percent of the weed coming in. So most of it gets through. I was in Florida when they copped eight hundred pounds of six tons of grass that was coming in. They knew that the shipment coming in from Colombia was six tons. Still, they only got eight hundred pounds—even with all their Intelligence information. They have forty agents at the Brooklyn docks, but they can't stop it coming in—even at the hottest docks, like the Grancolombiana. [A notorious shipping line owned principally by the Colombian Government.]

"The whole trick is clearing Customs. Once you've done that, you're home free. Customs is thorough. Six or eight guys can really do a number on a ship. Whether they've got a tip or not, they'll search a ship right down to the bilges. They're very together, these Customs people. Like they can detect a little difference in a shade of paint that indicates something has been repainted. Then they start diggin' around in there. They're clever as hell, these guys. But long as you give them credit for that and maintain that level of intelligence, you can stay even with them at least. You can't ask for more than that.

"The one big drag in this business is that you can never hang on to any of your money. There's so much turnover all the time. Fuck it! You sit down and say, 'I blew two hundred thousand last year just living!' I'm a fucking one-man business boom. I put a lot of people to work: waitresses, shoeshine boys, bartenders, barmaids, hookers. I've flown more people to California than TWA. The President's always trying to put me out of business, but I'm doing more for his trip than anybody. Me and a couple of hundred thousand like me! We put a lot of bread into circulation. There's at least one dealer in every block in New York. And at least one wholesaler in every ten blocks."

Wholesalers like Goldy get their goods from smuggling syndicates that go down to Jamaica, Colombia, Mexico, Costa Rica, Nicaragua or even more remote regions and buy up whole fields and warehouses full of dope. These big syndicates have to be sure in the first instance that the grass they are buying—and spending a fortune to smuggle into the U.S.A.—is not only top-grade marijuana but just the sort of grass that their customers are seeking. For as consumption of marijuana has become a common feature of middle-class life in sophisticated cities like New York, all the familiar snobbism and consumer one-upism of the big-city shopper has manifested itself in the grass market. People not only want to get high, they want to be able to drop heavy names like Acapulco Gold and Panama Red that are the Guccis and Hermès of the smoke trade. People want dope that not only smokes good but looks good. They want a spicy aroma or a plump seedless bud or a beautifully wrapped Thai stick that is an oriental artifact. To assure that the customer gets exactly what he wants, the big syndicates have started to employ professional dope tasters. Men who look at grass the way a diamond dealer looks at a rough-cut stone, gazing through the crude surface to spot the essence of the gem and assess its suitability to the market where eventually it must be sold. The most interesting man I met in the first seven months on this story was the Ph.D. among these smoke tasters: the guy I call Mike the Marijuana Maven.

I got on to this man through *High Times*, the journal of dope hedonism and adventure. Back in 1975, *High Times* was a kooky novelty. It looked like an elaborate put-on put out by the *Harvard Lampoon*. Imagine a glossy slick with a campy cover photo of a Thirties vamp, long sucky cigarette holder in hand, standing amidst jardinieres filled with flowering pot plants, gazing at the crescent moon (humming, doubtless, "How High the Moon?"). Inside were a dozen articles dealing with such familiar topics as "Hash Rubbing in Kashmir" or "Pot, Peasants and Pancho Villa." The service sections featured "Trans-High Market Quotations," viz.: "Johannesburg: Durban Poison sticks (top grade) $4.50–$14 bundle of 20." The ads were for pipes, rolling boards, cigarette papers and sieves. The centerfold was not the usual girlie fingering her private parts, but a stunning full-color photo of a peyote cactus "at the rare moment of flowering."

Like most of the biggies in the grass game, Mike is very paranoid. He lives in professional seclusion, and he doesn't like to come out and play. Rarely does he grant an interview, and when he does, there are conditions—many conditions. When he comes into my apartment, he is engrossed in conversation with the editor of *High Times*, who had arranged the meeting. While I bustle around like a suburban matron setting out drinks, ash trays, making small talk, he is still engrossed in the conversation that he brought into the room. Only when I interrupt him to request permission to tape the interview does the Marijuana Maven look me in the eye. Then he blink-blink-blinks like a computer spinning its reels.

Like all compulsive talkers, the Maven can start anywhere and slowly unreel his whole rap. It would take about 200 hours of straight talking, accompanied by continuous smoking. But don't fool yourself; it could be done. On this night, for example, he kicks off by remarking that most dope experts examine the ring of oil that accumulates on the joint as you smoke it. Good dope is supposed to create a heavy ring of oil and even drip down the joint. Mike is a little more advanced than most connoisseurs. He knows that dripping oil may be a sign of good dope; but then, again, it may just be a sign that the dope is full of cannabinol. CBN is what scientists used to think was the active ingredient in marijuana. That was before they discovered THC—tetrahydrocannabinol—with its various isomers, like the delta-3, 4-*trans* isomer, which is really the active ingredient in pot. Or delta-7 or delta-9. Hell! There are so many different isomers of dope that most haven't yet been identified. What's more, each of these isomers can give you a different head. So the idea that poor old cannabinol is the "active principle" belongs back in the Dark Ages of dope research, before infrared spectroscopy and nuclear magnetic resonance unlocked the deep secrets of hemp.

Most experts would put cannabinol down. Not the Maven! He follows every convolution around to its counter-convolution—then he follows that track around in turn. (When you smoke what he smokes, you can follow an idea around in circles for a long time.) He knows that good old cannabinol *is* an active principle after all! It's the thing that gives you the *munchies*.

When he hits the punch line, "*munchies!*," his academic manner cracks and a sly little Terry Southern titter escapes from his frozen face. It's a dissociative, *goyische* giggle, like you'd get off if someone were to tickle your toe while you were carrying on an important conversation on the long-distance wire. *"He-he-he!"* he snickers out of the side of his mind as his eyes blink-blink-blink and the computer tape reels give another little spin.

But, heavens! The Maven has been speaking for many minutes and his joint has been consumed. He has brought along for this ordeal a Baggie filled with his favorite brain food. Removing a botanically perfect specimen from the bag, he explains that this is a particularly desirable species of Colombian Gold from the mountains near Santa Marta on the Caribbean coast. It is the most beautiful piece of dope I've ever seen. The Golden Bough, no less. A big, fat, lustrous, superbly arched bud with the color and shape of a peculiarly abundant and glorious wheat head. The Maven prefers to have his joints rolled for him. He looks up now and says, with just a trace of sarcasm: "Weren't you going to assemble that joint for me?" But first he has to demonstrate how a real dope connoisseur relates to a fine bud.

Contrary to the practice of the callused palms, the true dope lover will never take a bud or a stick and pulverize it between his hands. Horrors! This gross practice obliterates totally from the leaf all the invisible pollen which is one of the finest constituents of the high. Pollen is where it's at with high-altitude dope. Only a schmuck takes the pollen off on his hands when he could be inhaling it into his soul. So the real dope lover disassembles the bud bit by bit, picking the seeds out of the goo, discarding the "lumber" while leaving the leaf.

Now the obvious question to ask the Maven, the question that has been asked of him hundreds of times from the East Village to Katmandu, is "What is good dope?" But the question sticks in your throat like a fishbone. It's like asking Picasso "What is a beautiful painting?" Only the sense of professional responsibility that makes interviewers act dumber than they are forces you to utter the icky syllables and receive the condescending stare. "Good dope? . . . The best dope? . . . Quality? . . . Ideal? . . . Perfection?" The Maven's eyes are blinking in a spasm of short-circuited synapses as he fastens his exquisite mandibles on this incredibly crude query. If you had asked him what gives Oaxacan its minty taste, he could have given you an answer consonant with his expertise and gone into the iron in the soil down there or the subtle distinction between menthol and mint.

Or if you had asked him, "What is *punta roja?*" he could have told you that it's Spanish for "red point" and refers to tiny red fibers in the buds that are invisible to the untrained eye but that emerge in the microscopic vision of the professional dope appraiser to tell him: "This stuff is dynamite shit!" But, no, like an asshole, you asked a dumb question; now he's got to backtrack to the most elementary distinctions, the freshman orientation lecture that he's always got to lay on fat-faced, balding, middle-aged intellectuals.

For the Maven there is no such thing as "good grass." From his point of view, all grass is great. As he sucks on his joint or holds it negligently, burning in his hand, as if it didn't cost $80 an ounce, he smiles a wan smile and talks for a moment like a Village rock critic, like a guy who really gets off on garbage. "I've smoked the humblest window-grown Kansas City weed and gotten off," he avers. "I would again. I never turn down any dope. I'm not a snob." Imagine that! A cat who commerces with weeds that cost up to $3,200 a pound! It's the counter-culture thing, the "bad is good" bit. He's also counter-culturish in the way he talks about his "hits": the dopes he's picked that have made it big on the American markets. "Oaxacan was one of my early hits," he reminisces. "Most of the Oaxacan weight that came in a few years ago was from what I chose. Then there's Culiacan. . . ." He's also a pop artist in his conviction that whatever he picks will go right to the cerebral cortex of America. As the man says: "I feel a tremendous responsibility. If I fuck up, I may fuck up America."

At this point, you're getting that fixated vision and total loss of the extremities—shall we call it decorporealization?—that is characteristic of potent weed. A warm inner sun is beaming from your midriff. Your head feels like a helium balloon on a long thin string. Your face is numb but your mouth is alive. Every time you say something it comes out a killer. You're like the Delphic oracle sitting over her fuming crack inhaling the vapors of prophecy. Everything that pops out of your mouth has the succinctness of a proverb. The Maven relaxes for a moment the rigor of the royal audience, which allows no questions to register upon the presence. He asks (more for courtesy than curiosity) your opinion, as a professional music critic, on the relation of rock to jazz. Without a thought, like a perfectly cracked fortune cookie, you reply: "Rock is the missing body of jazz." Wow! Did I say that?

Now you force yourself to focus your wandering mind on the Maven so that you can record his never-photographed countenance. What does this underground genius look like? When he first walked into the room and sat beneath your Noguchi lantern, he looked like a wasted, blinking, hippie scientist with a pale mushroom face and an eroding hairline. Now that he has moved a little into the light and offered his profile for your inspection, you're astonished to see that he's very good-looking: a young Brian Donleavy, with a neatly trimmed mustache, fine features and the delicate pink lips of the pot smoker. My, how you look at people's mouths when you live in a world of passing joints!

The Maven is now explaining to you that every grass has its "head." Some are good for creative work and some for procreative. Some will take you up to the stars and some will dump you on your ass. Being a stone intellectual, the Maven's private preference is for brain grass. He also has some kinky theories about dope and sex.

"The best grass is the mountain-grown, high-altitude grass that generates a lot of fresh thinking in the brain. Dope grown at sea level is narcotic; high altitude works like LSD because it causes the production of seratonin, which enables more random connections of synapses and makes more possibilities for connections and information retrieval. Smoke is a signal to your mind to do this. Yoga is another signal, as are various other things. Marijuana is a very effective one.

"According to at least one theory, marijuana produces a lot of estrogen in the body. You've heard these stories of men growing breasts? The estrogen causes the male to take on feminine characteristics—more mentally than physically. There's not really enough of it to affect one physically. But I think it causes men to become less aggressive, potentially. That doesn't mean they won't pick up a gun and kill you in a second. It just means there's less raw material for aggression there: less machodom generally.

"Also, in women, it supposedly makes them more animalistic. It could be said to make them more like men, if you define macho and male tendencies as more like an animal, more aggression, more paranoia, more forcefulness, et cetera. So it makes men more like women and women more like animals. And animals are more like men. It's a very unisex drug."

The Maven is eager now to do something that lies on the frontier of marijuana hedonism: blend two super-grasses to make a super-doper grass. He's pulled out his black pill case, with its vials of hash stones, mushroom flesh and labeled weeds. He selects a Red from Panama to mix with his Colombian Gold. His roller obediently combines them in a fresh joint swathed in the Maven's favorite paper: Zig-Zag Slow Burning. Hard to get and small in size but silky in consistency, Slow Burning is reluctant to incinerate. It's so thin that it contributes nothing to the taste of the smoke—a vital point to a smoke taster.

I ask the Maven what he thinks about New York as a dope town. He relishes the question. New York is his base. "If you're in New York on a good day," he smiles, "you can get *anything!* Mexican, Colombian, Nepalese hash—whatever. There's more money ready to buy dope here than anywhere else in the world. There are some very very wealthy dealers in New York because enforcement's very lax. It's a tough town to patrol, you know. A thirty-floor apartment building is pretty hard to case. They've pretty much given up here. And because it's a very anonymous town, it's very easy to deal in. So it just keeps growing and growing and growing.

"The need for marijuana is not a faddish thing but is very real. An organic need, a need of the times. A lot of people have stopped smoking over the last few years, but a lot of people have started too! And while a lot of people have stopped smoking, a whole lot more haven't stopped at all. Even the ones who say they have stopped—I'll bet you that most of them will be smoking again within five years! To stop for a few years is a wise thing, I think, because it gives you a reference point for what the experience is like so that you'll really know when you're stoned.

"The society of grass dealers is functionally the equivalent of the New York Stock Exchange. The aggregate opinion of everyone is what sets the price. There's much faddishness in dope dealing, which is true of the stock market, too. Thai is a fad in dope right now, but there's a lot of bad Thai around. Colombian used to be a fad here, and I'm sure that outside New York and in some circles here, it's still a fad. It's a spreading fad, like rock music was in the Fifties. Believe me, there's a world of difference between what will happen to America on Colombian or Mexican. Colombian is just more powerful. You're talking about a different drug, a much stronger potential to take you in whatever direction you might go. It can be like a nod-out, that's one type of Colombian; or it can be a very creative drug, good for physical activities, listening to music and all kinds of things. The more Colombian spreads, the more people will be smoking marijuana. Because it's much more satisfying. A lot of people who gave up smoking Mexican did so because they just weren't getting that high! You could smoke joint after joint, and it wasn't worth the hassle of all that sucking! Of course there are certain other grades of Mexican that are highly psychedelic. Colombian has a lot of psychoactive affects, but Mexican has this psychedelic factor. Then there is also the pure power factor, which simply means how great a distance it removes you from your consciousness when you started. But that might not necessarily be in a worthwhile direction. Like being unconscious—it's a long way from where you started but that's not so great, is it?

"Also, today, with the commerce and the fads, cosmetics— the appearance of dope—has become a big factor in whether dope will sell. A few years ago people didn't look at the dope, they *smoked* it! 'Did you get high?' 'Were there a lot of seeds?' Those were the questions then. Now they ask a lot of things in order to identify the product that aren't even necessarily worthwhile to know because what you know about one grade of Colombian might not apply to, let's say, a certain grade of Mexican grown in some back valley somewhere.

"A really good dealer is someone with quite a bit of knowledge. If you are a professional cannabis merchant, you have to be familiar with many types of commercial dope. You're familiar with Afghani hash, but then there are four or five different kinds of Afghani! There are twenty different kinds of Mexican easily! Like five or six different kinds of Colombian. And within each category, you have to spot the grades of that. About a year and a half ago a lot of Hawaiian grass started hitting New York. So Hawaiian started becoming a very highly prized thing. But not long after that we began to realize that not all Hawaiian was very good. Stuff coming from Maui was great but from some of the other islands, it wasn't so great.

"Another thing that happens is that a popular grass will be overplanted and become less desirable. A few years ago the big thing was Acapulco Gold. But in the growing areas where that was coming from, they kept planting it and planting it, until now Acapulco Gold isn't that good. It's still Acapulco and it's still Gold, but you can't say any more that this stuff will completely knock you out.

"These things matter eventually to anyone who smokes grass. Everyone's a dealer because everyone's some part of the distribution chain: whether you're at one end growing the marijuana or at the other end smoking the joint. Once you're a part of that chain of distribution, then you're as intimately involved as anybody at any point. If you're somebody sitting there with fifty tons in your possession, you're no different from the guy sitting there smoking the joint because there's got to be somebody to get the fifty tons in order for the other guy to smoke a joint. If they decriminalize and make one ounce legal, then what will that mean for the guy holding a ton except that he possesses 32,000 legal ounces?

"The sad thing," concludes the Maven, looking disconsolate, "is that there's so much ignorance about growing dope. That's what kills you as a smuggler: the realization that the natives you're dealing with—the people who've been growing this stuff for thousands of years—don't know shit about it. Look at the difference between the Colombians and the Mexicans. The Mexicans throw the seeds in the ground and trust to luck. Thank God their seed is well adapted to the conditions under which it must grow. The Colombians are light years ahead. They may nurture the plants in forcing boxes. They trim the bottom leaves from the start, forcing the resin to the top of the plant. Instead of a great big twelve-foot lopper, they harvest at six feet, giving them two and three crops a year. When the time comes to harvest, they drive a stake through the base of the plant. The trauma makes the resin rush to the top leaves. Then one sunny afternoon, when the sap has been drawn up to its fullness by the sun, they chop off the tops. Most agricultural people haven't the faintest idea how to pack grass. They bail it and crush it to death. Or they get modern and let it rot in plastic. It's hard to get intact buds like these, and everybody wants to see buds because when you see the bud you can tell that the grass hasn't been cut with some cheaper grade.

The difference between a Colombian bud and a Mexican—why, it's like the difference between an American Beauty rose and a dandelion.

"Still, we've got a big business here. Five to six billion dollars a year, and a pretty progressive element of society. According to a serious study made by *High Times,* there's over forty tons of marijuana consumed in the United States each day! Still, it will be so much better when people know what they're doing. There's nothing wrong with smoking any kind of marijuana—it's all good for you—but the better grades can do so much more for you. If you need energy, smoke some good marijuana and get energy. If you need to relax, smoke marijuana and relax. You need some creativity? Some insight? Want to meditate? Or use it as an aphrodisiac? It's a tremendously flexible drug."

One of the most interesting points the Maven made in his long rap (which I was too loaded to recall until I played back the tape the next day) was that many people today are growing their own dope as an alternative to paying the extravagant prices charged for weed in the underground marketplace. I knew this was true because I had uncovered many instances of little private-stash gardens flourishing in closets and on rooftops and at week-end hideaways. What I had never encountered in New York was a full-fledged underground marijuana plantation. Then one day I discovered such a basement farm.

Picture late afternoon on an old residential block in Manhattan. A Puerto Rican neighborhood. I meet Che outside his building, the five-story apartment house that he and his friends are buying with the money they earn from New York's biggest underground marijuana farm. Che is a short muscular cat who always wears a stocking cap over his kinky hair. He greets me with the outlaw's handshake, thumb up and hard squeeze. Then he leads me into the lobby and down the basement stairs. The basement door has been sheathed with galvanized iron and heavily padlocked. It looks like it hasn't been opened in months. It bears an official Fire Department sign reading: "Danger. Do Not Enter. Condemned Premises." Underneath is a crudely hand-lettered note that says: "In event of emergency call 877-3795." Smiling his guileful smile, Che leads me back upstairs to the lobby and into the back apartment on the first floor.

Shouting a greeting in Spanish to his wife and giving one of the children playing in the corridor a pat on the head, Che takes me into the back bedroom. He opens the door to a closet, drags out a couple of cartons, peels back a piece of rug from the floor and lifts up a trap door. Light gleams below. Squeezing through the narrow opening, I descend the steep wooden stairs. When I reach the bottom and turn about to look at the room, my eyes pop out of my head!

Standing before me is a magic forest of tall green plants— marijuana plants—growing under artificial lights. There are hundreds of them and they stand about six feet high. The ceiling is ablaze with fluorescent grow lamps. The walls gleam with silver foil. The hot tropical atmosphere is rank with the smell of hemp and fertilizer.

"Two hundred fifty plants!" Che smiles as he takes in the plantation with an expansive proprietorial gesture.

Then he's into his guided tour of the premises, pointing out the squat Westinghouse humidifier in the corner, the automatic timers on the wall (with directions in Spanish pasted above the switches) and the narrow catwalks that lead up from the cellar floor to the terraced forcing boxes where the young seedlings are started. A guy is working right under the ceiling as Che talks, balancing in sneakers on a narrow board and snipping busily at the bottoms of the plants. He's a graduate of an agricultural school, Che explains, the very man who set up this farm and now supervises the labor of the families that till it. He got the finest Colombian seeds, determined the ideal soil composition, the correct light, temperature and humidity. Now the crops are being planted and harvested on a rotating basis, with new plants replacing the old ones at regular intervals so that the flow of grass never stops.

Che takes me over to the cutting table, where the plants are hung upside down after being cut so that the resin accumulates in the tops. He shows me the infrared lamps for curing the grass, the blocks for chopping it and the sieves for taking out the stems and seeds. The last step is packaging the product. When the marijuana comes out of this basement, it's ready to go into circulation as first-quality, high-resin-content reefer.

After marveling over the arrangement at the farm, I quiz Che about the security for this very vulnerable establishment. He tells me that everything has been done to protect the farm, which is supporting so many families. He concedes that eventually there will be trouble. "Hey, man," he says with a resigned shrug, "sooner or later, they pop us. Somebody got to take a bust." Then smiling his little guileful smile, he adds, "We already picked the guy to go."

INTELLECTUAL INTERLUDE

My interview with the Marijuana Maven made me realize that I didn't know the first damn thing about dope. Here was this stuff that people had been cultivating and consuming for thousands of years, a legendary substance that informed ancient myths and current folklore, that figured in classic works of literature and famous historical episodes, that was regarded in one culture as a vile criminal racket and in another as a sacred sacrament—and I was just discovering it! It was a lesson in scholarly humility. At the same time, it was a challenge for a man who was accustomed to thinking that if one read long enough and deep enough, he would find the answer to all his questions in books. Hying myself down to my old haunt, the South Reading Room of the New York Public Library, I started making out call slips and worming my way through scores of books and articles. I commenced my library research at what struck me, a former English professor, as a logical point of departure: the origin and meaning of the word "marijuana."

The Word

Spelled variously "marihuana" (official U.S. government spelling), "marajuana" or "marijuana," the word is a Mexican-Spanish term applied originally to a kind of wild tobacco, *Nicotiana glauca*. The etymology is disputed: some derive it from the Portuguese term for an intoxicant, *mariguano;* others analyze the word as a euphemism composed of two of the most common Spanish Christian names, "Maria" and "Juan," comparable to our own slang term "Mary Jane." In other languages, times and cultures, marijuana has borne a great variety of names; in fact, if the number of names which a substance carries is any index of its importance, marijuana must be one of the most important substances known to man. In the *Multilingual List of Narcotic Drugs under International Control,* published by the United Nations, the list of 202 names for marijuana is mind-boggling: *bhang, canape, diamba, ganja, grifa, hanf, kif, maconha, mota, Rosa Maria* et cetera. In American vernacular, marijuana has many names that do not appear on the U.N. list; names that belong to particular periods of history or suggest certain effects of the drug or are word plays or puns on the drug's proper name. Back in the Thirties, when marijuana was being introduced to American society, it was called "muggles" and "muta," "grefa" and "tea." During the Forties in New York, it was called "boo" or "goo," "grass" or "gauge," "pot" or "shit." Today, the favorite word in the white world is "dope" and in the black, "herb." The scientifically correct term for marijuana is *cannabis,* which is Latin for "hemp"; or *Cannabis sativa,* which means "sown" or "cultivated" hemp; or *Cannabis indica,* which tacks on the country of origin. (Sometimes the word is followed by a capital "L," which is the abbreviation for Linnaeus, the great classifier of plants.)

Though names don't alter substances, it makes a world of difference whether you call dope cannabis, marijuana or hemp. Cannabis sounds like a disease of dogs, a typically opaque scientific cypher lifted from a dead language and totally meaningless to a layman, who may not even know how to pronounce this arcane-looking word. Marijuana, on the other hand, summons up the image of a leering Mexican *bandito* twirling his luxuriant mustache and gazing at you with lubricous delight. Hemp is another world again: fourth-grade textbooks, George Washington's farm, sails and cordage on Yankee clippers. Hemp is a square-toed, woolen-stocking word that is pure dumb Anglo-Saxon, like bump or lump. If Americans had always called marijuana "hemp," as do the English, it is doubtful that the drug could ever have incurred or sustained such a reputation for wickedness.

The Herb

Marijuana is a very special kind of hemp, not very well suited for making cordage and sails but botanically in the same species as the rope makers' plant. Being one of the oldest cultivated plants, perhaps the oldest plant cultivated for purposes other than nutrition, hemp has proven extremely adaptable over the 10,000 years during which it has been found. Through crossbreeding, genetic mutation and the natural variation of its germ essence, something like 200 varieties of hemp have evolved across the course of civilization. This extreme plasticity and variability is one of the most significant features of hemp. It explains why one type of grass can get you almost as high as LSD while another type can barely give you a buzz. It explains why countries that really care about grass raise the best grass and countries that don't care produce stuff that is of such poor quality. It also suggests that with modern plant-breeding technology, it should be possible to produce strains of grass that are more potent than anything hitherto known and to make the common weedlike strains that grow wild over the Midwest into powerfully hallucinogenic drugs. Hemp is one of those wonderfully cooperative plants that will do virtually anything it is bidden. Now that it is no longer prized as an aid to human survival, it is prized as an aid toward human happiness.

Marijuana plants, seen growing in a field, resemble a stand of bamboo. The long slender stems, attaining a maximum height of 18 to 20 feet, and the clusters of delicate, dependent leaves give the plant an air of tropical profusion. The leaves spread in clusters like the fingers of an open hand. Each cluster comprises five to eleven leaflets resembling serrated spear tips. Ridged down the middle and veined diagonally, the leaves are covered, as is the entire plant, with tiny hairs. The leaves are connected to the branch by a delicate, grooved stalk. In the wild these branches will grow densely from the thick, hollow, squarish central stalk, which terminates underground in a thick, divided taproot.

Marijuana grows best under the same conditions of soil and climate that favor corn: lots of water, especially in the early seedling stage; lots of light; and a soil or loam that is high in nitrogen and potash, moderate in phosphorous and containing little or no clay. The seeds sprout in three to fourteen days, depending on the variety. The life cycle of the plant is clocked by the length of the day. The male plant flowers in three to five months no matter what the photoperiod; the female plant will not blossom until the light drops below thirteen hours a day. At that point, the plant reacts as if the season were ending: within two to three weeks, it flowers profusely.

The male plant produces clusters of yellow or yellow-green flowers that contain five pendulous stamens. These stamens open lengthwise to allow their thin, yellow anthers to wave in the wind and release the minuscule grains of pollen. The female plant anticipates its fertile period by putting forth large, thickly packed clusters of flowers that stay hidden within its dense foliage. Each female flower contains a green tubular sheath that surrounds the ovary: the bract or calyx. From the bract extend the stigmas, which catch the airborne pollen. The bracts are coated with tiny hairs and glands that produce a light resin, which is thought to protect the ovary and maturing seed from sunlight, moisture, birds and insects. (Very few pests or insects attack marijuana, but many animals love it.)

The female plant begins to produce this resin just before pollination and continues to produce it until the termination of the growing season. The highest concentration of psychoactive substance is in the bract and the resin, with lesser concentrations in the flowers, leaves, small stems, large stems, roots and seeds, in that order. To achieve the highest concentration of the most valuable portions of the plant, some cultivators will remove the male plants from the field prior to pollination. The female plants, failing to be fertilized, produce a superabundance of resin and no seeds. This highly potent and much-prized marijuana is called *sinsemilla* (Spanish, "without seeds").

After pollination, the stigmas are dropped, and inside the bract-sheaved ovary, the fruit, a hard shell containing one dicotyledon seed, develops. The male plant, its pollen expended, withers and dies. The female thrives until its seeds are mature or the first frost arrives. The seeds are small, elliptical, flat, smooth, olive, brown or gray in color. They yield a good deal of oil when pressed. (Cooking oil and soap bases were among the early uses of the hemp plant.) Once the female plant has dropped its seeds, they lie dormant in the ground awaiting the onset of a new growing season. They are hardy and will germinate readily whenever suitable conditions are present. Marijuana grows wild all over the world as a weed.

The preferred moment for harvesting fertilized marijuana is when the plants are in bloom. Cultivators often pinch or bend or pierce the stalk at its base about two weeks before harvesting. Though there is no scientific proof that these practices increase potency, any kind of stress tends to increase the THC concentration in the tops and leaves. The plants are next uprooted or chopped close to the ground and taken to a large shed where specially constructed boxes are used for curing. The finest specimens are separated and cured in the sun in long, troughlike bins constructed of chicken wire, wood and burlap. The grosser portions are either baled quickly and shipped or suspended upside down from the beams of the shed in the mistaken belief that the resins will seep down the stalk and into the leaves. Heat will convert the inactive cannabinolic acids into potent THC; small-scale farmers will sometimes place the best portions in an oven at low temperature to force this conversion.

Hashish is concentrated marijuana. Many traditional techniques are employed for making hashish. The simplest method is to rub the leaves and flowering tops of the female plants with the bare palms. Under the blazing midday sun of India or North Africa, the resin fairly shimmers off the rows of plants. After hours of vigorous scraping of flesh upon plant, the process produces stringy, turdlike lumps of coagulated resin. Other methods entail shaking the pollen off the plant tops onto sheets or crumbling and sieving the dried tops to a fine powder, which is then molded with moisture and heat into little balls. The most prized hashish comes from the Himalayan countries of Kashmir, Nepal and Bhutan. Dark brown in color, resinous in texture, it is molded into sticks, fingers, disks, slabs and "temple balls." Middle Eastern hashish is stamped with various fanciful emblems: the elephant, the lion, the cobra. The refuse from the hash-making project is given to beggars—or sold to Westerners who, it is said, will smoke anything.

The Essence

The psychoactive ingredient of marijuana was for long thought to be cannabinol (CBN); then, in the early 1930s, researchers decided (mistakenly) that cannabinol was essentially inactive and turned their attentions to the task of extracting or synthesizing the isomers of tetrahydrocannabinol (THC). The ultimate success of this research turned out to be largely dependent on the development of more sophisticated chemical technology. Finally, on July 20, 1965, an Israeli scientist, Raphael Mechoulam, announced in a letter to the editor of the *Journal of the American Chemical Society* that he had performed the feat at which so many others had failed. "We wish to report," his landmark paper begins, "that we have completed the first total synthesis of *dl*-cannabidiol and *dl* ¹–3, 4-*trans*-tetrahydrocannabinol, the psychotomimetically active constituent of hashish (marijuana)." (Two numbering systems are in use for describing the tetrahydrocannabinoids; Mechoulam's delta-1 is delta-9 *trans*-tetrahydrocannabinol in the more commonly used nomenclature.)

Since Mechoulam's synthesis, the chemistry and pharmacology of marijuana have been revolutionized and great strides have been made in the study of cannabis. THC has been pronounced "a unique chemical not found anywhere else in nature." An oily substance insoluble in water but soluble in alcohol, it is rapidly inactivated by exposure to oxygen, light, humidity or elevated temperatures. Its molecular structure has been correlated with that of other hallucinogens such as LSD and psilocybin. Because delta-9 THC is so hard to work with, experimenters often substitute for it a nearly identical isomer, delta-8 THC, which is more stable and can be produced 98 percent pure.

It is recognized today that there are a number of other psychoactive ingredients in cannabis. (The subject is much too confused at the present time to permit a simple statement of what these chemicals are or how they operate either independently or in connection with delta-9 THC.) Therefore, the National Institute of Mental Health has authorized, for experiments which are meant to reproduce the actual effect of smoking or ingesting cannabis, an extract of the whole plant which contains 15 percent delta-9 THC.

The production of this extract and the growth of marijuana plants for scientific experiments all over the world are concentrated in a unique government institution: the National Institute of Drug Abuse Marihuana Project at the University of Mississippi School of Pharmacy. The government's grass farm at Ole Miss is the most scientific cultivator of weed in the entire world. Its director, Dr. Carlton E. Turner, boasts that his gardeners can grow grass to .1 percent of the desired THC content. They book orders from laboratories and foundations all over the world and cultivate each batch of grass according to the desired potency. As the world's best-educated dope farmer, Dr. Turner has made some very provocative observations on the weed he grows.

Testifying in 1975 before the Eastland Senate subcommittee,

he explained that the potency of weed depends much more on genetic factors than it does on conditions of cultivation. The typical THC content of the grass seized by the police of Mississippi in 1974, for example, was 1.46 percent, which is virtually the equivalent of commercial-grade Mexican pot, probably what most people smoke in Mississippi. By contrast, some specimens of Brazilian *maconha* which the lab analyzed registered a heavy 6.8 percent. What's more, in assaying the THC content of grass growing on the farm, Dr. Turner discovered that the THC content fluctuated both by the week and by the *hour*. "I do not know what happens to it. . . . Mexican female plants at an age of 13 weeks may contain 1.52 percent, which is average THC content, and the next week, at 14 weeks, may contain 3.77 percent. A particular Mexican cannabis plant . . . may contain as high as 4.61 percent delta-9 at 8 A.M. and at 9 A.M. that same plant will contain 2.17 percent delta-9 THC."

Dr. Turner's work has also gotten him into the study of hashish—with remarkable results. It has always been assumed that hash is a much more potent substance than grass, perhaps on the order of 10 percent THC. The Brave New World farmers at Ole Miss have poked a great big hole in this classic dope myth. When questioned about the THC content of hashish, Dr. Turner replied, "I have checked with the U.S. Customs Laboratory in Washington and recently with other researchers, as well as the United Nations. Those individuals found hash to be between 4 and 5 percent. At a recent U.N. meeting in Athens, Greece, a standard hash preparation was recommended for distribution by the United Nations' narcotic laboratories, and the recommendation was for a THC content between 4 and 5 percent. . . . So in the major market . . . that has been the average we have seen."

Subsequent study of hashish has shown that this preparation does not contain much more THC than a fine grade of marijuana, but it does contain a very high proportion of cannabidiol (CBD). Though not enough is known as yet about the relationship between CBD and THC to pronounce with certainty, it would appear that the character of a dope "high" is determined by the balance between these two psychoactive agents. THC produces the effect of exhilaration, CBD the narcotic effect. If you have a lot of THC and little CBD, you get a jittery high. Raise the concentration of CDB—as in hashish—and you get a high that is slow to come on and which is stuporous and long lasting. The ideal marijuana high, therefore, would entail a carefully engineered balance between THC and CBD.

On the subject of hash oil, Dr. Turner testified: "Liquid hash is just another name for a crude drug made from cannabis. We have analyzed liquid hash from slightly above 5 percent to greater than 88 percent. The more potent came from Brazil with the weaker coming from the Dallas DEA Lab and appearing to have been diluted with vegetable oil."

Perhaps the most remarkable findings of the botanists at Ole Miss were presented to the committee by the director of the Research Institute of Pharmaceutical Sciences, Dr. Coy W. Waller. Questioned about the growing potency of grass on the American market, Dr. Waller responded with a statement that had prophetic overtones:

The importance of genetic variation in marihuana as to its THC content is all important if we are going to determine what marihuana or THC does to man long range. . . .   There are no barriers to crossbreeding of the various strains, and it seems that the progeny from crossbreeding resulted in plants with higher THC content. . . . It is most rational that by strain selection a high producing strain should be genetically possible. How high is high? . . . Dr. Itsuou Nishioka at the University of Kyushu, Fukuoka, Japan . . . has shown that the THC producing strains are genetically dominant; [therefore] the crossbreeding of the wild stands of marihuana in the Midwestern part of the United States with a few high producing THC plants would convert our wild stands, which are now low THC producing [0.02–0.2 percent] to high THC producing marihuana.

It is reasonable to expect that marihuana can be produced to contain 5 to 6 percent THC, with present knowledge of strain selection and proper harvesting of selected parts of the plant. By using this more potent type of marihuana to make liquid hash, it is possible to obtain liquid hashish with a 50 percent THC content. We know from experience that synthetic THC can readily be purified to 100 percent material. The question is really what will THC do to man toxicologically, psychologically and sociologically. We have essentially arrived at a point where we can make any grade of THC that is desired or undesired.

As marijuana has been used by millions of people and for thousands of years, the first and most important evidence of the drug's effects is not that provided by recent laboratory experiments, but that furnished by marijuana's millennial history. Unfortunately, much of this history is inaccessible because it has never been drawn together by Orientalists from the primary sources, which are the documents, traditions and physical remains of ancient Chinese and Indian culture. Lacking a comprehensive survey of cannabis in the Orient, the most a student of Western civilization can do is to sketch out the history of marijuana as it gradually spread over our half of the world.

2 *The Threefold History of Hemp*

The history of marijuana is really three histories rolled into one. First, there is the history of hemp, a plant whose cultivation can be traced back thousands of years before the birth of Christ. Second, there is hashish, the preferred form of marijuana throughout the drug's long and colorful history in the Middle East and in India, the real homelands of dope. Finally, there is marijuana as we know it, a substance that has assumed importance in the Western world only in the past few decades.

The first indubitable reference in Western literature to getting high on hemp appears in the *Researches* of Herodotus, the Greek traveler, anthropologist and anecdotalist, known traditionally as the "Father of History." Writing in 450 B.C., at roughly the same date as Sophocles, Herodotus describes the Scythians, whom he met in Thrace, northeast of Macedonia. Famous already in the West for their prowess as mounted archers (the familiar Greek mythological image of the centaur drawing the bow is a travesty of the Scythian archer), these nomadic barbarians had many customs that were strange to the Greeks. One practice in particular completely escaped the comprehension of Herodotus. As the passage in question possesses such great historic interest and is customarily distorted by being quoted out of context, I shall reproduce it in its entirety:

All the other Scythians [except the kings], when they die, are laid on wagons and carried about among their friends by their next of kin; all receive and entertain the retinue hospitably, setting before the dead man about as much of the food as the rest are served. All but the kings are carried about in this way for forty days and then buried. After the burial the Scythians cleanse themselves as I will show. First, they anoint and wash their heads; then, for their bodies, they set up three poles leaning together in a point and cover these with woollen mats; then, in the place so enclosed, to the best of their power, they make a pit in the center beneath the mat-covered poles and throw red-hot stones into it.

They have hemp growing in their country, very like flax except that the hemp is by far thicker and taller. It grows both by itself and also by their sowing it, and from it the Thracians even make garments that are very like linen. . . .

The Scythians then take the seeds of this hemp and, creeping under the mats, they throw them on the red-hot stones; and, being so thrown, they smolder and send forth so much steam that no Greek vapor-bath could surpass it. The Scythians howl in their joy at their vapor-bath. This serves them instead of bathing, for they never wash their bodies with water. But their women pound, on a rough stone, cypress, cedar and frankincense wood, mixing water also with it, and then with the thick stuff so pounded they anoint all their bodies and faces, whereby not only does a fragrant scent linger about them, but when on the second day they take off the ointment their skin has become clean and shining.

This report might serve as a textbook illustration of the familiar phenomenon of cross-cultural incomprehension. As a Greek, Herodotus placed a great value on cleanliness. He interpreted the practices he observed as a form of bathing. The Scythians' tent was, he assumed, that familiar hygienic facility, a steam bath. Yet, in virtually the same breath that he describes the bath, he reports the technique by which the Scythians actually cleaned their bodies, by applying to them a paste like a modern mud pack. Now, if the Scythians cleansed their skin with a pungent poultice of macerated cypress, cedar and frankincense, what need had they of a steam bath? Why did they keep the paste on their bodies for a whole day? Why does the steam bath make them howl with joy? The answer is, of course, that Herodotus fails completely to comprehend the scene he is witnessing.

The "vapor" he observed was not steam but smoke. The Scythians were not cleansing themselves in a sauna but getting high in a temporary smoking lodge. The goo they applied to their bodies, though it did make their skins shine, was composed of

woods and spices that have always been employed in religious rit-
uals. For, like most modern students who quote and discuss this
passage, Herodotus fails to explain these practices in terms of the
occasion that prompts them. Neither the "vapor-bath" nor the
body pack are hygienic measures. They are rites of ablution, employing charismatic substances, to remove from the mourners the
taint of the dead. Hence, the proper inference from this famous
passage is not that the Scythians were "heads," but that they were
a people who employed hemp, like the Indians and many other
races in the East, to obtain that state of religious exaltation and
joy appropriate to the wake of a dead warrior.

Though Herodotus has long enjoyed the title "Father of History," his frequent inaccuracies have also earned him the so-
briquet "Father of Lies." Until recently, there was no way of
knowing whether his account of Scythian hemp smoking was fac-
tually accurate. Then, in the Sixties, Russian archeologists uncovered some frozen Scythian tombs in central Siberia and veri-
fied the 2,500-year-old report. According to the paper of the
Soviet scientists: "One particularly interesting apparatus was a
kind of cone-shaped miniature tent, covered with a felt or leather
rug, standing over a copper censer. Hemp seeds found on the
spot suggest that this contrivance was a special enclosure that
could be filled with narcotic smoke from the burning seeds." As
the seeds of marijuana are precisely those parts of the plant that
are the least intoxicating, it has been suggested that the Scythians
actually threw the tops of the plants on the fire, where they were
consumed entirely save for the seeds, which are the parts most
resistant to combustion.

The implications of the Scythian episode are not exhausted
with these few observations. The manner in which these tribes-
men, as celebrated today for their extraordinary art as gold sculp-
tors as they were in antiquity for their skill as warriors, employed
hemp to attain intoxication is just as significant as the purpose for
which they employed the herb. Smoking hemp—as opposed to
eating or drinking it—is the very best way to transfer the intoxicating essence of the plant into the bloodstream and hence into
the brain. Smoking is not, however, the most obvious way of
ingesting a plant, nor is it a technique that would suggest itself to
a primitive people making their first experiments with a new
drug. Unless one postulates some happy accident, like that de-

scribed by Charles Lamb in his droll history of roast pig, a chance conflagration that got the whole tribe loaded, the Scythian custom must have had behind it a long history of experimentation and usage.

Consider for a moment what is involved in the simple act of smoking dope. First, someone has to discover by some means that ingesting a particular substance will get you high. Agronomists have concluded that hemp was first brought under cultivation between 5,000 and 10,000 years ago in central Asia. As this is the region from which the Scythians stem, we may suppose that this people had long cultivated hemp, as Herodotus describes them doing, for the purpose of obtaining textile fibers. All hemp possesses some psychoactive properties; even where the strains under cultivation are weak in THC, harvesting great quantities of the mature plant may produce in the reapers a sense of giddiness and intoxication. This, we may assume, would be the first step in the process of cultivating the plant for purposes of consciousness alteration. A vast amount of work would have to be done, however, particularly in a society that knew nothing of the principles of genetics, to separate the more potent strains from the feebler varieties and to improve the plant to the point where it could dependably produce a psychoactive substance. At the same time that this work of selective cultivation was going forward, the cultivators would have to learn when to harvest the plant for their special purpose, how to cure it for maximum effect and, finally, how to ingest it.

To a reader who is not familiar with the mystique of marijuana, the idea of filling even a tiny tent with smoke just to get high must seem as barbarous as the notion of burning down the barn just to eat roast pig. To an experienced pot smoker, however, the image of the smoke-filled tent will not seem preposterous; for what every real head wants is not just a few puffs from a pipe or joint, or even a great many puffs. The ideal "hit" is a massive, nearly suffocating inhalation, a "shotgun" blast or "supercharge" that will infuse so much THC into the lungs in a single instant that the resulting high will be a "rush" that carries the smoker's head up into the clouds. It is the craving for this asphyxiating super-toke that explains the existence of all those bizarre-looking engines, those bongs and "bombs" and "power-hitters" that fill the lavishly illustrated pages of *High Times*. Judged in the light of modern scientific knowledge and massive contemporary usage, the dope-smoking technology of the ancient Scythians must be pronounced "jam-up!" If the day ever comes when dope is legal in America, there should certainly be a brand called "Scythian Gold."

The other line of thought that springs from the Scythian story is the paradoxical conjunction of marijuana and warfare. The Scythians were mighty warriors. Their record of conquest, from Siberia to the skirts of Eastern Europe, was unsurpassed in their day. On the other hand, no idea about dope has been more frequently attacked and ridiculed in modern times than the once-familiar notion that marijuana is a "killer weed." Thousands of words, hundreds of pages, whole chapters in carefully researched books have been devoted to debunking the notion that there is any natural link between grass and aggression. Indeed, the modern dogma inculcates precisely the opposite idea: that marijuana is a pacifying plant that makes its users mellow and mild, laid back and reflective, prone to be prone. Marijuana was, after all, the "Flower" in "Flower Power." Yet, here, on the very threshold of Western dope history, in the very first chapter of the Gospel according to St. Herodotus, we find ourselves stumbling over the awkward fact that the earliest dope smokers in the West were just like Attila's Huns, a discovery almost as embarrassing as would be the revelation that Custer's cavalry were all pot heads. What makes this association especially provocative is the fact that the very next page in the history of dope in the West is occupied by the story of an even more frightening band of dope killers: the Assassins.

The Assassins were a heretical sect of Muslims that flourished in the eleventh and twelfth centuries, first in Persia, then in Syria, where they came into contact with the Crusaders by trying to kill the prince who later became Edward I of England. The sect sought to establish control over the Muslim world by murdering its political opponents. To commit these high crimes, the Assassins had to be very cunning as well as fanatically courageous. They had to worm their way into carefully guarded palaces and observe the habits of their victims until they were ready to strike with deadly precision. Usually they were caught and cut to pieces. Naturally, such kamikaze daring prompted people to seek special explanations for the Assassins' superhuman powers. The most common tale associated the Assassins with a drug that had been familiar for centuries in the Muslim world: hashish. In the *Arabian Nights* hashish is treated generally as a visionary and aphrodisiacal drug. Carnal delights, hot *houris* and cool sherbets, were the hallmark of the Muslim paradise; hence, it takes no great flight of the imagination to surmise that through the crafty administration of this powerful drug to young and naïve minds the idea might be inculcated that if the fledgling killers died in the performance of their sacred duty, they would be transported at once to the erotic paradise whose pleasures they had already tasted while under the influence of hashish.

The first appearance of this idea in the West occurs in the little-known history of Arnold, Abbot of Lübeck (*circa* 1210), who summarizes the report of an agent who was dispatched to Syria in 1175 by Frederick Barbarossa. He describes how the Assassins' leader selected and educated the sons of the local peasantry so that they became totally obedient to his commands. The most important feature of this education in blood was the inculcation of the belief that the leader held it in his power to dispatch his disciples to paradise if he were pleased with their services. How was the lesson taught? He "intoxicates them with a potion, so that they are plunged into ecstasy and oblivion, and he shows them by means of his magic some fantastic dreams, full of pleasures and delights . . . and he promises them these things eternally as the rewards for such works."

The concept of the magic potion that offers a foretaste of paradise is elaborated much further in the next and most famous statement of the story in a celebrated passage in the travels of Marco Polo. The Venetian merchant passed through Persia on his way to China in the years 1270 through 1272; there he learned the story, he avers, from the lips of several men of that country. According to this version, the master of the Assassins—called by the Crusaders the "Old Man of the Mountain" because his stronghold was an impregnable mountain fortress—would drug groups of disciples with a nameless "brew" and then have them carried inside a walled garden that had been contrived to resemble in every detail the description of paradise given by Mohammed in the Koran. The garden contained "the most beautiful houses and palaces . . . all gilded and decorated with beautiful frescos. There were also canals filled with wine, milk, honey and water. It was full of ladies and maidens, the most beautiful in the world, who knew how to play every instrument, to sing marvelously and to dance so well that it was a delight to see them." When the Old Man desired to dispatch a particular Assassin on a mission, he would put him back to sleep and remove him from the garden. When he awoke, he would be distressed at the loss of paradise. Then the Old Man would say, "Go and kill this person, and when you return, I will have you carried by my angels into Paradise. And if you die on the mission, I will command my angels to take you up into Paradise." Either way, the young Assassin was sure of obtaining his heart's desire.

Passing from the crabbed and mystifying account of the German abbot to the flowing oriental imagery of the Venetian traveler is like leaving the confusions of the real world for the clarity and beauty of a fairy tale. Polo's account is poetry and the inspiration for poetry. It is a classic statement of a classic human dream: the same dream that appears in the Hebrew Garden of Eden, the Greek Elysian Fields, the French *Romance of the Rose* and in countless other literary documents and masterpieces down to its Romantic epiphany in Coleridge's enchanting opium dream, *Kubla Khan*. The thought that anyone could have ever taken this folktale as a document of history seems strange to a modern reader. Yet it was so taken not just by naïve readers but by some of the greatest European orientalists and intellectuals down to modern times. The most influential interpretation of the tale was that of the great French Arabist, Antoine Sylvestre de Sacy. In 1809, Sacy offered an explanation for the name Assassin that has never been refuted. Pointing out that the proper name for the Assassins was Ismailis, he argued that their other name was earned by "their using an intoxicating liquid or preparation still known in the East by the name of hashish."

Associating "Assassin" with "hashisheen," the plural form of "hashish," meaning one addicted to hashish (literally, "dried herbage") was a brilliant stroke of scholarship. Not content with forging this link, Sacy went on to argue, with no compelling evidence, that either the account offered by Marco Polo was correct or the drug may have sometimes been used "to produce a state of frenzy and violent madness." The Malays, he noted, prepare another narcotic, opium, in such fashion that the drug makes them run amok and kill one another with the frenzy of madness.

Many pages of learned argument have been devoted to debunking every feature of Marco Polo's story and its customary interpretations. Archeologists have examined the mountain fortresses of the Ismailis and concluded that they could not have held the sort of pleasure gardens evoked so fondly in the story. Etymologists have disputed the derivation of the word for "killer" from the word for "hash eater." The argument seems destined to go on forever; however, what is at issue is not primarily the veracity of the story but the authority it provides for what has long been a standard folk belief; namely, that there is some causal link between hemp and murder. Before one rejects this idea out of hand, it should be understood that hemp functions as a mood intensifier. If the user approaches the drug in a serene and pleasure-oriented manner, he is likely to have a blissful experience; if, on the other hand, he is depressed or angry or anxious, the effects are apt to be very different. What is more, the power of culturally endorsed associations is such that, like self-fulfilling prophecies, they tend to dictate the character of the experience they are meant to describe.

To leap from the dawn of history with the Scythians or from the world of the *Arabian Nights* with Marco Polo to events that occurred almost within living memory and on our own borders, one could cite the example of Pancho Villa and his peasant army. This army was comprised of peons and Indians who smoked so much dope that they couldn't live without it, a fact commemorated humorously in one of the many verses of the army's favorite song, "*La Cucaracha.*" The Cockroach—the peasant soldier—"can no longer walk," sings the song, "because he hasn't, because he hasn't, marijuana to smoke." When *la Cucaracha* did get enough to smoke, he demonstrated how marijuana got its reputation for being "killer weed." Describing the Battle of Agua Prieta, Haldeen Braddy writes: "The intrepid Indians acted like wild men completely out of their heads from inhaling marijuana. They rose from a crouch and headed for the barbed wire. The marijuana gave them superhuman strength. So frenzied were they with the drug that some of them succeeded in breaking the wire with their hands."

In this country we smoke almost invariably under conditions of recreation and leisure; in other cultures men may smoke just as commonly under conditions of great stress or hostility. In Latin cultures, for example, with their macho code of honor, their sudden explosions of rage and the universal availability of firearms, the effects of smoking marijuana can be drastically different from what they are in a West Coast hippie commune where everybody is laid back, cooled out and intent upon his private thoughts and feelings. The doctrine of set and setting—the notion that how a psychoactive drug affects us depends as much on the persons and circumstances involved as it does upon its biochemical character—is invoked always by drug apologists to explain away bad drug experiences. A more impartial application of this perfectly sound principle would allow it to explain how in many circumstances marijuana acts not as a tranquilizer but as a device for nerving men up to perform aggressive and even murderous deeds.

To cite one more example, in the late nineteenth century, the explorer Hermann von Wissmann visited a Bantu tribe in the Belgian Congo and discovered that they had conquered all the neighboring tribes and publicly burned their fetishes. They had replaced the worship of these idols with a new ritual which consisted essentially of the smoking of hashish. According to W. Reininger, writing in *Ciba Symposia:* "On all important occasions, such as holidays or the conclusion of a treaty or alliance, the Balouba smoke hemp in gourds which may be as much as one meter in circumference. In addition, the men gather each evening in the main square where they solemnly smoke hemp together. But hemp is also used for punishment. The delinquent is compelled to smoke a particularly strong portion until he loses consciousness." Here you have a total inversion of the hippie rhetoric of the counter-culturish Sixties: dope as the idol of warriors, not men of peace; dope as a factitious religious ritual imposed upon conquered people against their will; dope as punishment instead of pleasure.

The moral is plain. Marijuana, like sex, is what we make of it. It is cultural putty. In one culture it will be the source of energy, the cause of rage, the psychological innervation for murder. In another culture it will function just as efficaciously as a tranquilizer, a wisdom drug, an inducement to love and erotic bliss. Even in our own highly homogenized culture, one observes dope producing contradictory effects; people who become depressed instead of elated, people who become panicky instead of relaxed, people who lose their appetite instead of getting "the munchies," people who voice their rage through clouds of marijuana smoke. So to those who tell us that marijuana will do such and such to our minds, we must always have the strength to reply: "Speak for yourself, Buster. It don't do that to me!"

THE ASSASSINS CLUB

Though hemp had been a familiar drug in the Orient for thousands of years, it did not enter the carefully guarded precincts of European culture until the nineteenth century. Then, it made a sensational appearance by being injected into the nerve center of the Western world: the brilliant and influential Paris of the 1840s. The discovery of the drug at that particular time and place can be associated with a number of factors: Napoleon's conquest of Egypt and the subsequent vogue of everything oriental; the blossoming of the French Romantic movement, with its addiction to exotic images and sensations; the influence of the first great drug writers, particularly Thomas De Quincey, whose *Confessions of an English Opium-Eater* was translated as early as 1828 by Alfred de Musset and whose disciples included Charles Baudelaire, who revered De Quincey as a Romantic genius, paying him the tribute of a second, more eloquent, translation, coupled with a commentary on the noble character of the English author. Yet despite all these favoring circumstances, there would have been no vogue of hemp in Paris at this time if a certain young French psychiatrist had not brought the drug back from the Middle East and begun to experiment with it for purposes that had nothing to do with getting high or having visions or writing brilliant pieces in the *Revue des Deux Mondes*. As this whole episode in cultural history depends so completely on the original French Connection, the most natural place to begin the story of dope in the West is by introducing the "seraphic doctor."

Jacques Joseph Moreau commenced his medical career by escorting wealthy patients on prolonged journeys to picturesque places, distraction being, as Dr. Johnson remarked to his fellow melancholic, James Boswell, the principal device for "the management of the mind." During one such trip that comprised sojourns in Egypt and Turkey, the young psychiatrist discovered hashish and was fascinated by its psychological effects. Observing that many of the symptoms of hashish intoxication were identical to those of madness, Moreau determined to experiment upon himself and others in a controlled setting to see if hashish would not offer a key to insanity. The experiments which he commenced in the early 1840s at Bicêtre Hospital outside Paris made medical history. By employing hashish as a psychotomimetic, a substance that mimics the effects of madness, Moreau established the branch of medicine known today as psychopharmacology. Like later experimenters with LSD, mescaline and other psychedelics, he was determined to capitalize on the fact that no matter how extreme the delirium, how vivid the hallucinations, how compelling the delusions of the hashish eater, he never loses his capacity for self-observation and communication. "To understand the ravings of a madman," Moreau was to write later in his remarkable book *Hashish and Madness*, "one must have raved himself, but without having lost the awareness of one's madness."

Moreau's method was audaciously simple: first, he would take the drug and submit himself to the observations of his interns; then, he would give the drug to one of the interns and become himself the observer. Moreau prepared his hashish in the manner he had observed among the Arabs. Using imported plants (his own attempts at cultivation on the hospital grounds did not produce plants of sufficient potency), he concocted an obsolete pharmaceutical preparation called an electuary. His recipe is interesting: "the flowering tops of the plant are boiled in water to which fresh butter has been added. When this concoction has been reduced by evaporation to a syrupy liquid, it is strained through a cloth. One thus obtains a butter of greenish color which contains the active ingredient. This extract is never absorbed in its pure form because of its obnoxious and nauseous odor. It is sweetened with sugar and flavored with scented fruit or flower extracts."

Moreau's basic dose of what the Arabs call *dawamesc* was a "lump the size of a walnut." According to the computations of a leading authority on the pharmacology of cannabis, Professor Gabriel G. Nahas, this 30-gram dose contained approximately 150 milligrams of THC, a very large dose indeed, considering that the average marijuana cigarette delivers only 4 to 5 milligrams. With one-half or one-quarter of this dose, writes Moreau, "one will feel happy and gay, and one might have a few fits of uncontrollable laughter." Only with the full dose, however, does one reach the state of transcendental bliss that the Arabs call "Al-Kief." Once during the experiments, the hospital's pharmacist took a triple dose. For three days he experienced all the symptoms of acute psychosis: hallucinations, incoherence and great agitation. Usually, however, the procedure was to take the normal dose, which produced a pattern of reactions that Moreau summarized in an eight-point list that stands to this day as the tersest and most telling description of the effects of hashish ever compiled. Arranged in order of increasing mental derangement, the effects of hashish eating are:

1. Feeling of happiness:

It is a feeling of physical and mental comfort, of inner satisfaction, of intimate joy; that you seek mainly to understand or analyze that for which you cannot find the cause. You feel happy; you proclaim it with exuberance; you seek to express it with all the means at your disposal; you repeat it to the point of satiety. But to say how and why you are happy, words are not enough. Imperceptibly, following this febrile and nervous feeling of happiness which shakes convulsively all of your sensitivity, there descends a soft feeling of physical and mental fatigue, a kind of apathy, of unconcern, an absolutely complete calm to which your mind abandons itself with great delight. It seems that nothing can impair this stillness of the soul and that you are inaccessible to sadness . . . the eater of hashish is happy not like the ravenous man who is famished and satisfies his appetite, or like the hedonist who satisfies his desires, but like the man who hears news that overwhelms him with joy, like the miser counting his treasures, like the gambler favored by luck, like the ambitious man intoxicated by his success.

2. Excitement, dissociation of ideas:

One of the first noticeable effects of hashish is the gradual weakening of the power that we have to orient our thoughts as we wish. Imperceptibly, we feel ourselves overwhelmed by strange ideas unrelated to those on which we want to concentrate. These ideas, which we do not want to recall, crop up in our mind, one knows not why or how, become more and more numerous, livelier and sharper. Soon one pays attention to them; one follows them in their most extravagant associations, in their most impossible and fantastic creations. . . . The action of hashish weakens the will—the mental power that rules ideas and connects them together. Memory and imagination then predominate; present things become foreign to us, and we are concerned entirely with things of the past and of the future.

So long as the disorder has not gone beyond certain bounds, one readily recognizes the mistake in which one is temporarily involved; there occurs an uninterrupted succession of false ideas and true ideas, of dreams and of realities, which constitute a sort of composite state of madness and reason and make a person seem to be mad and rational at the same time.

We undergo the most contradictory influences. We turn in all directions. . . . From irritation, one can pass rapidly to fury, from discontent to hate and desire for revenge, from the calmest love to the wildest passion. Fear becomes terror, courage a dedication that none can stop and that ignores danger.

3. Errors of time and space:

Under the influence of hashish, the mind can fall into the strangest errors concerning time and space. Time seems at first to drag with a slowness that exasperates. Minutes become hours, hours, days. Soon, with more and more exaggeration, all precise ideas of the duration of time escape us, the past and the present are merged. The speed with which our thoughts follow one another and the resulting dream state explains this phenomenon.

4. Development of the sense of hearing, the influence of music:

Pleasant or unpleasant, happy or sad, the emotions that music creates are only comparable to those one feels in a dream. It is not enough to say that they are more vivid than those of the waking state. Their character is transformed, and it is only upon reaching a hallucinatory state that they assume their full strength and can induce real paroxysms of pleasure or pain. At that moment, the immediate, direct action of the harmonics and the actual auditory sensations are combined with the most varied and fiery emotions which result from the associations of ideas created by the combination of sounds.

5. Fixed ideas (delusions):

With hashish, unless intoxication is excessive, the delusions are very short-lived. You catch yourself at times imagining the most incredible things, the strangest monstrosities, to which you surrender body and soul. Then suddenly, on the stroke of lightning, conscious thinking returns: you take hold of yourself, you recognize the error in which you had indulged. You were crazy and you have become reasonable. But you remain convinced that in pushing things a little farther the delusion had a good chance of completely dominating you, for a period of time which cannot be foreseen.

6. Disturbance of the emotions:

With hashish, the emotions display the same degree of overexcitement as the intellectual faculties. They have the mobility and also the despotism of the ideas. The more one feels incapable of directing his thoughts, the more one loses the power to resist the emotions they create. The violence of these emotions is boundless when the disorder of the intellect has reached the point of incoherence.

7. Irresistible impulses:

Seeing an open window in my room I got the idea that if I wanted I could throw myself from that window. Though I did not think I would commit such an act, I asked that the window be closed: I was afraid I might get the idea of jumping out the window. Deep down in my fear, I felt a growing impulse, and I had an intimate feeling that I might have followed it with a stronger "excitement."

8. Illusions and hallucinations:

Progressively, as "excitement" grows, our mind shuts itself off from external impressions to concentrate more and more on subjective ones; as this kind of metamorphosis takes place, we are drawn away from real life to be thrown into a world where the only reality is the one created by our memories and our imagination; progressively, one becomes the toy, first of simple illusions and then of true hallucinations which are like the remote sounds, the first lights, which are coming to us from an imaginary and fantastic world. . . . It has happened to me many times that being in a rather lively state of intoxication and looking attentively at a portrait I saw all of a sudden the portrait come to life. The head moved slightly and seemed to want to detach itself from the canvas. The entire face took an expression that only life may confer; the eyes especially were alive; I saw them turning in their orbits to follow all my movements. The first time I had such an experience without expecting it I could not retain a cry of fear. I retreated several steps, crying, "It is prodigious! That portrait is alive!."

The social and literary effects of Moreau's work were no less impressive, though considerably less edifying, than his scientific observations. In 1843, two years before the publication of his book, Moreau offered some hashish to a young writer of his acquaintance named Théophile Gautier. One of the most flamboyant of the French Romantics, Gautier had distinguished himself first by leading the historic demonstrations that accompanied the initial performance of Hugo's *L'Ernani*—the first shot of the literary revolution that was French Romanticism—shouting: "Death to the old wigs!" He had then composed a novel, titled *Mademoiselle De Maupin*, which recounted the adventures of a female transvestite. A phrase maker, he authored the Romantic's battle cry: "Art for Art's sake." Gautier was also an unblushing hedonist. In the preface to *Mademoiselle De Maupin* he wrote: "[I would] give a large prize to anyone inventing a new pleasure, for enjoyment appears to me to be the end of life and the only useful thing in the world."

Giving Gautier his first taste of hashish produced startling effects, which he reported soon in the Parisian press. He records three distinct episodes of consciousness alteration. In the first, he hallucinated torrents of gems in floral kaleidoscopic patterns, a classic drug image with many counterparts both in the subsequent literature of mescaline and LSD and in the ancient religious writings of the Hebrew and Oriental races. He also experienced great hilarity and began to toss pillows in the air like an Indian juggler. Half an hour later, the second wave of intoxication hit him; this time he saw "billions of butterflies with wings fluttering like fans," as well as giant flowers that exploded like fireworks. His hearing was heightened fantastically and he experienced synesthesia: "I heard the sounds of colors. . . . A whispered word echoed in me like thunder. . . . I swam in an ocean of sound." He had never felt such bliss; his basic image is that of sponge soaking up delights, joys, sounds, perfumes, lights. The experience seemed to last 300 years, but in fact it occupied only fifteen minutes. The third bout was the most intense. He became completely mad. He hallucinated every sort of grotesquerie: "goatsuckers, fiddle-faddle beasts, budled goslins, unicorns, griffons, incubi fluttered, hopped, skipped and squeaked through the room." Seizing a pencil, he sketched Moreau from behind playing the piano while dressed in a Turkish costume with a sun on the back of his waistcoat—the drawing survives. The musical notes are visualized flying off the instrument as in a modern comic strip.

What happened next is a clear anticipation of Timothy Leary and his cenacle or Ken Kesey and his Merry Pranksters. The young cultural revolutionary decided to spread hashish around like a new sacrament and to organize its devotees into a secret society. Taking a hint from Sacy's lecture on Marco Polo, Gautier called his new organization, "The Assassins Club." The original members included Gerald de Nerval, who was writing oriental romances and was subsequently to travel extensively in the Middle East; Fernand Boissard, a painter; F. B. de Boisdenier, a sculptor; Dr. Moreau; and, six years later, Baudelaire. Honoré de Balzac visited the club but would not touch hashish, fearing the loss of mental control, though subsequently he confessed in a letter to a female friend that he had tasted the drug under other auspices. Alexandre Dumas is sometimes listed as a member, but he belonged to another world entirely; his account of hashish in *The Count of Monte Cristo* is highly factitious.

The monthly meetings of the club were Bohemian parodies of conventional club meetings. The dessert—*dawamesc*—and coffee (Turkish) were served before the main course so that the slow-acting drug could take effect by the end of the meal. The table settings and utensils were a bizarre conglomeration of chipped antiques and exotic weapons: krises, poniards, daggers. The company itself was a motley crew of bearded and queerly costumed men whose faces assumed strange appearances in the light of the flickering lamps and candles. When the meal concluded, the members repaired to the immense salon, whose ceiling was ringed with a frieze of satyrs chasing nymphs and whose walls were covered with faded paintings and moldy hangings. Then the real fun would commence. Music would be played while the members engaged in stoned conversations or monologues. They would nod out in corners or experience in trancelike states overwhelming hallucinations.

For nearly three years the club's activities remained a secret until Gautier printed a dazzling description of the whole scene in France's most celebrated literary and cultural journal, the *Revue des Deux Mondes* (February 1, 1846). The article applied an extravagant style to an extravagant experience. Modern readers have treated it with skepticism or assumed it was merely the product of the Romantic imagination. Moreau, the best judge of such matters, regarded Gautier's descriptions of the hashish experience quite differently: allowing for the "stylistic exaggeration" of the author, he concluded, "the effects of hashish could not have been better described." Indeed, when one subjects this famous article to close literary analysis, what one discovers is that every one of Moreau's eight categories has been brilliantly realized in passages of hyperbolic but essentially authentic imagery. Though it would be naïve to read the account as a literal transcription of a single experience, the piece must be pronounced an excellent rendering of the archetypal hash trip.

Throughout the remainder of the nineteenth century, many other authors both in Europe and America contributed to the swelling literature on hashish. Late in life, Baudelaire made his final statement on the subject. Addicted to opium and alcohol like his hero, De Quincey, Baudelaire is not likely to have been a great hash eater. He had tasted the drug, however, in the most interesting circumstances in which it could have been consumed, and he had compiled his little store of hashish anecdotes; so when the occasion arose in the course of his journalistic career to contribute a paper on the topic, he must have felt himself well qualified for the task. The work that emerged, "The Hashish Poem," is a deeply jaundiced treatment of its theme. The general impression is that of an exhausted but dutiful lecturer eager to close up his notes and go home. Home, in this case, appears at the end of the piece, when Baudelaire sinks, almost gratefully, into a very somber meditation upon the evil of this paradisiacal drug. Sermonizing with the echo of the pulpit around his words, he excoriates the Romantic aspiration toward human divinity. Having denounced the drug as conducive to the ultimate sin of pride, he turns finally to destroy the myth of its Faustian powers of inspiring the imagination: "Let us grant," he reasons, "that hashish gives, or at least increases, genius, yet it cannot be forgotten that it is the nature of hashish to diminish the will; thus it gives with one hand what it takes away with the other; it gives imagination without the ability to use it." With these pessimistic words, the annals of the Assassins Club close.

The nineteenth-century literature on hashish comprises the most vivid and compelling accounts of drug usage in the history of the West. If one concentrates on the facts and lets the moral judgments slide into a separate category, every account harmonizes perfectly. Basically what this literature teaches us is that eating hashish will drive you crazy. Though the first part of the experience is blissful and fascinating, the latter stages are a nightmare. A characteristic turn, like a psychic modulation from major to minor, is found in every narrative. At this point paranoia takes hold. The hashish eater sinks into profound melancholy and guilt or is driven to frenzy. In the most extreme cases, the writers report that they would do anything to end the experience, including murdering someone or themselves. When one has read through all these accounts, a basic question comes to mind: how is it that the drug that is for orientals the key to paradise is for occidentals the gate to hell? The customary answer in our Freudian age is that the Westerners who took the drug were guilty, self-hating, self-destructive creatures who got, to put it bluntly, just what they deserved. The implication is that if one is a noble hippie soul or a really "good" and groovy person, eating hash can only be a ball.

Faced with such a doctrinaire answer, there is little that an earnest seeker after truth can do but add his personal testimony to the reams of corroborative evidence that have already been put into the record. As so much of the classic literature dates from a long time ago, there is at least the value of contemporaneity in any current account of the effects of eating hashish.

HASH BURNED

Several years ago, I was on assignment for a travel magazine in Miami. I had some friends down there, nice respectable middle-aged people, who had been given a lump of hashish. The woman was a good baker, so she decided to prepare some hashish brownies according to the classic recipe of Alice B. Toklas. She prepared a tin of brownies and gave one to her husband. He ate the pastry and an hour later fell sound asleep. Next day, he thought: "This stuff is too much for me. I'll give it to Albert. He writes about Lenny Bruce and drugs and all that stuff. Al will know what to do with it. Al can handle it." The fact is that I had never eaten any hash in my whole life. The Sunday after I got the brownies, I and three friends—Valery, Annette and Keith—were visiting an engineer and his wife in Coconut Grove, the most lushly tropical neighborhood in Miami. It was lunch time and Keith, a big, powerful athlete who loves to eat, began complaining he was hungry. Whispering in my ear, he hissed: "I knew, I just *knew* these people wouldn't serve any food." He was getting restless, so I said: "Keith, here's the key to the room. Why don't you go back to the hotel and get that box of hash brownies. We'll eat a few and then we won't care about lunch."

The brownies were delicious. But there was a lot of hash in them. You could taste it with every bite: a strange chemical flavoring that would have been repulsive if it hadn't been disguised by the chocolate. Meanwhile, we had all sat down at the table in the dining room and were starting to enjoy ourselves. As the mood brightened, I ate one brownie, then another and another. In all, I must have consumed at least three. Everybody else ate one or two, except Keith. A glutton, he put away *four*.

Nothing happened for quite a while except that the conversation grew more amusing. When I start feeling high, I want to run my mouth, tell my favorite stories, get everybody laughing. That afternoon I was really hitting my stride. I wrapped up one story with a hilarious punch line and sat back to enjoy the laugh. Hahahahaha! It was music to my ears, until it died. Then, for the first time, I noticed that something was odd. Everyone was silent. They were sitting there around the table, their faces wreathed with smiles, but with an odd, fixed look, like people in a painting. Suddenly, something clicked in my head. I flashed: "These people are whacked out of their minds! Gonged to the gills!" Then, I thought: "Jesus! You must be loaded too!" Now, when you're performing, you're not in your own head, not in touch with your feelings—you're out there on stage. Only now, when I stopped blithering and began to concentrate on my own sensations, did I feel the soft glow of the hash. "Yeahhh," I mused, "I am a little drugged. That's nice."

Just at that moment, I heard a loud persistent rapping from the garden. TONK! TONK! TONK! TONK! "What the hell is that?" I asked myself. Turning to survey the scene, I was stunned by the beauty of the picture that presented itself. The engineer had had the happy thought of making the back walls of his house huge two-story screens that offered an unlimited view of his garden. Now I was looking out onto this astounding VistaVision of tropical swamp land. Mangroves, palms, tropical vegetation and flowers, little canals and docks—a fascinating picture. I couldn't have picked a more perfect setting in which to enjoy the sensory enhancement of dope.

Running my eye around this lovely landscape, redolent more of Manila or Bangkok than of Miami, I finally located the source of that loud persistent hammering. It was a little bird pecking in a feeder. It couldn't have been making more than a slight tapping sound, but the hash had so exaggerated my sensations that it struck my ear like loud hammering. "That's funny!" I said to myself in a dopey, bemused fashion, delighted to have found the source and to be able to figure out that it was me and not the bird that was responsible for the loudness of the noise.

Without saying a word, I got up from the table and wandered out of doors to enjoy the spectacle of the garden at first hand. I always wander off when I'm high because I hate the interruption of my thoughts and fancies that occurs when I'm among people. No sooner had I sat down on the back steps to the house, than out came Valery, a beautiful, spiritual-looking girl molded from the same exquisite porcelain as Katherine Hepburn. She was looking very frail and haunted, like the heroine of a Gothic novel. She kneeled beside me and spoke in her pretty British accent. She said she was afraid. She felt strange. She wanted reassurance. I said, "Don't worry, it's nothing. Just a little hash." But at that moment, I caught the chill of her anxiety. Panic is notoriously contagious. Now that she had put the bug in my head, I began to think: "Perhaps we've taken too much. Now we're in for it. Who knows what's going to happen?"

As I moved my lips and uttered the reassuring phrases, I began to do a backward zoom from the lovely scene before me to that dark mental cell where we sit all hunched up when we're scared and obsessing like mad. The tensions in my mind made me restless. I got up and went back into the house. Now I was seeking reassurance. What I saw was not comforting. Everybody was still sitting around the table as if in a trance. I don't think they had spoken one word since I had left. How long had it been since I had left? I was getting disoriented. Normally, I have a marvelous sense of time. I can measure hours even when I'm asleep. A mental alarm clock. Now I couldn't tell whether I had been out in the garden a couple of minutes or half an hour. Keith was drowsing. Annette, his French girl friend, was staring dumbly. Our hosts had the same foolish smiles on their faces. They were nodding like signifying dolls, as if to say: "We know. . . . We know!" It was like one of those science fiction movies in which the spaceship sprays the city and everybody goes into a freeze.

Now I was getting nervous. I could see that this stuff hit you in waves. It reminded me of when I was a child at Atlantic City. My father was trying to teach me to swim. He would take me in the water and hold me horizontally in his arms. I was calm as long as my feet were on the shingle. The moment I felt my legs go up into the surf, I would start to scream and kick and fight to get back on the beach.

At this point, Valery came up to me again. Now she was looking extremely upset. I decided that the best tactic would be distraction. Engage her in serious conversation so she wouldn't notice how strange she felt. Talking is my natural tranquilizer. Even in my moments of greatest fear, talking to someone about anything always acts to calm me. As it happened, Valery and I had known each other for years. We had shared many experiences. We began to speak very seriously of our relationship. The conversation was deep and frank. She told me things that I had never imagined. Suddenly, in the midst of this revealing discourse, she toppled over and fell at my feet. I stared at her recumbent body for a moment and thought: "Damn! Just as I was making my point!" Without a moment's hesitation, without the slightest effort to aid her, I turned away and followed the train of my thoughts out into the street.

At that moment, I began to have the first intimations of the horrible delusion that would gradually gain upon me until it practically drove me out of my mind. My throat and mouth were very dry. I wanted to swallow, but I couldn't swallow. I felt a spasm in my throat. Slowly, I became convinced that if I tried to swallow, I would *strangle*. The saliva would catch in my windpipe, I would gag, I wouldn't be able to breathe! The more I was obsessed about it, the more I began to panic. The more I began to panic, the more I began to think: "I'm trapped! I'm caught! What can I do to escape?" I kept testing my mouth. "Can I swallow now? Can I take just a little swallow?" "No!" The answer was "No! if you swallow, you asphyxiate!"

So I'm standing out in a nice quiet suburban street confronting death. My mouth is parched. I would give anything for a sip of water. "That would be *instant death!*" the minatory voice in my mind booms. "The first swig would be like a knife in your esophagus. You would gasp and blanch. You would fall on the floor. You would asphyxiate and *nobody would help you!* These people are all *helpless!*"

Now I'm practically at my wit's end. I'm the character in the horror story with the walls closing on him. I decide to make one last effort to control my mind. "I'll go out into the street and walk—not walk but *march!* I'll raise and lower my feet like a soldier on parade. One, *two*, one, *two*. With military discipline I'll conquer this thing. Walk it off the way you walk off drunkenness." But it doesn't work. The heat of the sun dries me out even more and the poundings of my heart send another rhythm racing through my body that contradicts alarmingly the steady tramp of the brave little soldier.

I turn back into the house one last time. Keith is now completely comatose. He's lobbed out in a chair like a giant cat sound asleep. Only it doesn't look like restful sleep. His neck is awry and his tongue is lolling out of his mouth. Annette is curled up in the fetal position on the sofa. For all I know, they may both be dead. Valery is now sleepwalking. Our hosts are wandering around in a wimpy way uttering inanities. I'm so distraught that I can't bear to talk to them.

Then a phrase suddenly pops up in my mind. "THE SWALLOWING REFLEX." "That's it!" I say to myself. "I've lost my swallowing reflex!" Suddenly, I'm a white-coated clinician. I'm receiving myself as a patient at the emergency room. I've got a clipboard in my hand. I'm making notations. "Patient has lost swallowing reflex—presents symptoms of acute disorientation—left lobar grunge inoperative—Pabrunski Syndrome—et cetera." The moment I visualize this desperate scene, I suddenly realize what I must do. I must get medical aid. At once!

I collar our host and tell him, affecting to be calmer than I am, "Look, man, this stuff is terribly strong. I myself am out . . . how are you feeling?" "Well," he says, "I just ate one and I'm feeling pretty good." "Oh yeah," I counter, "well, I ate three and Keith here ate *four*. We're really in trouble, and I think it's time we did something about this situation." "Like what?" he says, looking at me in astonishment. "Like getting some medical help," I reply sternly. "Well, it's Sunday," he *fumffers*—but I was way ahead of him on that track. "We could go to a hospital," I snap. "A hospital!" he exclaims breathlessly, as if I had said, "a charnel house." "Why not?" I persist, getting a really hard edge on my voice. "Well, how would we get there?" he puzzles. "I wouldn't dare to drive! Can you drive?" "Me, *drive?*" I scream. "Are you crazy?" "Please," he begs, "I don't want any scenes around here. Everybody knows me. This could hurt me." "Do you mean to say that you would imperil the lives of four innocent people just because you're afraid of what the neighbors would say? Do you want to have the responsibility for four lives on your hands?"

Finally he cracks and backs down and goes off into the kitchen with his tail between his legs. I never dreamed that when he got into that kitchen he would pick up the phone and dial the *emergency number!*

Five minutes later as I'm sitting out on the front steps of the house brooding over my swallowing reflex, I hear a siren screaming up this quiet, genteel, residential street. The siren gets louder and louder until it comes swinging into the driveway in the form of a white fire department emergency vehicle. It screeches to a halt and three firemen come running out like they're going to put out a fire. They're toting oxygen tanks and medical gear. One big, curly, klutzy fireman comes running up to me and grabs my pulse with one hand while he gapes at the watch on his other hand. I'm so spaced that I sit there like he was shining my shoes. Then he pulls out a sphygmomanometer and whips it around my arm. Pump, pump, pump. A stethoscope in the ears, and a *psssssst!* He turns around and shouts, "Hey, chief! Come over here. This one's took real bad!" When the chief comes over, the medic riddles off the data: "Pulse, 140; blood pressure, 210; marked tremor; blah, blah, blah."

The chief stares down at me and says, "What did you people eat?" Then, for the first time, it hits me that I've got my ass in a jam. Here we are out of our nuts on hashish, and the law is staring us in the face. If I were a long-haired kid, I would have been a goner. It's marvelous, though, how the middle-class middle-aged can fake their way out of a bust.

"I don't know, chief . . . we ate something . . . some cookies that a guy gave me at the hotel . . . he was, umm, a musician." "Well, who is he? Is there any way we can find him?" "I don't know . . . he prob'ly left . . . he gave me those cookies . . . I thought they were just brownies. Now I realize they must have had drugs in them. He was a *rock musician.*"

The firemen run around the house and grab the remaining brownies. They put them in a plastic bag as if they were radioactive. Then they get on the phone and call two ambulances. More sirens scream down Honeysuckle Lane. The neighbors are all over the place. The guy who owns the house is going crazy. As we learned later, he's a consulting engineer for Dade County.

I'm put in the first ambulance with Annette. A medical attendant rides in the back with us. As the ambulance starts racing toward Jackson Memorial Hospital in Miami, which has a special drug ward, I turn to the attendant, practically with tears in my eyes, and tell him that I've lost my swallowing reflex, that I can barely breathe, that I'm terrified that if I try to swallow, my tongue will stick in my throat and I'll strangle. "What shall I do till we get to the hospital?" I beg him, reaching out instinctively to hold his hand. He struggles to come up with the answer. Finally, he hits it. "If you're so frightened of swallowing your tongue," he says, "maybe you should hold it with your hand." "Right!" I exclaim. Without a moment's hesitation, I reach up and take hold of the tip of my tongue with my left hand while I continue clasping his hand with my right. In this bizarre fashion, Professor Albert Goldman, A.M., Chicago; Ph.D., Columbia; Phi Beta Kappa; *Who's Who in the East*—the whole schmeer— rides to a drug clinic in an ambulance, tongue in hand.

The atmosphere of a drug clinic is not designed to soothe the mind. People are screaming with hallucinations, ODs are nodding out in chairs, people are throwing up with loud, retching sounds. No sooner do we appear then a gaggle of bright, young Jewish doctors pounce on us. "All right," says the one with the clipboard (I wasn't wrong about that part), "what's wrong with these people?"

"I can't swallow . . . I've lost my swallowing reflex," I blurt out, brushing off the poor ambulance attendant who held my hand. "What are you talking about?" says the doctor, looking at me in astonishment, not recognizing at first that I'm clinically insane. "Doctor, I ate three hash brownies and now I can't swallow. You've got to give me something to restore my swallowing reflex." I'm relieved to be telling my story to somebody I trust. Seeing him staring at me without reacting, I throw my sinker: the other symptom that has been gaining on me for the past hour. "Another thing, doctor, I keep reaching up to take off my hat —and I'm not wearing a hat!" He smiles and says: "Well, that's hash. It sort of produces a tightening around the head. That's why you keep reaching up for your hat."

Next, he decides to test us and see how far gone we are. He goes over to Keith, lobbed out in his wheelchair, and says,

"Hello, what's your name?" Blurred answer. "All right, Mr. Kean, I want you to count backwards from fifty by sevens. Could you do that for me, please?" Mumbles. "Just start now—fifty? Then, the next number would be . . . what?" Pause. "Umm, forty—forty—forty-three!" "Good. Right! Now the next number counting backwards from forty-three by sevens would be . . . what?" "Thirty—thirty—" Silence.

Finally, the doctor comes over to us and offers his solution. "Look, there's two things you people can do. We can give you an emetic and you can throw this stuff up. . . ." Before he gets the word "emetic" out of his mouth, I'm protesting. "Throw up! That's the worst thing I could do! I can't swallow and you want me to throw up! I'll suffocate, strangle on my own vomit! You won't catch me throwing up!" "O.K., O.K.," he soothes, "you don't have to do it. The other thing is, you can just sit here in this little chair and be quiet and it will pass over."

I couldn't believe my ears! Here I come into this clinic presenting the rare symptoms of classical Mideastern hashish intoxication, like you read about in books—if you can *read*, that is—and this asshole is telling me to be quiet and sit in a little chair. "Look, doctor," I try one last time. "I can't swallow, I can't breathe!" "You're swallowing and breathing as you talk to me," he chants like a little girl going "ta-ta-ta!" "You've had a dose of hash that has probably peaked already. If you don't make a fuss and get yourself all agitated, it will pass over. So, please, stop worrying and just be quiet."

With that, he turns on his heel and walks away. I'm feeling utterly exhausted and haven't the energy to dispute the issue. A quarter of an hour later, the chief of the clinic breezes by. He calls the young doc over, asks him what gives with the odd-looking crew in the corner. I hear the young doc tell the older doc: "That one [meaning me] was very paranoid when he arrived; that one . . ." blah, blah, blah. So there I was, sitting in a clinic full of sick junkies on a Sunday night in Miami, listening to some little twerp of an M.D. describe me as "paranoid"—and all because I ate one or two hash brownies too many. Goddamn Alice B. Toklas!

3 Marijuana in the New World

Marijuana, as opposed to hashish, commenced its Western history not in Europe but in the New World. Instead of entering the main portal of Western civilization, the weed slipped through the carelessly guarded back door of Europe's colonies in South America. It was in eighteenth-century Brazil that the practice of smoking dope first became popular. There can be no question that the drug was introduced into the Americas through the slave trade. All the Brazilian names for marijuana—*maconha, macumba, diamba, liamba, pungo* et cetera—are African words from the various languages and dialects spoken by the original slaves. Most likely, the slaves brought the seeds of the marijuana plants with them on the slave ships, as they brought the seeds of certain other African plants, such as the sesame. Once a considerable number of slaves became freedmen, they established a trade across the South Atlantic with their brethren in Africa, which brought them many commodities and implements which they required for their special social and religious practices. In this connection, it is interesting to note that in Bahia, the most African of the Brazilian provinces, the word for marijuana, *macumba*, is also the name of the voodoo religious cult. Just as the Bantus (highly prized by the Portuguese slave masters) smoked great pipes of marijuana as the principal sacrament of their religion, so these Baienese Negroes smoked marijuana as a sacred intoxicant and burned it as incense during the rites of the cult.

In view of Brazil's primacy as the first marijuana culture of the West, it strikes one as being both natural and appropriate that this country should still produce the most potent and valuable dope grown in the Western hemisphere. Brazilian Black, the name by which this drug is known in the United States, is actually a mistranslation of *Cabeça de Negro* or "Nigger Head," the allusion being not to the color of the dried plant but to its characteristic shock-headed appearance on the stalk.

Perhaps the most significant feature of marijuana's debut in the West is the way the new euphoriant was greeted by the local authorities. Though the Portuguese were generally far more tolerant—or lax—toward African culture than were their Anglo-Saxon counterparts in North America, the officials of the provinces affected were moved to publicly condemn and ban by law the practice of marijuana smoking. As early as 1823—when no one in Europe, save for a few travelers and scientists, had so much as heard of hemp intoxication—the chamber of Rio de Janeiro entered laws on its statute books stipulating fines for dealing in *maconha* and jail sentences of three days for any slave caught smoking. Compared with the penalties that were imposed until recently in America, not on slaves, but on the sons and daughters of the "best" families, these provisions of the slave code seem mild. Yet it is prophetic of the whole future course of marijuana in the West that on its very first appearance the new drug should have been met with hostility and outlawed.

Marijuana's popularity in Mexico has already been noted. Just prior to World War I, marijuana appeared on the Texas border, where it was called *Rosa Maria*. The demand for it in the U.S. was satisfied by bulk imports, which were made up into one-ounce packets that were sold over the counter in drugstores. One druggist in Floresville, Texas, established a mail order business with customers all over Texas, Arizona, New Mexico, Kansas and Colorado.

Meantime, New Orleans was becoming the first great American entre-pot. In those years, the Crescent City was a pungent melting pot where West Indian and South American sailors brought their coca and *ganja*, where Mexicans who had just slipped over the border arrived with their "grefa" and "muta" and where the black and creole jazz men blew their horns and sticks of "tea" as they entertained the local population with street parades, saloon serenades, sporting house recitals, funeral dirges and weekend barbecues and picnics. Gradually, the history of smoke wreathed around the history of jazz until the two highs went forth together to conquer the Western World. The conquest might have taken longer if American society had not been convulsed at this moment by the outbreak of the Great War. In 1917, the U.S. Navy decided to keep our boys in blue lily-white by shutting down Storyville, New Orleans' legendary red-light district. The most important effect of this cleanup was to drive jazz and all its joyous ways up the Mississippi to speakeasy Chicago, thus planting marijuana right in the heartland of America.

The great symbol of the jazz and marijuana culture of that day was Louis Armstrong, the king of both New Orleans and Chicago jazz. Armstrong was a pot head till the day he died. The last great interview with him in *Harper's* was procured by Larry King by offering the septuagenarian unlimited access to some very fine gauge. John Hammond, the well-known record producer, recalls Armstrong as a fellow passenger aboard the S.S. *Homeric* in 1933:

In those days Louis swore by two cures for all that ailed him. One was marijuana, the other Abilene Water, which was a violent purgative. . . . He considered alcohol evil and marijuana virtuous, and he smoked it constantly, to my horror. It never led him to try anything stronger, however, but in my opinion it did hurt him, for it enabled him to become the exhibitionist he became to the detriment of his genius. "It makes you feel good, man. It relaxes you, makes you forget all the bad things that happen to a Negro. It makes you feel wanted, and when you're with another tea smoker it makes you feel a special sense of kinship."

Armstrong, according to Hammond, was "introduced to marijuana by the white clarinetist Mezz Mezzrow." The first part of this statement is dubious: Armstrong and Mezzrow did not get tight until 1929, by which time the famous trumpet player had been on the jazz scene for so many years that it is unthinkable that he was still ignorant of the weed. The second part of the statement—the identification of Mezzrow as a "white clarinetist" —is hilarious; for referring to the Mighty Mezz in this fashion is equivalent to introducing Timothy Leary to a subsequent generation as a "psychology professor."

Milton Mezzrow was, is and shall always be the single most

important figure in the history of marijuana in America. Like Leary, the Mezz turned on a new generation to a new drug. Unlike Leary—who went from being a respected intellectual to being a quack, a mountebank, a fink and the author of some of the most dreadful hippie prose of the "Love Generation"—Mezzrow progressed from being a street tough and speakeasy jazz tootler to being: 1) the first white Negro, 2) the Johnny Appleseed of weed, 3) the author of a great American autobiography, *Really the Blues,* the finest eyewitness account of American counter-culture ever published. The book is, likewise, the masterpiece of the counter-culture's most characteristic literary medium: the slang-laced, jazz-enrhythmed, long-breathed and rhapsodic street rap and rave-up. When Henry Miller finished reading *Really the Blues,* he exclaimed: "I really ought to put up a monument to this day, for . . . [this] perfectly marvelous book conveys a powerful, vital message of unadulterated joy. At whatever page I open the book, it makes me feel I have just struck a new seam in a gold mine."

The key to everything the Mezz accomplished in life and art lies in the fact that he was a classic cultural transvestite: a person who harbors a profound conviction that he was born in the wrong time or the wrong place or—as with the Mezz—in the wrong *race.* Alienated from the jittery world of the Twenties and dissatisfied with even the finest white jazz musicians of that day, including his friend, the legendary Bix Biederbecke, the Mezz left his native Chicago and embarked, while still in his twenties, on a spiritual pilgrimage. Never did he rest until he was firmly ensconced in Harlem, where he became the strong right arm of Louis Armstrong.

During his early years in Harlem, the Mezz got hooked on opium. For four years he did nothing, literally, but lie inside a mattress-lined coalbin in the basement of a tenement smoking hop and talking trash with a couple of congenial colored janitors. Not reborn but revitalized, he returned eventually to his accustomed activities as a jazz musician, reefer peddler and record producer. In the mid-Forties, he encountered an intellectual journalist named Bernard Wolfe, who delivered the veteran jazz hero of his life story, which was published in the year 1946.

It is *Really the Blues*—and this book alone—that enables us to understand the rise and spread of marijuana in America. For marijuana did not come to New York any differently than hashish came to Paris in the 1840s. One lone man was responsible for the introduction of the weed into the greatest city of modern times, as one man alone was responsible for bringing hashish to the cultural capital of nineteenth-century Europe. In each case the drug was injected into the very heart and brain of a culture by being offered to some of its most creative spirits. The great difference is that in the case of Dr. Moreau and the *Club des Hashischins*, the first experimenters were literary intellectuals who recorded instinctively their reactions and reflections, leaving us a relatively full account of what happened. In the case of the Mezz turning on Harlem, the situation was much different. Though there were many writers, both black and white, who were trying to capture the Harlem of this period, not one of these men or women ever produced anything that could compare with *Really the Blues* either for documentary or literary quality because none of them participated in the street life of their community, which was the soil out of which this culture sprang.

The Mezz first smoked dope in the men's room of a roadhouse at Indiana Harbor in the year 1924. He was handed a cigarette wrapped in brown wheat-straw paper by a jockey who told him: "You got to hold that muggle so it barely touches your lips, see, then draw in the air around it. Say *tfff, tfff*, only breathe in when you say it. Then don't blow it out right away, you got to give that stuff a chance." The Mezz gave it a good chance: he smoked it down to the butt. Then he returned to the bandstand.

The first thing I noticed was that I began to hear my saxophone as though it was inside my head, but I couldn't hear much of the band in back of me, although I knew they were there. All the other instruments sounded like they were way off in the distance; I got the same sensation you'd get if you stuffed your ears with cotton and talked out loud. Then I began to feel the vibrations of the reed much more pronounced against my lip, and my head buzzed like a loudspeaker. I found I was slurring much better and putting just the right feeling into my phrases—I was really coming on. All the notes came easing out of my horn like they'd already been made up, greased and stuffed into the bell, so all I had to do was blow a little and send them on their way, one right after the other, never missing, never behind time, all without an ounce of effort. The phrases seemed to have more continuity to them and I was sticking to the theme without ever going tangent. I felt I could go on playing for years without running out of ideas and energy. There wasn't any struggle; it was all made to order and suddenly there wasn't a sour note or discord in the world that could bother me. I began to feel very happy and sure of myself. With my loaded horn I could take all the fist-swinging, evil things in the world and bring them together in perfect harmony, spreading peace and joy and relaxation to all the keyed-up and punchy people everywhere.

Having discovered that blowing pot helps a man blow jazz, the Mezz turned his talents for hustling to procuring a steady supply of "golden leaf" from some of the 30,000 Mexicans resident in Chicago.

What Mezz discovered about the basic effects of weed and the marijuana sensibility reads as freshly today as when it was dictated thirty years ago:

It's a funny thing about marihuana—when you first begin smoking it you see things in a wonderful, soothing, easygoing new light. All of a sudden the world is stripped of its dirty gray shrouds and becomes one big bellyful of giggles, a special laugh, bathed in brilliant, sparkling colors that hit you like a heatwave. Nothing leaves you cold any more; there's a humorous tickle and great meaning in the least little thing, the twitch of somebody's little finger or the click of a beer glass. All your pores open like funnels, your nerve ends stretch their mouths wide, hungry and thirsty for new sights and sounds and sensations; and every sensation, when it comes, is the most exciting one you've ever had. You can't get enough of anything—you want to gobble up the whole goddamned universe just for an appetizer.

Finding himself in Harlem in the year after the Great Crash with nothing in his pockets but some Prince Albert cans or Diamond matchboxes filled with "grefa" from his Mexican connection in Chicago ("little Pasquale used to sell his muggles six for a dollar but he gave us a cut-rate price, a tobacco tin full-up with "muta" for two dollars, or a Diamond matchbox full for four or five"), the Mezz fell into the practice of mixing business with pleasure by pushing a little gauge. Bear in mind that this was the legendary Harlem of Ellington and Armstrong, of Bojangles Robinson and the Hoofer's Club, of Fats Waller and James P. Johnson, of the first black reviews, like *Shufflin' Along* (by Eubie Blake) and *Hot Chocolates*. This was the Harlem that was a mecca for serious white artists, like George Gershwin, or for frivolous slumming parties of nitwit socialites, like those who ran up every night for the midnight jungle show at the Cotton Club (a mob-operated joint where Negroes were not admitted). Anyone who got into Harlem's head, who provided it with a new high, a new source of energy, insight or inspiration, was performing an act of almost unimaginable cultural, intellectual and artistic impregnation. "Overnight," Mezz writes, "I was the most popular man in Harlem. On the Corner I was to become known as the Reefer King, the Link between the Races, the Philosopher, the Mezz, Poppa Mezz, Mother Mezz, Pop's Boy, the White Mayor of Harlem, the Man about Town, the Man that Hipped the World, the Man that Made History, the Man with the Righteous Bush, He who Diggeth the Digger, Father Neptune."

The Mezz took his stand at the very heart of Harlem, dispensing his favors on a classic bit of turf known locally as the Stroll: the block between 131st and 132nd streets on Seventh Avenue, which contained an extraordinary concentration of theaters, cabarets, rehearsal halls, entertainers' hangouts, bars, rib joints and a famous alley that was the inner sanctum of Harlem's jazz life. Here, in front of the marquee to a famous nightclub called Connie's Inn, stood the "Tree of Hope" (later just a stump and today a bit of wood that is brought ritualistically onto the stage of the Apollo Theater on amateur night). The custom was to slap or hug or kiss the tree while you wished for success. Like a tribal witch doctor at the foot of a sacred tree, the Mezz received his people.

FIRST CAT: Hey there, Poppa Mezz, is you anywhere?
ME: Man, I'm down with it, stickin' like a honky [loaded like a millworker on payday].
FIRST CAT: Lay a trey on me, old man.
ME: Got to do it, slot ["slotmouth," a humorous name for any black, suggested by the recently introduced coin vending machines, whose mouths are always open waiting to be fed]. (*pointing to a man standing in front of Big John's ginmill*) Gun the snatcher [dig the plainclothesman] on your left raise—the head mixer [bartender] laid a bundle his ways, he's posin' back like crime sure pays.
FIRST CAT: Father grab him! [God kill him!] I ain't payin' him no rabbit [no more attention than you'd give a rabbit jumping over a fence]. Jim, this jive you've got is a gasser, I'm goin' up to my dommy [domicile] and dig that new mess Pops [Louis Armstrong] laid down for Okeh [Records]. I hear he riffed back on *Zackly* [a hit of the day: "Exactly Like You"]. Pick you up at The Track [Savoy Ballroom,

headquarters for Lindy Hoppers] when the kitchen mechanics romp [on Thursday, the maids' night off].

SECOND CAT: Hey Mezzie, lay some of that hard-cuttin' mess on me. I'm short a deuce of blips [pair of nickels = a dime] but I'll straighten you later.

ME: Righteous, gizz, you're a poor boy but a good boy—now don't come up crummy. [Complicated pun here on gizzard, which is stuffed with bread crumbs. The meaning is "don't give me any stuff, i.e., bullshit, when it's time to pay."]

SECOND CAT: Never crummy, chummy. I'm gonna lay a drape [a suit of clothes] under the trey of knockers [three pawnshop balls] for Tenth Street [ten dollars] and I'll be on the scene wearin' the green.

THIRD CAT (*coming up with his chick*): Baby, this is that powerful man with that good grass that'll make you trip through the highways and byways like a Maltese kitten. Mezz, this is my new dinner and she's a solid viper.

GIRL: All the chicks is always talkin' 'bout you and Pops. Sure it ain't somethin' freakish [faggy] goin' down 'tween you two? You sure got the ups on us pigeons, we been on a frantic kick tryin' to divide who's who [who plays which role]. But everybody love Pops and we know just how your bloodstream's runnin'.

FOURTH CAT (*coming up with a stranger*): Mezz, this here is Sonny Thompson, he one of the regular cats on the Avenue and can lay some iron [tap dance] too. Sonny's hip from way back and solid can blow some gauge, so lay an ace on us and let us get gay. He and Pops been knowin' each other for years.

ME: Solid man, any stud that's all right with Pops must really be in there. Here, pick up Sonny, the climb's [the "high's"] on me.

SONNY (*to his friend*): Man, you know one thing? This cat should of been born a J.B. [jet black], he collars all jive and comes on like a spaginzy [black]. (*turning to me*) Boy, is you sure it ain't some of us in your family way down the line? Boy, you're too much, stay with it, you got to git it.

FIFTH CAT: Hey Poppa Mezz! Stickin'? ["Holding?"]

ME: Like the chinaberry [elderberry] trees in Aunt Hagar's [any old black mammy's] backyard.

FIFTH CAT: Lay an ace on me so's I can elevate myself and I'll pick you up on the late watch.

SIXTH CAT (*seeing me hand the reefers to Cat Number Five*): Ow, I know I'm gonna get straight now, I know you gonna put me on [turn me on].

FIFTH CAT: Back up, boy, forty-five feet. Always lookin' for a freebie.

Jim, why don't you let up sometime? Hawk's [winter's] out here with his axe [icy wind] and me with this lead sheet on [the lead sheet has only the melody line and so can symbolize a skinny top-coat], tryin' to scuffle up those two's and fews [hookers were paid two dollars a trick but when business was bad they went for fewer than two] for uncle [the pawnbroker] so's I can bail out my full orchestration [winter overcoat].

SIXTH CAT: Aw, come on and bust your vest [be big about it], what you goin' to make out of sportin' life? [Don't spoil our fun.] You know you took the last chorus with me. [You know I treated you the last time.]

FIFTH CAT: Look's like he got me, Mezz, but this cat wouldn't feed grass to a horse in a concrete pasture. He's so tight he wouldn't buy a pair of shorts for a flea. Man, just look at him, dig that vine all off-time [that old-fashioned suit] and his strollers look like he's ready to jump [his pants are so baggy that he looks like he's bending his knees to jump]. This cat's playin' ketch-up [even the score] and I got to tighten his wig. Hold it down, Jim [speaking now to Mezz], and I'll come up with a line two like I said. [The price is one dollar but numbers were often doubled—"line two"—to fool outsiders.] Come on, Jack, let's final to my main stash [his main home, i.e., where he lives with his *main* woman].

These cats had the fastest metaphors in town. To find anything like this lingo, you'd have to page back to the time of Shakespeare, when another illiterate population, the "groundlings," exhibited a similar relish for playing with words. These Harlem vipers had a culture so potent, so pure, so original and yet so perfectly in tune with the times that eventually it called the tune for most of American society, white or black, down to the end of World War II and the petering out of the real Jazz Age (as opposed to the corny, literary "Jazz Age" of Scott Fitzgerald and the flappers).

"Marihuana took Harlem by storm," recollects the Mezz, going on to explain that "new words came into being to meet the situation. *The mezz* and *the mighty mezz*, referring to me and to the tea both; *mezzroll*, to describe the kind of fat, well-packed and clean cigarette that I used to roll (this word got corrupted to meserole and it's still used to mean a certain size and shape of reefer, which is different from the so-called panatella); the *hard-cuttin' mezz* and the *righteous bush*. Some of these phrases really found a permanent place in Harlemese, and even crept out to color American slang in general. . . . In Cab Calloway's *Hipster's Dictionary,* mezz is defined as 'anything supreme, genuine'; and in Dan Burley's *Original Handbook of Harlem Jive* the same word is defined as meaning 'tops, sincere'!"

Eventually, the Mezz was approached by the local boys, by the Mob and even by legitimate businessmen from downtown to commercialize his dealings, even to establish a nation-wide trade in marijuana. He turned a deaf ear to all these proposals, explaining that he just wanted to spread the weed around among his friends and make enough money to survive. Thus, he established himself in the history of the Dope Game as the first Good-Guy Dope Dealer, the prototype of thousands of college kids two generations later who would draw the distinction between "pushing"—getting someone to buy something they didn't want or need—and "dealing"—providing a useful service for a legitimate profit.

The marijuana trade was very primitive in this period. The Mezz, for example, sold his dope by the joint, rolling it himself in a distinctive manner, which for some reason he fails to describe in his book. His distinctive trademark was a hexagonal tuck at each end of the reefer to keep the loosely packed weed from trickling out. Made with the end of a big square kitchen match, this tuck was folded in such a way that when the smoker was ready to light up, all he had to do was run his thumbnail down the length of the joint and the drag end would pop open. Stories are told of how the hip would look at such a joint and exclaim, "Oh, you've got the mezz!" Such a little world was marijuana in the Thirties.

Buying tailor-made joints from local dealers became such a popular method of scoring that by the end of the decade, when an undercover survey was made for the *La Guardia Report,* there were 500 dealers in Harlem alone. Joints were sold, in the words of a pop song, "three for a half, four for a dollar." The cheapest dope was called "sass-frass" and was probably American-grown hemp with little potency. The more expensive grade was the "panatella," to which Mezz refers; this was, most likely, Mexican weed. The highest quality available was called "gungeon" and sold for a dollar a joint. Dealers insisted this stuff came "right off the boat from Africa"; judging from the name, it was probably Jamaican *ganja.*

Another method of scoring was to buy an ounce for six to

eight dollars. In the days when a working man made sixteen dollars a week, an ounce was a big buy, which is why most people bought dope by the joint. One old head interviewed for this book told me that he and two other young men would buy their ounce in Harlem, then rent a cheap hotel room for a dollar and spend part of Saturday night cleaning, rolling and tucking. If you didn't want to roll, you could buy a package of Crescents: gold-tipped cigarette casings. All the smoker had to do was fill them up.

Buying a joint for private consumption would do very well in some circumstances, but the social proclivities of the ghetto have been ever such that the prospect of private pleasure pales always before the delight of "hanging out." As smoking dope in bars was never a practice tolerated by saloonkeepers, an institution sprang up at this time that strikes us moderns as being both odd and quaint. This was the smoking lounge or "tea pad." According to the *La Guardia Report* (published in 1944 but reflecting conditions at the end of the Thirties, just after marijuana was declared illegal), there were in Harlem approximately 500 tea pads. Second-story establishments above stores or parlors in tenement apartments, these smoking bars had, according to the *Report*, a conventionalized type of decor:

The tea pad has comfortable furniture, a radio, Victrola, or, as in most instances, a rented nickelodeon [juke box]. The lighting is more or less uniformly dim, with blue predominating. An incense is considered part of the furnishings. The walls are frequently decorated with pictures of nude subjects suggestive of perverted sexual practices. . . . The marihuana smoker derives greater satisfaction if he is smoking in the presence of others. His attitude in the tea pad is that of a relaxed individual, free from the anxieties and cares of the realities of life. The tea pad takes on the atmosphere of a very congenial social club. The smoker readily engages in conversation with strangers, discussing freely his pleasant reactions to the drug and philosophizing on subjects pertaining to life in a manner which, at times, appears to be out of keeping with his intellectual level. A constant observation was the extreme willingness to share and puff on each other's cigarettes. A boisterous, rowdy atmosphere did not prevail and on the rare occasions when there appeared signs indicative of a belligerent attitude on the part of a smoker, he was ejected or forced to become more tolerant and quiescent. One of the most interesting setups was a series of pup tents arranged on a roof-top in Harlem. Those present proceeded to smoke their cigarettes in the tents. When the desired effect of the drug had been obtained, they all emerged into the open and engaged in a discussion of their admiration of the stars and the beauties of nature.

Though nothing is said in this description about the music that played on the juke boxes of the tea pads, there were enough dope records in the old catalogue to fill a whole machine.

Contrary to the hippie mythology of the Sixties, songs about dope were not an invention of the Rock Age. If anything, they were less characteristic of that age than they were of the early Thirties. To get an idea of how common such songs were once, one has only to run his eye over the sales brochures of a current specialty label called Stash Records. In three years this company has marketed no less than six albums of old party records, each averaging sixteen songs, almost all of them about dope. This is an astonishing number, especially in view of the depressed condition of the recording industry in the early Thirties, the victim not only of hard times but of the recently introduced radio, which offered endless amounts of music free. Nor is it any less surprising to look at the personnel on these cuts and discover instead of the antici-pated nonentities many of the most famous singers and musicians of the day, commencing with Ella Fitzgerald, Fats Waller and Jack Teagarden and including New Orleans veterans like Sidney Bechet, folk music heroes like Leadbelly, New York sophisticates like Larry Adler, country primitives like the Memphis Jug Band and the famous orchestras of Cab Calloway, Benny Goodman, Chick Webb, Jimmie Lunceford and Gene Krupa. Most of these old reefer songs were written, evidently, for the race record mar-ket or for the black-and-tan reviews staged at Harlem night spots. Though the songs weren't broadcast as widely as were the deeply encoded messages of the Doors or the Jefferson Airplane in later times, reefer songs were performed frequently on the air. Fam-ous musicians, like Louis Armstrong, delighted in those days, just as they do today, in slipping references to drugs past the censors and out into the finely tuned ears of the heads and hipsters.

Between the dope songs of the Thirties and the Sixties, there are, to be sure, some notable differences—though not of the sort one might anticipate. The older songs are far more explicit be-cause marijuana was not illegal when they were composed. In-stead of alluding to drug use obliquely, the old songs describe their theme head-on. You hear the singers making sucking sounds

and bursting into "laughing jags." You visualize the dopers waiting impatiently—"gaudy frails chewin' their nails"—for the appearance of the dealer. When the Man arrives, everybody turns
on and starts to Lindy. All the standard clinical symptoms are
noted, ranging from dryness of throat to "the munchies." The
psychological effects are no less exhaustively described by the
songs than they were by Dr. Moreau, though the phraseology is
certainly different. Getting "high," feeling "mellow," getting
"gay," even the extreme effects of torpor and delusion are
evoked: "If he trades you dimes for nickels and calls watermelons
pickles, then you know you're talkin' to the Reefer Man." The
song writers crack jokes: "Here's smoke in your eyes!" They make
puns: "When I get low, I get high!" They also struggle to one-up
the clichés in the style of jive-talking hipsters: for the trite expression, "get high," they offer the hipper phrase, "get tall" or
"climb." In these songs, the whole modern vocabulary of dope
smoking and dealing makes its public debut. Though some of the
words sound quaint, practically all of them are still in use, including phrases that most people would surmise to be of much more
recent origin. When it comes to dope lingo, we see now that the
Sixties were just a replay of the Thirties.

The most popular of the old reefer songs paid tribute, appro-
priately, to the Mezz. Written by the jazz fiddle player Stuff
Smith, this tune became the theme song of all the little jazz joints
along 52nd Street. Recorded several times by different musicians, the best performances are those by the song's author,
with vocals by Jonah Jones. Titled "You'se a Viper" (from the
biblical imprecation "You are a generation of vipers!") and set to a
fast-steppin', finger-poppin' jump tune, this old favorite runs:

> Dream about a reefer, five feet long,
> The mighty mezz, but not too strong.
> You get high, but not for long,
> 'Cause you'se a viper.
>
> Now I'm the king—of everything!
> You got to get high, to have that swing.
> Light a tea, let it be,
> 'Cause you'se a viper.
>
> Now your throat gets dry,
> You know you're high,

Everything is dandy.
Truck into the candy store,
Bust your conk on peppermint candy!

Then you know—your body's sent!
You don't give a durn if you don't pay rent.
Sky's high . . . *you* high!
'Cause you'se a viper.

"Viper" appears in many song titles of the period: "Viper's Moan," "Viper Mad" et cetera. The most important code word, however, is not "viper," "reefer," "tea," "gauge," or "weeds" [sic]—though all those terms were employed: the key word is "jive." This little monosyllable is so suggestive of the whole complex of attitudes that developed around marijuana in the Harlem of the Thirties that it deserves special scrutiny.

The first thing to grasp about a word like "jive"—or "number" in carny slang—is that it means anything its speaker wants it to mean. As semanticists say, the meaning is determined "contextually." Such blank words are very useful in underground cultures; they enable the speaker to communicate easily with those he wants to understand him, while keeping everyone else in the dark. Though manifold in meaning, the word "jive" is rooted in a single concept, *falseness*, that ramifies into "fake," "insincere," "playful" or "teasing." "He's jive" means "He's a phoney." "Don't jive me" means "Don't kid me." "Jive talk" is jazz slang, the teasing, taunting way the hipsters speak when they're "jiving" each other. Calling marijuana "jive," therefore, is a way of both concealing and revealing this illusion-producing drug.

The other great difference between the dope songs of the Thirties and the Sixties lies in the different moods and attitudes of the respective eras. Marijuana was embraced by Harlem as just another kick, another way of getting high, along with jazz, jitterbugging, fast-talking jive patter—the whole spillover of the euphoria of the Twenties. Nobody thought that writing a song about marijuana obliged him to develop some new "spacey" type of music. Nor did it cross anyone's mind that just because he was getting high on something that was a mystery to the squares, apocalypse was just around the corner. Portentousness—the nuclear-bombing run of a song like the Byrds' "Eight Miles High," one of the best dope songs of the Sixties—was totally alien to the dope culture of the Thirties. Sometimes, it's true, the older songs do exhibit a certain hot, swirling, dusky strain or a "let-me-take-you-down" seductiveness that conjures up Sportin' Life tempting Bess; but, for the most part, the tone of the old reefer songs was simply, "Let's light up and have a ball!"

Reefer songs do contrast forcibly with songs of the same period made about other drugs, like opium ("kickin' the gong around") or cocaine ("happy dust") or heroin ("junk"). Songs like "Jerry the Junker" or "Minnie the Moocher" are in the minor mode, full of sardonic humor, and they mince no words in describing the victims of heavy drugs. The songs reflect clearly, therefore, the street-wise experience of the people of Harlem, who drew a sharp line between tea, which was just a fun drug, and opium and heroin, which were deadly. Alcohol was treated pretty much as were the death drugs. *Really the Blues* contains the classic statement, by a musician friend of Mezzrow's, on the superiority of marijuana to liquor:

You just dig them lushhounds with their old antique jive, always comin' up loud and wrong, whippin' their old ladies. . . . Just look at the difference between you and them other cats, that come uptown juiced to the gills, crackin' out of line and passin' out in anybody's hallway. Don't nobody come up thataway when he picks up on some good grass . . . then for instance you take a lot of ofay liquor-heads, when they come up here and pass the jug around. Half of them will say they had enough 'cause some spade just took a drink out of it. . . . Now with vipers it's different. . . . Them Indians must have had some gauge in that pipe of peace that they passed around, at least they had the right idea, ha ha! Now, far as hurtin' anybody is concerned, you know and I know that we can wake up the next day and go on about our business, marihuana or mary-don't-wanna.

The Mezz's dedication to the weed made him one of the first martyrs to the federal ban on the drug, which was instituted in 1937. Characteristically, the Mezz was busted not for selling dope but for trying to give it away. In 1940, while entering the back door of a jazz club at the World's Fair (the club was called, ironically, the Gay New Orleans), Mezz was collared by a detective, frisked and found to be carrying a pocketful of joints—which he planned to lay on the band. He was indicted, convicted and sentenced to one to three years on Riker's Island. It wasn't the first bum rap he had taken, and he served his seventeen-month stretch in fairly congenial surroundings in a colored cell block and playing in the prison band. But his days of dealing were over.

When he got out of the can, he worked for a while as a record producer, putting together some now legendary dates with the surviving members of the original New Orleans school. Eventually, he left the United States for Europe. In 1972, at the mellow age of seventy-three, the Mighty Mezz died in Paris, always a haven for jazz musicians—and Negroes.

As the Thirties turned the corner into the Forties, the mad *Totentanz* of wartime America kicked off. Rosie the Riveter, bored shitless after eight hours on the midnight-to-eight swing shift, began to look around for some new way to get high. Though marijuana was now illegal, a neon-lit no-no, plenty of young people all over the country were turning on. They were encouraged to try dope by the example of their culture heroes: the jazz musicians. Though the uptight jazz press (comprising, needless to say, people who are not jazz musicians) has struggled valiantly for thirty years to deny the all-too-obvious link between jazz and dope (just as Jewish organizations struggled for years to overcome the idea that Jews were better off than anybody else—God forbid!), practically every jazz musician who ever breathed has sucked marijuana smoke into his lungs. The older jazz men smoked dope because they had always smoked it; the younger players smoked dope because it was the fashionable thing to do in a world where everything turned on being "hip" and because pot was supposed to make you play better.* (This became a hotly debated issue and even led some unimaginative psychologists to administer to stoned jazzmen the standard Seabrook Musical Aptitude Test—given, typically in those days, to grade-school Johnnies to determine whether they should receive trombone lessons. Naturally, the tests proved that the jazz musicians showed "reduced proficiency" when high, precisely the same conclusion they would have drawn if Toscanini got loaded, the point being that what constitutes a musician, especially a creative musician, and most especially an *improvising* musician, is an enormously

---

* In 1954–55, the sociologist Charles Winick interviewed 357 jazz musicians in New York. Sixty-nine percent were white; 31 percent black—a curious disproportion for an art that has always been dominated by black players. Eighty-two percent had smoked marijuana; 54 percent were "occasional" smokers; 23 percent smoked regularly. Seventy-two percent of the marijuana smokers were drinkers. Fifty-three percent of those interviewed had used heroin. Only 2 percent used both heroin and marijuana at the same time.

complex combination of factors that have never been so much as identified let alone codified into a constrictive format like a standard performance test.)

One of the many reasons why musicians objected to going out on band tours during the war years was the impossibility of scoring for dope at a senior prom in Des Moines. To overcome this objection, band managers made a regular practice of allowing the boys to stock up on drugs before they left the "Apple." When the band bus would leave the Broadway–52nd Street area to begin the tour, it would make a pit stop in Harlem so the players could score for "goo." Then, as the buses rolled along the great highways of the U.S.A., the air inside the vehicles would become as thick with smoke as the inside of a Scythian's tent. When the tours ended with the musicians alighting in midtown, no matter how late the hour, they would be met by the pushers, who kept tabs on the bands' schedules and always appeared in time to cut into the musicians' pay checks.

In those years, weed sold in New York for fifteen dollars an ounce: twice what it cost before it was outlawed. The preferred brand was called Red Cross; Charlie Parker honored it with a tune of that title. You could buy grass in the rough or clean-picked. There was no problem in scoring for as much as a pound. Old hipsters who have been hanging around Times Square for forty years look back on the "dynamite shit" of the old days with keen nostalgia. They never seem to realize that smoking dope for a lifetime raises your tolerance level so high that no grass in the world can still get you off in three tokes.

One of the best places to score for dope in those days was a jazz club. This fact inspired the old hipster gag about the guy who lives outside New York and can't find any way to score. When he calls a cynical bebopper in the Apple and complains that he can't connect, the musician tips him to the secret. "Cut out the ad for the jazz club from your local paper, man. Roll it up and light it. It'll get you out of your kug!"

Having made marijuana their secret badge of identity, it was inevitable that jazz musicians would become the special targets of the old Bureau of Narcotics. Harry J. Anslinger wanted to make examples of the big men, like Louis Armstrong, and even lock up whole bands. The only notorious bust, however, was that which bagged Gene Krupa out on the West Coast in 1948. To the average

American living anywhere but in New York, marijuana was an exotic drug used only by way-out hep cats and movie stars. If it hadn't been for an occasional sensationalist article in the Hearst press, nobody would have known the stuff existed.

In New York marijuana always enjoyed a special status. The Apple was the only city in the country where marijuana had penetrated deeply into the white middle-class neighborhoods: the Jewish and Italian districts of Manhattan, Brooklyn and the Bronx. When I arrived in Brooklyn in 1950—coming from the University of Chicago, where in three years I had never heard the word "marijuana"—I was astonished to discover that all the hip kids in the neighborhood were into dope. They called it "tea," "boo," "grass" and "pot," but the preferred word was "shit." That the word for heroin in the black ghetto had been appropriated by the sons and daughters of Jewish storekeepers and garment-center workers for the milder drug is suggestive of the passion with which these young men and women admired the black culture of jazz. This was the moment in modern urban history when thousands of kids all over the country had finally come to the point the Mezz had reached twenty years earlier when he moved into Harlem and became a "white nigger." Many of the young men in these Brooklyn neighborhoods were more or less talented jazz musicians. The girls were mad about Billie Holiday. Smoking tea was their way of identifying with the dark and tainted lives of their heroes. Calling dope "shit" was the next best thing to shooting the real shit, which few of them dared try.

Nineteen forty-six, the publication year of *Really the Blues*, is also the commencement year for the Beat movement. The Beats are, perhaps deservedly, a neglected passage in the history of American counter-culture; but they are important figures in the history of drugs in this country, for with the Beats marijuana comes out of the underground world of jazz and the urban ethnic ghettos and goes into the mainstream of American culture. Kerouac, Ginsberg, John Clellon Holmes, most of the Beat writers, were white, middle-class, college-educated young men who had a great longing for the ecstatic and transcendental experiences symbolized by jazz. They lived in a time of remarkable spiritual aridity and dreariness, a time when any sensitive person felt *beat*. Instinctively, they sought avenues of escape, including the classic romantic avenue of drugs. Grubby caricatures of Blake,

Baudelaire and De Quincey, the Beats found in a potent amalgam of the exotic, the mystic and the erotic the antidote for their dreary fate as postwar Bohemians and artists. All of them were characterized by a remarkable adhesion to the enthusiasms, dreams, spiritual gestures and even the physical appearance of adolescence. To the day he died, a middle-aged man ravaged by drink and despondency, Jack Kerouac resembled nothing so much as a disheveled and dissipated college boy. Yet, it was precisely this refusal to mature, to go along with the game plan of the middle-class American professional man or careerist, that made Kerouac (and Ginsberg and Corso) the real prototypes for the hippies of the following generation. In the mental and physical slovenliness of the Beats, in their rather pathetic devotion to the life of "kicks," was prefigured precisely the raunchy human sea that crested at Woodstock.

Beat literature contains numerous allusions to marijuana, but there is one passage in particular that singles itself out and rises like an apotheosis of the Beat Soul or, as Kerouac says, like a "pornographic hasheesh dream in heaven." The narrator along with his hero, Dean Moriarity, and another buddy, Stan, have driven down over the border of Mexico in search of whatever kicks they can run into. They end up in a typically dusty and sleepy Mexican town called Gregorio and tie in with some of the local youths who, as they'd hoped, are in possession of some of the local weed. Not one of the three *gringos* can speak a word of Spanish, but once the dope is broken out and the smoking begun, the problems of communication disappear. What ensues is a stoned binge that combines all the stimulants their Beat imaginations and combined fortunes can conjure: a foreign country, a mysterious language, booze by the buckets, screaming, pulsing mambo music, the sexual heat of a whorehouse and, above all, the sweet beguiling intoxication of marijuana.

The Beats were the first visible social fallout of the Atomic Age. Uptight Fifties America was for them *ultima dull*. Their hopes lay in being on the road, being stoned, raving fractious poetry and chasing ecstasy with a manic frenzy that fairly begged for either scorn or "Go, man, go" approbation. Beats like Kerouac and Ginsberg clung to the few artifacts of hipness that had survived Hiroshima intact and used them as totems to poke in the eye of the squares. They were the first children of white America to smoke openly at the dinner table, the first to howl in insolent rage at their elders, the first to live in unwashed, unmarried splendor, the first to elevate the Dionysian above the straight. They were the pitch men for a consciousness that was a direct affront to everything America was supposed to be in the era of Ike and Mamie. And their example was not unnoticed by the young.

The same rundown corners of San Francisco and New York where the Beats had congregated became the places where dope and Rock 'n' Roll took hold in the early Sixties. These seedy enclaves began to fill with a generation that had grown up in the shadow of instant annihilation and considered getting high a birthright and not an existential challenge. It was a generation raised on instant foods, Walt Disney, Mattel toys and constant war, on radioactive mutants from the sea and Muzak, on assassination, worldwide hunger and bullshit. The Beats had prepared a home for these kids to retreat to when the music they wanted to play became too loud for the folks in Islip, Shaker Heights and Redwood City; when the dope they wanted to smoke kept putting them in some honky courtroom; when the acceptance they needed so badly was missing. Haight-Ashbury and Greenwich Village became filled with renegades who weren't in search of poetry and revelation so much as solidarity and a feeling that they "belonged."

The hippies soon forged an autonomous culture—a loose, trendy melding of a hundred different influences that sustained itself far better than the Beat culture before it. These kids belonged to the Sixties more than the Beats had ever belonged to the Fifties. Beat subterraneousness was supplanted by a public openness that entailed the enthusiastic embrace of anything that could be smoked, snorted, swallowed or shot into the skin or veins.

Marijuana posters appeared on tenement walls and in hand-me-down shops, marijuana cookbooks were sold in natural-food shops, smoke-ins became instant street festivals, rock stars dropped veiled references to marijuana in their songs. Marijuana was grown in window boxes in Haight-Ashbury and hawked openly on the streets. As the kids began to question the right of the government to take their lives in war, they rebelled likewise against the old drug laws. Finally, the ragged joyous army of rockers gathered itself at Woodstock in 1969. Nothing in that age of Puerile Wonders made such an impression on America as the sight of its young stoned on every forbidden drug at Yasgur's farm, zonked and deliriously happy for those three days that signaled the onset of the new Age of Pot.

When you review the history of marijuana in Western civilization—a very short history of little more than a century—one thing strikes you before all else; namely, how the drug has conformed with the spirit of the age no matter what the spirit or the age. For the French Romantics, voyagers in strange seas of exotic imagery and oriental delirium, hashish was the essence of the oriental sublime. It inspired profound reveries and startling hallucinations and awesome transcendental flights cloaked in the imagery and language of that hyperbolic age. For the cats and kitties of the Jazz Age, marijuana was kicks, climbs, jollies and high times jumpin' to the beat of a hot horn or a mean licorice stick. For the hipsters of the Bop era, marijuana was a cool head, a slow take, a deep dig, the hipster's aid to thought and reflection. With the Beats the pendulum swung back toward the exotic and the ecstatic as Dean Moriarity and Jack Kerouac plunge into the jungle of Mexico with their American road skills and their faith in the infinity of the soul, a latter-day revival of the arch-Romantic spirit crossed with freshman party kicks. Eventually, the ardors of the Beats were extinguished in the spacey age of Rock, which restored dope to its position as the food of thought, the drug for heads, the stuff of stone.

At every point in this history, marijuana was treated as if it were the cause of that of which it is purely effect. So the history of dope reduces eventually to the history of culture, and at last it becomes clear that instead of man being the slave of drugs, drugs are the slaves of man. Because wherever man's head lies in a given time, drugs will simply intensify that posture of the soul, whether it be active or contemplative, cool or ecstatic, hip or hippie.

4 *The Persecution of Marijuana*

The persecution of marijuana began in the Thirties. Prior to the passage of the Marihuana Tax Act in 1937, the legislation that outlawed the drug in America, marijuana had suffered for years from a bad press, being cited constantly as the cause of murders, rapes and family massacres. What's more, the drug had been outlawed in twenty-nine states, including every state west of the Mississippi, when in 1930 agitation commenced to ban it by federal law.

There were many precedents for such legislation: the Opium Act of 1909; the Harrison Narcotics Act of 1914, which outlawed cocaine and opium derivatives like heroin and morphine; and the Eighteenth Amendment, ratified in 1919, which launched the prohibition of alcohol. All of these earlier drug acts sought to bring under control substances that were clearly damaging to the user's health. Marijuana was regarded not as a medical problem but as a social menace. As usage of the drug was at that time limited to a very small portion of the population, a campaign had to be waged to persuade the American public that this obscure weed posed a danger sufficient to justify a federal ban.

The man who led this irrational crusade, overriding the opposition of the AMA and the druggists (who resented the intrusion of the government into an area that had traditionally been the province of medical professionals), was the newly appointed commissioner of the recently established Federal Bureau of Narcotics, Harry J. Anslinger. A bull-necked, bald-headed, slab-shouldered cop with the bureaucrat's talent for wheeling and dealing behind the scenes, the demagogue's flair for sloganlike phrases and the crusader's unquenchable fire of moral indignation, Anslinger was the perfect man to marshal America behind the New Prohibition. Seizing on the reports he found in local papers of crimes and acts of violence under the influence of marijuana, exploiting the myth of the dope-crazed reefer smoker and the evil Mexican or Negro criminal, he concocted a witches' brew of misinformation, superstition and racial prejudice that came to a foaming boil in a notorious magazine article titled "Marijuana: Assassin of Youth." Published in 1936, this article did more than anything else to push through the Marihuana Tax Act of 1937. As the tone and technique of the article is the best introduction one could have to the man who dominated drug enforcement in this country and abroad for the next thirty years, and as the substance of the article sums up the whole marijuana myth of the first half of this century in America, it is incumbent on anyone who wants to understand why marijuana is illegal in this country today to read these fateful pages. The article commences in the style of the Hearst newspapers of that day or the old *Daily Graphic:*

The sprawled body of a young girl lay crushed on the sidewalk the other day after a plunge from the fifth story of a Chicago apartment house. Everyone called it suicide, but actually it was murder. The killer was a narcotic known to America as marijuana, and to history as hashish. It is a narcotic used in the form of cigarettes, comparatively new to the United States and as dangerous as a coiled rattlesnake.

How many murders, suicides, robberies, criminal assaults, holdups, burglaries, and deeds of maniacal insanity it causes each year, especially among the young, can only be conjectured. The sweeping march of its addiction has been so insidious that, in numerous communities, it thrives almost unmolested, largely because of official ignorance of its effects.

Here indeed is the unknown quantity among narcotics. No one can predict its effect. No one knows, when he places a marijuana cigarette to his lips, whether he will become a philosopher, a joyous reveler in a musical heaven, a mad insensate, a calm philosopher, or a murderer.

That youth has been selected by the peddlers of this poison as an especially fertile field makes it a problem of serious concern to every man and woman in America.

Having lined up the target with his contention that marijuana produces acts of uncontrollable violence, Anslinger starts to wheel out his heavy artillery. He escalates from the pathetic to the horrific:

It was an unprovoked crime some years ago which brought the first realization that the age-old drug had gained a foothold in America. An entire family was murdered by a youthful addict in Florida. When officers arrived at the home they found the youth staggering about in a human slaughterhouse. With an ax he had killed his father, his mother, two brothers, and a sister. He seemed to be in a daze.

"I've had a terrible dream," he said. "People tried to hack off my arms!"

"Who were they?" an officer asked.

"I don't know. Maybe one was my uncle. They slashed me with knives and I saw blood dripping from an ax."

He had no recollection of having committed the multiple crime. The officers knew him ordinarily as a sane, rather quiet young man; now he was pitifully crazed. They sought the reason. The boy said he had been in the habit of smoking something which youthful friends called "muggles," a childish name for marijuana.

Marijuana makes young men into assassins. The pun is intended; Anslinger recounts in the course of his piece the Marco Polo story with all the customary distortions. The only question is: where do the kids get this deadly stuff? Anslinger explains that marijuana grows everywhere and is sold by all sorts of people, from the old man who pushes the *tamale* cart down the street to the lady who sells sandwiches to school kids to the shadowy gangsters who run dope dens. The word "den" summons up the sinister atmosphere of the opium den, which is precisely the effect that Anslinger intends. According to Anslinger, there are dope dens in every little American town. Consider this case:

In a small Ohio town, a few months ago, a fifteen-year-old boy was found wandering the streets, mentally deranged by marijuana. Officers learned that he had obtained the dope at a garage.

"Are there any other school kids getting cigarettes there?" he was asked.

"Sure, I knew 15 or 20, maybe more. I'm only counting my friends."

The garage was raided. Three men were arrested and 18 pounds of marijuana seized.

"We'd been figuring on quitting the racket," one of the dopesters told the arresting officer. "These kids had us scared. After we'd gotten 'em on the weed, it looked like easy money for a while. Then they kept wanting more and more of it, and if we didn't have it for 'em, they'd get tough. Along toward the last, we were scared that one of 'em would get high and kill us all. There wasn't any fun in it."

This account suggests that marijuana is addicting, like morphine or heroin. In fact, the only accusation against marijuana that Anslinger fails to rehearse in his famous article is the notion that marijuana leads on to hard drugs. In later years, when Anslinger decided to play down the notion of killer weed because it offered every murderer a built-in excuse if he could prove that he was high, the resourceful propagandist changed his pitch and said that the principal danger of dope was the step up it offered to heroin.

The most contemptible feature of Anslinger's propaganda against dope was his playing on the heartstrings of his audience. His cases always turn in the telling into corny Thirties movies. (A couple of B movies were actually made out of this material; one of them, *Reefer Madness*, is often shown today to raise camp laughs— and money for reform of the marijuana laws.) Consider the way Anslinger winds up the article. After the yellow journalism of his opening and the psychopathia of his heaviest horror stories, he needs something special to sink the last putt. With a good eye for a sob story, he comes up with this gem:

In Los Angeles, California, a youth was walking along a downtown street after inhaling a marijuana cigarette. For many addicts, merely a portion of a "reefer" is enough to induce intoxication. Suddenly, for no reason, he decided that someone had threatened to kill him and that his life was in danger. Wildly, he looked about him. The only person in sight was an aged bootblack. Drug-crazed nerve centers conjured the innocent old shoeshiner into a destroying monster. Mad with fright, the addict hurried to his room and got a gun. He killed the old man, and then, later, babbled his grief over what had been wanton, uncontrolled murder.

"I thought someone was after me," he said. "That was the only reason that I did it. I had never seen the old fellow before. Something just told me to kill him!"

Anslinger's only comment is: "That's marijuana!"

After years of building support for one or another anti-marijuana law; after extensive correspondence with lobbying groups like the YWCA, the National PTA and the National Councils of Catholic Men and Women, all of whom he panicked into action by opening his files and spewing forth their most lurid tales; after dueling clumsily with representatives of the AMA and pharmacists; after testifying before congressional committees; and, most important, after making common cause with the Hearst press, which put the talented Winsor McKay (creator of Little Nemo) to work drawing minatory editorial cartoons, Harry Anslinger finally attained his goal with the passage of the Marihuana Tax Act.

The law stipulated that to grow, transport, sell, prescribe or use marijuana, the citizen had to pay a special occupational tax of one dollar. Furthermore, every transaction had to be accompanied by a written form; and, most important, every transfer of marijuana was to be taxed at the rate of one dollar per ounce to registered persons (i.e., doctors) and a stunning $100 to unregistered persons. Should anyone seek to avoid these levies, he then became subject to the full fury of the law: five years imprisonment or $2,000 fine or both punishments concurrently. Though marijuana per se was not declared illegal, the tax law ended for all practical purposes the traffic in marijuana. (The law remained on the books until 1970, when it was declared unconstitutional by the Supreme Court in the Timothy Leary case. The judges ruled that it constituted a case of double jeopardy. "How," demanded the Court, "can one file for a tax stamp to partake in business that is already deemed illegal in every one of the 50 states?")

Once Anslinger triumphed with his tax act, marijuana went underground and remained outside the realm of controversy for an entire generation. When the hippies started blowing smoke in everyone's face in the Sixties, the dope issue was broached again. This time the drug's persecutor was no less a person than the President of the United States: Richard Milhous Nixon.

In 1971, Nixon declared that drug abuse was the Number One Problem facing the United States. He declared a holy war on drug dealers and smugglers. He escalated the drug budget a staggering 1,100 percent, from $69 million in fiscal year 1969 to $719 million in fiscal year 1974. Most important, he established by his side in the White House a special office to direct the crusade, appointing as his special aide in this campaign the keen young zealot Egil Krogh.

Krogh was an energetic and dedicated administrator. He

began to transmit the President's urgency in every direction. He put the heat on the State Department to use diplomatic leverage on countries that supplied drugs to the U.S. He tried to get J. Edgar Hoover to use his FBI agents to crack down on domestic drug business. He even tried to get the CIA, with its shadowy network of operatives and spies and "special project" designers, to join forces in the Dope War. At the end of a year's hard .work, however, Krogh had to report disappointing results to his boss. The dope problem was a lot harder to solve than anybody had anticipated.

To start at the supply end of the line, there were all sorts of hang-ups with foreign governments. Invariably, the governments expressed their abhorrence of the drug trade and pledged themselves to use every effort within their capacity to stamp out the accursed weeds. Some governments even went beyond promises to action and dispatched military units into the field and made arrests and seized and burned crops or loads. Yet these measures seemed to accomplish nothing in the long run. The seizures were only a tiny proportion of the total amount of contraband, the men arrested were soon replaced by other men and the raids into dope-growing territory would leave a few scars that were soon healed—or they would drive the dope growers further into the hills.

Some countries, like Turkey, which was eager to cooperate in exchange for American military aid, found that they could not deny their farmers the income that growing drug plants brought them. Turkish farmers complained that the problem was not theirs but America's. They had been cultivating poppies for centuries, and their people were not murderous addicts. Why should *they* pay the price for America's problem? Other nations, like Mexico and Colombia, simply did not have total control over large areas of their own countries. Control could be achieved temporarily by military expeditions, but when the soldiers retreated, conditions reverted to what they had been before. The people who lived in these remote regions were generally desperately poor *campesinos* or totally alienated peasants who had never viewed themselves as part of the nation.

The worst rub of all was the growing awareness of the extent to which the governing class was motivated by the same greed that characterized the peasants. The connections were not only shady businessmen out to make a buck or lowly officials looking for their *schmeer;* members of the leading families were in the Game. The very government officials with whom the American diplomats were negotiating could be profiting from the traffic they were supposed to be putting down. The list of ambassadors, ministers, generals and even heads of state who were in the dope business was appallingly long. What hope was there of gaining these people's cooperation when their family fortunes were so closely tied to dope?

On the other end of the line, in the U.S., the problems were just as great. There were special interdiction units working constantly on drug cases: the Bureau of Narcotics and Dangerous Drugs, the Customs Service, the narcotics squads of the big cities and the states. They made buys on the streets and worked their way up the chain of customers and dealers until after an immense amount of work and money and time, they knocked off a few schmucks who thought themselves the kings of the ghetto. It was always the tip of the iceberg, the little guy, not the boss, the surface of the problem, not its depth. Most drug arrests were young college-age kids of good families who were caught with a little dope or a few pills in their possession. Their arrests, trials and imprisonment costs the government a lot both in enforcement costs and in political good will. If you took the sophisticated professional view of the matter, these kids were the victims, not the instigators, of the crimes. Why punish the victims when the real perpetrators were going free and waxing wealthy?

To get the big men in the drug game would take the most skillful and costly kind of enforcement effort. The FBI could do it, but Hoover was wary of implicating his agency in the corrupting medium of drug police work. The temptations to corruption in this form of crime were too great for any but the most dedicated agents and cops. The strategy of buying and/or posing as a drug dealer brought the men right down to the level of the criminals they were seeking to apprehend. After a while, even the most dedicated agent might start asking himself: "Why am I taking all the risks of a big drug dealer when I'm not making any of the money?" At that point, he might become a double agent. It had happened time and again, not only with the narcs of the big city undercover squads (like the French Connection case in New York) but way up in the hierarchy of the federal drug enforcement apparatus.

The old Federal Bureau of Narcotics, Harry Anslinger's

agency, was the most notoriously corrupt department of the federal government. In testimony offered the Senate subcommittee on investigations on July 29, 1975, John E. Ingersoll, director of the Bureau of Narcotics and Dangerous Drugs between 1968 and 1973, testified that in the FBN, "corruption reached high levels, especially in the New York office. . . . Key informants were killed. Other law enforcement organizations did not trust the FBN. Someone was selling out. . . . Because of arrest quotas and poor controls over the use of informants, informants had too much freedom and too much influence in determining who would be arrested . . . there was no particular security over the files that revealed the identities of informants . . . some [agents] resorted to bartering narcotics for information." Anslinger, forced to retire by John F. Kennedy in 1962, is said to have known nothing of this dirty work. Hoover knew it all.

Finally, Krogh and his aides were forced to go outside the normal channels of approach to the drug problem and try solutions that were neither legal nor moral. It is now well known that the scandalous activities revealed by Watergate did not have their inception in the establishment of the Plumbers. Quite the contrary, it was Nixon's all-out War on Drugs that first revealed to his political lieutenants the possibilities for conducting a secret war on their political enemies. If Hoover wouldn't cooperate and the CIA was playing hard to get, there was yet another way the game could be played. The administration could create a new super-agency which would be to the world of drugs what the FBI was to other forms of crime and what the CIA was to international intelligence gathering and counterespionage. The new agency would be, in effect, Nixon's secret police force.

In 1973 Nixon created by presidential fiat the DEA, the Drug Enforcement Administration, the most powerful, resourceful and costly drug police apparatus ever assembled in the history of civilization.* To some the DEA is the closest America has ever come to a Gestapo: a shadowy army guarded from surveillance and control by the secrecy of its operations and the moral cloak which it casts over its illegal and murderous activities. To others the DEA is the one organization in America that promises relief from the curse of drugs, its occasional excesses being viewed

---

* The DEA has more than four thousand employees, of whom about half are agents. Its budget is currently about $190 million, roughly one-third the cost of the FBI.

tolerantly as the inevitable consequences of any war against an enemy who is as ruthless as the international drug syndicates. Certainly no agency in recent times has been the object of more controversy, nor has any department of the government been subjected to such a consistently bad press. It is incumbent, therefore, on anyone who wants to understand the new Age of Pot to get a clear idea of the prime government apparatus in the War on Drugs. For whatever conclusions one forms about the DEA, one thing is certain: if the solution to the drug problem lies in all-out warfare, this agency is the closest we have come to an antidrug commando army. What it has done or failed to do is the measure, the ultimate measure, of the police approach to drugs.

The first thing to understand about the DEA is that it was born under a bad sign. Created not by Congress but by administrative reshuffling, cobbled together from bits and pieces of several predecessor agencies, fleshed out with men and machines taken from services like Customs, which had always been competitive with the narcotics bureaus of the past, the DEA was born with the germs of dissension and administrative discord planted deep within its core.

In the old days, back in the Thirties, drug enforcement, which was, admittedly, a very minor function of the federal government, was all under one administrative umbrella. The Federal Bureau of Narcotics and Customs were both arms of the Treasury Department. If, as organizations dealing with what was generically the same problem, they came to blows, the dispute could be ironed out within the family. Customs, which has the responsibility for stopping the flow of narcotics over our borders, has always been the government's most effective antinarcotic agency. There are many reasons for this good record, but the most important one is the simple fact that when drugs are brought into this country, they are brought in large quantities and at high purity. If they can be seized at that moment, the efficiency of the interdiction effort is greatest. To nab the smuggler at the border, however, it is necessary to have information that comes from his foreign bases; hence, Customs had long maintained an intelligence network that comprised special agents whose task it was to gather information overseas, especially from the agents of other nations' customs services, who traditionally have engaged in a reciprocal exchange of information with the U.S. Another way of learning about impending shipments of contraband is to develop informers inside the U.S. Here Customs was bound to step on the toes of the FBN; hence, the ancient quarrel between the two organizations that was going on thirty years ago and that goes on to this day in a far more bitter and exacerbated form between Customs and the FBN's descendant, the DEA.

When Nixon created his superagency, he destroyed nearly as much as he created. First of all he drastically reduced the effectiveness of the Customs Service by stripping it of its intelligence-gathering function. Without paid informants no narcotics interdiction apparatus can succeed; yet the only way to develop informants is to go out into the field, either here or abroad, and make advances to potential sources. This soliciting of information was denied to Customs, though the practice never ceased entirely. Furthermore, by putting the DEA into the Justice Department, Nixon created an administrative conflict that soon began to seriously disturb and distract him. Instead of the squabbles of the bureaucrats being resolved by the secretary of the treasury, they were now carried by the secretary of the treasury, and his opposite number, the attorney general, John Mitchell, straight into the White House, where Nixon himself had to act constantly as umpire. Nixon invited this kind of take-it-to-the-top attitude by making the control of the drug program a matter in which the White House staff held direct responsibility derived from the President; he also increased the complexity of every important decision by creating a cabinet committee on narcotics on which served a whole array of other top government officials, ranging from the secretary of state to the attorney general to the secretaries of defense, treasury and agriculture, plus the director of the CIA and the U.S. representative to the U.N. As every one of these powerful men had his pet ideas on drug law enforcement, the division of opinion often reached the point of administrative anarchy.

On the moral level Nixon's new scheme had many troubling features from the outset. One of the basic principles of American law is the separation of police power from prosecutional authority. By placing narcotics under the attorney general in the Justice Department, Nixon tacitly encouraged federal prosecutors to collude with federal narcotics agents in actions that could easily result in the violation of individual rights and liberties. U.S. attorneys began to function like Mr. District Attorney, playing crime buster before the local press and directing the enforcement of the law instead of confining themselves to the prosecution of those who were arrested by the law enforcement personnel.

On the practical level, Nixon adopted two drastic strategies that were destined to boomerang. In the great world of international diplomacy, he became embroiled in a whole series of international power plays designed to dry up drug supplies at the source. These geopolitical maneuvers produced invariably results that were either nugatory or embarrassing to this country. He talked the Turks out of producing opium; then the American medical profession woke up one day to find themselves faced with a severe shortage of opiates. He thrust himself into the witches' kitchen of Southeast Asia but succeeded only in making the heroin manufacturers much wealthier by offering them immense bribes to keep their products off the U.S. market. Everywhere Nixon turned diplomatically in his War on Drugs, he made enemies for the U.S. and did not advance his own cause one whit.

On the street level, the same record was repeated. When Nixon felt that the local police officials of the major American cities were not doing a good enough job cracking down on the pushers, he sent federal officers into the cities to work on street-level crime. The result was that the local police felt they were being relieved of some of their responsibilities. No longer did they operate with the same zeal. (One notable exception was the bust of Frank Mathews, America's biggest heroin dealer, which was made by a team of New York police working under a federal agent.) DEA agents were likewise encouraged to get down into the street and buy drugs and bust sellers. This practice was supposed to lead up the ladder of the criminal hierarchies into the nerve centers of the international drug-smuggling apparatus. It did no such thing, even though it was funded with millions of dollars of federal money—money that went either into the pockets of the criminals or, in some cases, into the pockets of the federal agents.

As if all that were not bad enough, the DEA soon began to get involved with scandals and become scandalous itself. A DEA agent testified before Congress that he had been hot on the tail of a major Corsican smuggler who was working a deal with Robert Vesco when for no good reason he was called off the case and subsequently dismissed. At the same time, two other DEA agents were sent to Vesco's home in New Jersey, not to bug the place but to sweep it of bugs.

Senator Charles Percy disclosed that the DEA's head of special projects, a legendary soldier of fortune named Lucien Conein, had been briefed by a firm in Cincinnati on some very sinister assassination apparatus: for example, a telephone that would explode when picked up. Later Conein admitted publicly that he was recruited from the CIA by the Bureau of Narcotics and Dangerous Drugs to command a unit that would have the capacity to assassinate drug traffickers.

How many traffickers were murdered by government agents or hired hit men, how many mysterious disappearances of major drug dealers were actually undisclosed assassinations and how many smuggling planes were fatally sabotaged or shot down is one of the deepest and darkest secrets of the whole drug enforcement program. The most intriguing question is to what extent these practices continue today.

The scandal that finally rocked the DEA to its foundations broke in the summer of 1975, when the agency's head, John Bartels, was summoned before a congressional committee, chaired by Senator Henry Jackson, and made to testify about an astonishing duel that was being fought behind the scenes between Bartels and two of his top administrators. These officials had gone to the Justice Department and accused their chief of covering up for his public information officer, who had compromised himself by appearing with a prostitute in a bar where known criminals consorted. Bartels accused the administrators of using the case to embarrass him and to cover up their own failure to weed out of the DEA all the corrupt agents who had long-standing cases pending against them. The DEA bureaucrats retaliated with even more compromising testimony about the administrator's angry and unprofessional behavior as he fought his lieutenants, often with the aid of specialists brought in from outside the agency. The case produced a clamor in the press, and even though the committee absolved Bartels of criminal activity, it censured him severely for administrative blunders. He was dismissed shortly after the committee hearings by Attorney General Edward Levi.

In 1976 the same committee reviewed to the length of 191 closely printed pages the entire history and conduct of the DEA.

Its conclusions were devastating. Discussing the "DEA's failure to adequately deal with the Federal drug problem," the senators censured the agency for relying on buy-and-bust techniques:

DEA has relied upon undercover work to an inordinate degree. The risks in this indiscriminate use of undercover agents outweigh hoped-for advantages. The danger to the agent is great. Conversely, the results have proven to be minimal. Major traffickers do not sell narcotics; they have other people to do that. The notion that it is possible to reach the highest rungs of the drug traffic by buying at the low level and advancing progressively to the highest stages is questionable. . . . DEA inherited many personnel integrity-related problems from predecessor agencies . . . top management has been at a disadvantage in dealing with personnel integrity problems because Federal narcotics enforcement personnel, unlike FBI agents, work under the rules and regulations of the Civil Service Commission. Adverse actions under Civil Service require stringent elements of proof in the transfer of suspected employees. Because of this, the DEA has not been able to exercise the degree of discipline . . . which the FBI enjoys.

Promising to continue the investigation of the organization in the context of a study of what should be the government's technique for dealing with narcotics violations, the committee indicated very clearly that it favored a return to the old assignment of responsibility that gave Customs control of smuggling and state and local police control over street crime.

Though the DEA is now very much on the defensive in Congress and before the press, it has on occasion achieved the purpose for which it was created. Perhaps the most effective and impressive of its antipot campaigns has been Operation Buccaneer, which completely knocked out the *ganja* trade between the U.S. and Jamaica, once the greatest supplier of dope to the eastern half of the United States. To understand what motivated this unparalleled paramilitary operation, one has to page back again to the period when drugs first became a primary issue in world politics.

When Richard Nixon declared drugs to be the Number One Problem, he directed his first major interdiction campaign at the Mexican border. Nixon closed the border completely for a week in 1969 during the notorious Operation Intercept. The results were appalling. Apart from the fact that the closing produced the worst traffic jam in history, soured our relations with the Mexican

government and subjected hundreds of thousands of perfectly innocent people to the moral and emotional pressures of being
treated as suspected dope smugglers, Operation Intercept had the
paradoxical effect of exacerbating America's Number One Problem. Though relatively little marijuana was confiscated at the
border—who would be crazy enough to run dope through such a
blockade?—it did slow down the normal rate of transport, with
the result that the traditional summer famine was worse in 1969
than at any time in recent years.

Dope is always in short supply during the summer for a great
variety of reasons, ranging all the way from South American growing cycles to the simple fact that the dealers, like everybody else,
like to go to the beach in the warm months and forget about their
work. Summer '69 found all the really heavy dope consumers
stocked up in anticipation of the drought. It was the occasional
smokers, the people with no stash, who were caught short. So
they stopped smoking grass, which is just what Nixon wanted.
But they started experimenting with other heavier and far more
dangerous drugs, which is just what Nixon feared. So by a curious
logic of stupidity, the most drastic effort ever made to kill killer
weed boomeranged and summer '69 is remembered today by
thousands of young Americans as the first time they ever tried
heroin.

OPERATION BUCCANEER

To the dope smugglers the logical answer to their Number One
Problem was to seek fresh fields on which to play the Game. If
Mexico was hot, why not go somewhere else? Where could they
go? Jamaica was famous for its red dope. The tourist paradise lay
so close to the Florida shore that a small plane could make the
round trip without refueling, bringing back a thousand pounds of
high-quality weed with every run. The island was provided not
only with dozens of sneaky little airstrips; it had 150 miles of quiet
bays and remote beaches and secret docking sites where the
yachting smuggler could follow his airborne comrade with equal
success. The best part of the deal was the attitude of the local
populace. Unlike the dour Mexicans, who regard the dope trade
as just another bloody campaign in their endless war with the
central government, or the Colombians, who think that three

puffs on a joint can make a man a homicidal maniac, the Jamaicans were groovy brothers who delighted to turn on everybody. When the hippies would bus out to the famous dope beach at Negril (where all the old Dorothy Lamour movies were shot), they would find that the bus drivers would take them into their shacks and turn them on. Jamaica was the kingdom of marijuana. Like the Peruvians, whose national emblem includes the coca shrub, the Jamaicans could have stamped their currency with a seven-frond dope leaf.

Dope, like rum, is a basic element of lower-class Jamaican life. Introduced from abroad in the mid-nineteenth century by indentured East Indian laborers who were brought over to bolster the work force after the abolition of slavery, marijuana was adopted by the rural blacks like some long-forgotten but fondly remembered African folk heritage—which it might have been. Not only the Indian technique of dope cultivation and dope preparation, but the oriental religious ritual, folk medicine and social attitude were taken over from the immigrants entire. To this day the Jamaican word for dope is a Hindi term: *ganja*. Hindi, too, are the words for the mature plant—*kali*—and the dope-smoking pipe—*chillum*.

Dope smoking is well-nigh universal among the rural labor force, and dope drinking, in the form of *ganja* tea, is a common practice among Jamaican women, including the old crones who are the most devout parishioners of the local churches. When a Jamaican child turns sickly, he is certain to be dosed with a syrupy drink that is prepared by boiling *ganja* leaves in spring water and then diluting the brew heavily with condensed milk. When the white child of the "buckra," the "Mass Lester" or the "Mass Herbert," remains ill despite the ministrations of the best local physicians, he too is encouraged to drink the medicinal tea that is prescribed for everything from asthma (where it probably is effective) to VD (where at least it takes away the pain).

Jamaica's famous religious cult, the Rastafarians, has exalted dope to a sacrament. Citing such biblical texts as "gather the herbs of the field," the Rastafarians have installed marijuana as the sacred bush, the "burning bush," in the very heart of their ceremony and their mystique.

With *ganja* growing in every backyard and social usage an accustomed thing, it was inevitable that marijuana consumption in

Jamaica should reach proportions that are natural for humans but astounding and "abnormal" by American standards. It was just because Jamaicans smoke so much dope in such a socially permissive setting that the U.S. government funded the study that was published in book form as *Ganja in Jamaica*. This study shows that marijuana is used in a much different way in Jamaica than it is in the U.S. Instead of being a recreational drug, its most characteristic function is as a source of energy for performing manual labor, just as coca (the source of cocaine) is used by the Indians of Ecuador, Peru and Chile.

When the Jamaican laborer gets up in the morning, he rolls himself a "spliff," a big conical-shaped joint made of brown wrapping paper and stuffed with a large quantity of marijuana and tobacco mixed together. In startling contrast to the skinny American joint, which holds maybe one gram, the Jamaica spliff is a bomber that contains perhaps as much as ten grams. (THC content of Jamaican dope is typically about 3 percent; this compares with 1.5 percent for Mexican and 3.5 percent for Colombian.) The laborer smokes his joint for breakfast and he smokes again at lunch and he smokes every time he prepares himself for some heavy task, such as cutting cane or building roads or carrying loads on his back. In the course of a day, he may consume as much as an *ounce* of strong marijuana.

When the scientists put their measuring instruments on the workers, they discovered that when the Jamaican laborer smokes his spliff and then starts cutting cane or hoeing or ditching, what he does, in effect, is to slightly reduce his coordination and work efficiency but to so improve his mental set that the burden of work is lifted from his shoulders and the task facilitated. As far as the long-range effects, both physical and emotional, of such heavy dope smoking, they are in no wise different from those found in chronic tobacco smokers. There are a few bronchial symptoms, but otherwise the workers seem as sound mentally and physically as can be expected from people who live in a primitive rustic society where malnutrition and bad sanitation are the rule. (It should be said in passing that the sample used in this study was too small to provide a basis for compelling generalizations. Like every study of marijuana to date, *Ganja in Jamaica* has been criticized by medical researchers and relegated to the vast repository of inconclusive investigations.)

In view of this widespread and heavy usage of *ganja* in Jamaica, it is safe to say the government of the country would never have moved against the drug if it had remained confined within its traditional patterns of growth and consumption. Indeed, one of the first acts of the current Jamaican government of Michael Manly, which took power in 1972, was to abolish mandatory prison terms for a number of crimes, including possession of *ganja*. (Jamaica is no less ambivalent about dope than is America about alcohol. Despite the fact that everyone smokes or drinks tea, there have been laws on the books since 1913 that treat this common practice as a crime.) What got the central government geared up to come down hard on the *ganja* trade was neither dope usage nor a desire to enforce laws that are usually scoffed. The reason why the Jamaican government struck the *ganja* trade a mortal blow was because American smugglers were rapidly transforming Jamaica from a poor but peaceful island into a rapidly boiling pot of revolution.

The fire under the pot was American money—and American guns. Jamaicans are gun freaks for reasons easy to understand. Throughout its 300-year history, the island has been always a giant slave plantation dedicated to growing sugar cane and bananas, distilling molasses and rum and, more recently, gouging bauxite out of the soil and entertaining tourists. The labor for this industry has been exacted from millions of hard-pressed blacks who have gradually built up, like their brethren all over the Western world, a profound longing to take their lives in their hands and end the oppression that has made them miserable. The simplest, purest and most perfect symbol of a man's determination to risk his life for freedom is a gun. Jamaicans always carry machetes; but what they long for are pistols. (That's what that enormously engaging movie, *The Harder They Come*, is all about.) When the dope smugglers recognized this fact, they instituted one of the most profitable and explosive commodity exchanges in the history of business. They began flying in loads of American-made weapons in exchange for loads of Jamaica-grown grass. It was a deadly deal, and soon it changed the complexion of Jamaican life.

In the hideous city of Kingston, a squalid tropical metropolis blanketed by a thick pall of smog, the desperately poor men who had come up from the country and lived in packing crates began to make waves—crime waves. Instead of the familiar Saturday-night shootings and machete maimings (all over Jamaica you find people with a couple of fingers or a whole hand missing from a machete fight), new and far more menacing patterns of crime began to appear. The police were attacked. Prominent business leaders were kidnaped and held for ransom. Finally, in a rash of assassinations, several members of parliament were killed. Every day the *Daily Gleaner* reported some new atrocity. The very foundations of Jamaican society appeared to be tottering.

Michael Manly, a charismatic political leader who has been compared with Fidel Castro, decided to take action against this menace, which might soon topple him from power and plunge the island into suicidal anarchy. He decided to disarm the Jamaican populace. As the first step in this direction, he moved to end the *ganja* trade with America.

Operating through a newly appointed minister of security and justice, Eli Matalon, Manly summoned to Jamaica some of the top brass of the DEA, including the director of international operations, John T. Cusack. The DEA was accustomed to bargaining with foreign countries that resented the demands being made upon them by the American government. It was as-tonishing to find a country that was eagerly soliciting the presence of American agents and making every possible effort to provide the agents with everything they needed to do their job. In the course of a series of meetings in Kingston in early 1974, an elabo-rate plan of action was drawn up to be implemented jointly by the U.S. and Jamaica.

Basically, the Americans were to supply the equipment and the specialists; the Jamaicans were to supply the troops. The aim of the operation was to shut down totally the *ganja* trade with the States; hence, it was decided that a comprehensive attack should be mounted on everybody involved in the trade, ranging from the farmers up in the hills to the dealers down in the towns to the smugglers out on the sea or high in the air. The operation was laid out in three parts: investigation, interdiction and eradication. The investigative effort would entail infiltrating the *ganja* trade and developing conspiracy and smuggling cases against the prin-cipal agents. The interdiction procedure would consist primarily of aerial and sea patrols. The eradication effort meant getting out on the land and destroying the crops and stockpiles.

The operation got going in early summer when a number of DEA and Jamaican constabulary undercover agents began to infiltrate the centers of the Dope Game in Montego Bay and Kingston. They set up buy-and-bust situations and extracted from those they busted deeper information about how the Game was being played and who were the principal players. Armed with this information, the authorities began to tie together everything they knew from the American end of the Game in Miami and New York with the new information they were gathering in Jamaica. Eventually, they got a clear picture of the *ganja* trade and a good idea of what would have to be done to suppress it.

The first and most urgent need was for a total surveillance network that would cover the island like an electronic lid and reach far out to sea in every direction. The ideal was to create a system of surveillance so perfect that not one ship or plane could arrive in Jamaica or its surrounding waters without being spotted by the task force. Jamaica is a small island and most of the smuggling traffic comes down through the Windward Passage between Cuba and Haiti and hence along the northeast shore, either heading west toward Montego Bay and Negril or south toward Kingston. It was decided, therefore, to set up a powerful radar station on the northeast coast and to connect the radar with every center of the operation from Kingston to Miami by means of a powerful and reliable radio-communications system—which could also be used to direct and control the movements of the planes, ships and troop formations that would be dispatched eventually against the smugglers.

On July 4, 1974, a jet cargo plane flew down low over the water north of Montego Bay and slid into Manly International Airport. From its belly a team of sweating stevedores extracted by hand a huge equipment pod containing a 5,000-pound radar unit. Next, they removed from the plane a 4,000-pound motor generator set to power the radar, and finally they took out the oddly shaped and carefully created antennae: the big dishes and towering masts that would pick up the smugglers far out at sea or in the air and then transmit the news of their arrival directly to the Jamaican authorities. That very night the massive equipment was trucked out to a remote tropical beach resort at Runaway Bay on the northeast coast. There, in an incongruously luxurious and hedonistic atmosphere of private pools and slope-roofed bungalows and waving palm trees, the American technicians began to set up the first DEA radar station ever established on foreign soil.

As this work was going forward, the Americans began to deliver to the Jamaicans a lot of military personnel and hardware: several Huey helicopters, familiar from service in Vietnam; a number of 31-foot Bertram cabin cruisers with machine guns on their front decks; some fixed-wing aircraft for reconnaissance and pursuit work; and, most important, the U.S. Coast Guard cutter *Hamilton*, a big imposing ship with a threatening gun turret on its forward deck and a long low helicopter ramp on its stern. For it had been decided that there could be no substitute for a real naval blockade of the Windward Passage. With its scout plane and its sophisticated electronic surveillance gear, the *Hamilton* could stick a stopper right in the neck of the bottle through which poured all the yachts and cabin cruisers and shrimp trawlers running down from Florida to pick up cargoes of dope.

From mid-August through November, Operation Buccaneer was in full swing. Every morning single- and twin-engine patrol planes would take off from the Jamaican Defense Force airstrip at Up Park Camp in Kingston. They would fan out and work over the coast, noting every fresh arrival during the night. After dark a whole fleet of cabin cruisers would begin to prowl around those parts of the coast where loadings and off-loadings were most likely to occur. On many occasions the smugglers fled and the gunboats pursued. It got to be a game in Jamaica that summer to sit up on top of a hill with a cold drink in your hand and watch the fireworks out at sea. Gradually, these tactics began to produce results. Yachts were seized loaded to the gunnels with dope. Caches of grass were uncovered in the slums of Kingston. Planes were chased through the air all the way back to Miami. Men were arrested as they stepped off airliners in Kingston or Montego Bay. The Game was getting hot.

Prime Minister Manly was stoking the flames even higher in the Jamaican parliament. Ramming through a whole sheaf of anticrime laws, he turned Jamaica overnight from an easygoing British colony into a modern Third World police state. Cornerstone and touchstone of his new legislation was the notorious Gun Court. The law against guns stipulated that anybody found with an unregistered weapon in his possession—or even *a single bullet*—could be hauled off to a barbed-wire concentration camp in the heart of Kingston called Gun Court (and painted bright red for effect), denied the right of *habeas corpus*, tried without benefit of jury or press and given an *indefinite sentence*. In 1976 the Privy Council in London ruled that the imposing of indefinite sentences was illegal. The Manly government complied with the ruling. Now if you're caught with a bullet in your pocket, you are given a mandatory sentence of life imprisonment.

Parallel to the gun law came other regulations, for example, those governing private airstrips. Owners of such strips were compelled to post guards on them twenty-four hours a day or fence them with chain-link fences or barricade them with sandbags or other obstructions when they were not in legitimate use. Where it was feared an airstrip's proprietor would not comply with the government's demand, special machine-gun crews were stationed at the strips with orders to shoot down any plane landing or attempting to take off without proper clearance. Some planes were gunned down; others crashed trying to land on narrow roads or pitted pastures. Soon the traffic by air and sea had been disrupted.

Next the government turned to the farmers. The Jamaican *ganja* crop cycle is twice a year, as in most hot countries. The spring crop is planted in April and harvested in August; the winter crop goes into the ground when the rains come down in June and is cut in November. When Operation Buccaneer first hit its stride, the crop was coming off the land. It was estimated that some 1,300 acres were under cultivation, with an average yield of 800 to 1,000 pounds an acre. The only way to be absolutely sure that none of this grass ever hit the American market was to go out to the fields and burn it. The problem was that the fields were mostly up in the Cockpit Country, a weirdly pocked volcanic mountain region in the center of the island that looks from the air like a cupcake pan covered with red dirt and green foliage. Access to this remote region was so limited by road that the only way to get there unannounced was by helicopter. The DEA made arrangements to fly four Huey troop-carrying choppers to Kingston, where they began ferrying armed teams of Jamaican army and constabulary up to the pot fields.

A couple of years later, the DEA put out a forty-minute color film of the operation, which has some interesting footage of the chopper operation. You see the helicopters scrabbling over the bowl-shaped valleys. The red dirt of the countryside. The soldiers in their berets and fatigues cutting the grass with practiced machete strokes. Then a final shot of conflagration as the dope soaked with kerosene goes up in flames. You don't see any farmers resisting or being arrested. You don't see any barns being broken open. You don't see anything, naturally, that would make for bad public relations. It is safe to assume, however, that the seizing and burning of 420 acres of Jamaican land by 4,000 troops produced some rural tensions.

By the fall of 1974, the Jamaican *ganja* crop had been destroyed and the island's drug traffic virtually halted. The final tabulation was impressive:

Ganja	730,000 lbs.
Ganja seeds	8,083 lbs.
Hashish	65 lbs.
Cocaine	20 lbs.
Vessels	17
Aircraft	10
Weapons	11
Cash	$143,000
Arrested	98

What were the lasting benefits to Jamaica from the suppression of the *ganja* trade? Frankly, it would be hard to state them. Jamaica's economy is now so totally wrecked that at one point in 1976 the national treasury had only a two-week supply of foreign currency. Tourism has fallen off badly, primarily as a result of the bad vibes emanating from the island. Unemployment has reached 35 percent. Manly remains in power, wearing African clothes and brandishing a white rod of correction bestowed upon him by Haile Selassie. Meanwhile, everybody who can flee the country is getting out. As for organized crime, it is now said that the two greatest sources of crime in the streets are the two major political parties, both of which maintain gangs of armed motor-biking bully boys who regularly ravage the neighborhoods of their political opponents. So flourishes law and order in the island paradise, blessedly free of privately owned guns and American smugglers. In point of fact, dope smuggling from Jamaica resumed in 1977, as the Manly government began to give serious consideration to a proposal to decriminalize *ganja*.

5 The Colombian Connection

After I had spent a few months reading about grass—and smoking lots of good weed—I began to feel restless. Studying all these historical documents was an interesting occupation, but the story I was after was not to be found in books. The simple truth was that nobody had ever written anything that cut to the heart of the Dope Game. Sure, there was a book called *Weed: Adventures of a Dope Smuggler,* by Jerry Kamstra, that chronicled a move from Mexico in 1963. The book has one good chapter that offers a revealing close-up of some tiny plantations hidden in the almost inaccessible mountains east of Acapulco. Otherwise, *Weed* is just a historical vignette of the days when dope running was part of the West Coast hippie mystique: a "noble" act conducted in a densely paranoid atmosphere by acid-dropping scions of Jack Kerouac who were always creaming at the thought of penetrating "age-old peasant cultures." By 1975, Mexico was yesterday's story. Though the country was still statistically the greatest dope exporter in the Western hemisphere, its days were numbered as *Número Uno.*

The Mexicans made the grave mistake of adding to their traditional market in marijuana a lucrative business in heroin, which had burgeoned after a series of American diplomatic and police maneuvers cut off the customary sources in Turkey and Marseilles. The new trade in Mexican Brown brought down the heaviest kind of heat from the Nixon administration: paramilitary heat that stopped at nothing in its commandolike attacks on the "enemy." Intensive surveillance from the air coupled with heavily armed land expeditions plus the large-scale dumping of Vietnam-type defoliants add up to a pretty effective program of suppression. The poppies bloom in the same fields that produce the marijuana. The heat was coming down on both alike. Not only were the Mexicans beginning to spill a lot of blood, they were being forced to do their farming the hard way: with thin mountain soil, inadequate water and premature harvests. Just getting up to one of their remote mountain farms required the skill of a stunt flier. The result of all these problems and pressures was that the quality of Mexican weed—never very high, except for a few remote regions—had declined precipitously. Famous names like Acapulco Gold were now jokes in the dope world. Soon Mexico would follow Jamaica as another fading chapter in the DEA's case books.

What most influenced my final decision—to go to Colombia—was the fad that developed in the summer of 1975 for Santa Marta Gold. Night after night, as the stereo poured out the jungle drums and erotic sacrificial cries and moans of Donna Summer singing *Love to Love You, Baby,* I would sit in my gorgeously costumed apartment, which was draped with pleated, multicolored, floor-to-ceiling hangings like the tent of Harun al-Rashid, smoking this marvelous new dope, with its spicy aroma, its mellow effect on the throat and its impressive repertoire of psychological effects. A real *high,* not a schluffy narcotic, a thinking man's weed that carried you up to the *O altitudo!* of your loftiest mind trips, a euphoriant that filled your soul with joy at the same time it filled your body with a delightful sensation—as if it were a bottle of soda water that had just been slightly shaken and uncapped so that the bubbles came streaming up from your toes to your head in an endless stream of psychomotive energy—Santa Marta Gold began to loom before me like the mysterious Golden Bough that Virgil held before him as he descended into the underworld.

EL DORADO

When I started reading about our nearest good neighbor in South America, the first thing I discovered was that the Game being played there today is merely the latest in a long succession of freebooting enterprises that go straight back to the discovery of the country in the sixteenth century. With the glee of an English professor discovering a new allusion in a classic text, I practically stood up and cheered in the South Reading Room the day I learned that Colombia was the original El Dorado and Santa Marta the first town the *conquistadores* had founded on the continent.

It was in 1525 that the Spanish, under the command of Alonso de Ojeda, a former shipmate of Columbus, landed at the site of Santa Marta. The city was established as a treasure-hunting base, pure and simple. The Spaniards were not prospectors. They had no intention of panning mountain streams or digging into rock formations. Their target was much more alluring. They were planning to discover and seize the most fascinating character that had ever loomed before their greedy imaginations: the fabled Indian chieftain who had been described by Columbus's earliest Indian guides as *El Dorado* or the "Gilded Man of Cundinamarca." The legend of this extraordinary figure has been summarized neatly by Ferrol Eagin in *The El Dorado Trail:*

Somewhere on a plateau in the high mountains of what is now the Republic of Colombia lived a king whose wealth was even greater than that of the Aztecs or Incas. The king's name was *El Hombre dorado*, or El Dorado. Once a year El Dorado was the central figure in a ceremony that required the covering of his body with gold dust. To accomplish this, his body was coated with resinous gums. Then it was liberally dusted with gold. When this was done, El Dorado was carried in a litter decorated with discs of gold. The first part of this procession consisted of men whose bodies were painted with red ochre, as this was a mourning ceremony for the wife of an earlier chief who had drowned herself in Lake Guativitá and became goddess of the lake. To pay tribute to the goddess, all those following the men painted with red ochre were dressed in richly adorned costumes of jaguar skins, bright feather headdresses, and all were decorated with gold and emeralds. Songs and music accompanied the procession; and when it reached the shores of the mountain lake, El Dorado and his nobles got into a canoe and paddled to the center of the lake. There the gilded king threw offerings of gold and emeralds into the icy water. Finally, at the close of the ceremony, El Dorado jumped from the canoe and washed the gold dust from his body.

The site of this ritual became the goal of many expeditions mounted from both sides of the Andes by Spaniards, by Germans—authorized by Charles V to "discover, conquer and populate"—and by Sir Walter Raleigh. Several of these heroic undertakings did find the plateau and the lake in the recesses of the mountains near Bogotá. They even found a few golden artifacts, but they did not find the golden kingdom. The greed of the *conquistadores* was sated instead on the wealth of the Incas and the Aztecs, while Colombia was relegated to the crown's less valuable conquests.

The ironic punch line to this first chapter of Colombia's history is that the gold *was* there in the sierras in prodigious quantity and worked with delightful art, the product of the Chibcha civilization that flourished in the fourth century A. D. The hoard simply eluded the rough and hasty searches of the foreigners. Four hundred years later, around the turn of the twentieth century, the gold was uncovered by a series of archaeological expeditions. Today, you can see the treasure in all its astonishing glory at the Bank of the Republic at Bogotá. No gold collection in the world can match it: 8,000 pieces of ingeniously worked and cast metal in the form of body ornaments, ceremonial vases, human and animal figures of great charm—150,000 grams of metal, five times the combined weight of all the gold ornaments in all the museums of the world!

The search for El Dorado commenced with the incursions of the Spanish, Germans and English. Next, it was the turn of the buccaneers, particularly the dread pirate Morgan. The Jesuits followed, controlling the country for centuries until their tenacious grip was broken by the great revolutionaries of the early nineteenth century led by Simón Bolívar, who lies buried on the outskirts of Santa Marta. Then, it was the politicians who squeezed the country until Teddy Roosevelt, a buccaneer worse than Morgan, ripped off Colombia's most valuable province, Panama, so that the U.S. could build the canal. Now the foreign capitalists arrived to exploit—in the manner so vividly described by Joseph Conrad in *Nostromo*—the minerals, crops and nascent industries, especially the growth of the coffee bean and the banana and the mining of emeralds. Eventually, the foreign and native capitalists organized themselves and the country into two great parties, the Liberals and the Conservatives. Then, one day, all the violence and injustice that had been perpetrated throughout Colombia's long and lamentable history, all the humiliation and disgrace that had been inflicted upon the national honor, all the rage that had been swallowed by this enslaved people, the vindictive madness that had been encoded virtually in the country's genes erupted in a cataclysm that for sheer horror and insanity has no parallel in the history of the Western hemisphere.

La Violencia raged for twenty years and claimed a quarter of a million lives. Abruptly, irrationally, irresistibly it broke out on April 9, 1948. On that day, the Liberal mayor of Bogotá, a popular leader named Jorge Eliécer Gaitán—a man of the people who has been compared with Fiorello La Guardia—was shot and killed in the street by a nobody named Roa Sierra. The assassin was instantly seized and lynched by an enraged mob. The act was interpreted, however, as the first shot of a Conservative coup. The Liberals rose spontaneously and, with the help of the local constabulary, took over Bogotá, triggering a reign of terror. In the midst of the ninth meeting of the Inter-American Congress, with the city full of distinguished foreigners, a bloody three-day riot, the *Bogotazo*, erupted, sending a large part of downtown Bogotá up in flames. In the classic newspaper photo, you see in the background the imposing neoclassic facade of the capitol bedecked with the flags of every American nation while in the foreground several overturned wooden streetcars are burning with such vigor that the smoke and flames appear to be rising like an immolatory pyre destined to consume the seat of government and the very reign of law and order.

A providential rainstorm extinguished the fire before the city was totally consumed: but nothing could restore law and order. Like a string of bloody firecrackers, one city, one province after another exploded into violence, until the whole country was torn to pieces in interminable and savage battles. Far worse than any ordinary war, *La Violencia* bore the hideous brands of fratricide, genocide and mayhem. Communities, friends and families turned on each other and committed unpardonable atrocities. Whole villages were massacred. Children and pregnant women were skewered on pitchforks. Men were castrated and their genitals stuffed down their throats. The gulf between the monstrous acts performed daily and the remote causes for all this violence grew so great that eventually the nation's actions assumed the form of a sanguinary and surrealistic farce, which is precisely how they appear in the novels of Colombia's greatest writer, Gabriel

García Márquez. Finally, the savage war of Reds versus Blues guttered out, and a formula for peace was discovered. When order had been at last restored, Colombian history resumed its natural course with the arrival of the next great wave of pirates and freebooters: the dope smugglers.

To understand why Colombia is today the number one country in the Dope Game, you have to add to the nation's history of violence and rapine a long list of predisposing factors, particularly the following:

1. *Geographical location:* Colombia has major seaports and 1,600 miles of open coasts on both the Caribbean Sea and the Pacific Ocean. It is ideally situated, therefore, for smuggling drugs to the east, west and gulf coasts of the U.S., to say nothing of Canada and Europe. To the south, Colombia has common borders with the coca-growing countries of Ecuador and Peru, making it the natural place for the processing and transshipment of cocaine to every consumer country in the world. A light plane can fly from a secret airstrip in the Guajira to southern Florida in seven hours. A fishing boat loaded with 40,000 pounds of pot can sail to the Florida Keys in three days. Regular commercial flights from Miami to Barranquilla take a mere two and a half hours.

2. *Topography and separatism:* Divided by three chains of the Andes and diversified climatologically by the tremendous extremes represented by the Caribbean coast, the Andean alps, the great plains of the interior and the steaming Amazonian jungle of the far south, Colombia has always displayed a very high degree of regionalism. To a Colombian from Bogotá, where there is lots of cold and rain, winter damp and fog and an elevation greater than Denver, *La Costa*, with its subtropical climate and maritime atmosphere, its sandy beaches and banana palms, its large numbers of blacks and Indians, seems like a distant and exotic land. These regional differences were further exaggerated during the civil wars, when many areas proclaimed themselves independent republics and successfully resisted the efforts of the central government to bring them under control. Even today, bands of guerrillas roam the interior, attacking military outposts and sacking towns. Efforts to subdue them are hampered by the inadequacy of the roads and the lack of good communications.

3. *Government:* Colombia's so-called democracy—which has been qualified for years by an official state of siege—is unitary and

highly centralized. The president appoints the governors of the departments, and the governors appoint the mayors and other local officials. Local government is, consequently, weak and corrupt. People expect very little from the central government and resent its intrusions into their affairs. The notion that the welfare of the state is every citizen's responsibility is totally alien to the *campesinos*.

Today, Colombia's democratic form of government is in jeopardy, owing largely to the moral and political corruption coupled with the economic disorder produced by the immense traffic in drugs. The Colombian government estimates the annual drug volume at *$8 billion*—three times the value of the country's most valuable export commodity, coffee. The rate of inflation has surpassed 50 percent per annum, the workers have staged general strikes—which have been met with military force—and the army, which has traditionally stayed clear of Colombian politics, is beginning to grumble about the decay of law and order. If Colombia, which with Venezuela is one of the two surviving democracies in South America, does turn into another military dictatorship, the blame will rest primarily on the American dope merchants.

4. Poverty and latifundia: The traditional South American landowning system, called *latifundia*, is even more outrageous than the old sharecropper system in the American South. Not only is the peasantry denied ownership of the land, it is compelled to migrate frequently so that it does not form any potentially dangerous attachments to the soil it works. (Bad as is the treatment of the peasants, it is generous compared with the way in which the Indians are treated. The latter are systematically exploited for their labor, robbed of their lands and condemned to brief lives of pain and disease by the substitution of alcohol and cocaine for proper nutrition.) With 60 percent of the Colombian population struggling to survive on only 9 percent of the national income, the common people are happy to embrace any enterprise that promises them a living. Rural Colombians in particular have been predisposed by the turmoil of the civil wars to a life of guerrillalike brigandage.

5. Oligarchy and feudalism: Any Colombian schoolchild can name the twenty families that own and rule Colombia. Though ostensibly divided into opposing political parties, these families are united, no matter what their political allegiance, by their greater allegiance to the feudal rule of the families. Until 1978 there was a regular rotation of government from one faction to the other, which did little to promote the strength or efficiency of the government but allowed both sides an equal share of the plunder.

6. *Corruption of government officials:* Bribery is a long-established custom in all South American countries, as it is in most parts of the world. The extent of the corruption of officials of the Colombian government by dope smugglers can be measured from a few items, culled from the Colombian press of the last two years.

Item: Colombia's consul in New York is caught at JFK with twenty-five kilos of cocaine in his diplomatic luggage. Freed on bail, he disappears and is last reported at liberty in Colombia.

Item: A notorious Colombian drug dealer is spotted by the federal police, who give chase. The crook runs to the headquarters of the drug police and puts himself into the custody of the commandant. Next day he escapes and is picked up later in Bogotá driving the commandant's own car.

Item: *La Gloria,* a sailing vessel that is the principal training ship of the Colombian navy, is dispatched to participate in Operation Sail. Before the vessel can dock in New York, word is received that it is carrying drugs. A search by American Customs turns up twenty-eight kilos of cocaine. The crew is put on trial in Barranquilla. Every officer and man goes free.

Item: A confidential report to President Carter accuses some of the highest officials of the Colombian government of complicity in the dope business. The Colombian government lodges a vigorous protest. An American official is obliged to admit publicly that the charges cannot be proven.

7. *The Mafia:* Though the aristocratic families hold themselves free for the most part from the gross criminality involved in the drug trade, the pattern of economic exploitation which they exemplify is aped by many middle-class families who cannot be so fastidious about the means they employ to rise on the social scale. Reasoning correctly that the dirty money they make today will be clean by the time it is inherited by the next generation, these middle-class families have developed into a Mafia that is even more ruthless and bloodthirsty than the Sicilian Mafia. The most dreaded families come from Medellín; considerable insight into

their operations was obtained a few years ago when one of the greatest of them, the crime family of Alberto and Carlos Bravo, was prosecuted in New York City.

The action which the federal attorney brought against the Colombians was one of the biggest drug cases of modern times. Twelve defendants were convicted after a three-month trial that entailed the testimony of 105 witnesses, the audition of 175 wire-tapped conversations and the examination of 500 exhibits, including fifty pounds of cocaine worth more than a half million dollars wholesale and three and a half tons of marijuana, worth about $2 million, as well as $330,000 in cash. Drugs were seized in Manhattan, Queens, Miami, Los Angeles, Toronto and San Antonio, Texas. The police investigation established that the gang's weekly flow of cocaine in New York alone was twenty pounds, worth at street level about $2.5 million!

Putting the whole story together from court transcripts and from interviews with the police officers involved, it appears that the Colombians got the idea of moving into New York—where hitherto the cocaine trade had been in the hands of the Cubans—when they realized that the Colombian community in the Queens neighborhoods of Jackson Heights and Corona had mushroomed to 200,000 immigrants. With a large number of local Colombians aiding in the distribution of the product and becoming customers for the cocaine, the smuggling ring developed an operation that boggles the mind. They moved the cocaine by every means imaginable: by human carrier or "mule" (one of the indicted conspirators ran a sewing shop in Medellín where special brassières and girdles for carrying cocaine were fitted to the mules); by means of hollowed-out coat hangers and furniture legs; in suitcases; even in a dog cage containing a live dog. The marijuana, a much bulkier commodity, was smuggled into the Grancolombiana docks on the waterfront in Brooklyn inside cargo containers that had false sides and ceilings. The vast sums of money that were realized in these enterprises were funneled back to Colombia by means of bank money orders and diamonds.

The most interesting and amusing insights into the case were given to me by a veteran New York undercover narc named Vinnie Palazzotto. After working for years on the American Mafia, Palazzotto was greatly impressed by the Colombians. He told me: "The old Italian Mafia has been ruined by Americanization. The younger men have no discipline and can't keep their mouths shut. Instead of being like the old Mafia guys, whose own wives didn't know what they were doing, these new punks are always surrounded by broads who know all their business. When we pinch one of these young guys, he may inform on his own boss—and *get away with it!* The Colombians are another story entirely. They're like the Italian Mafia used to be. They're hard as nails and care nothing for human life. They'll not only snuff a guy who rats but his *whole family!* I saw a picture recently in a Colombian magazine that showed a family whose members had been chopped to bits—the limbs hacked off the bodies with machetes. One guy who got sent to prison here before the big bust went down was deported back to Colombia. When all the other people up here got hit, the Colombians figured he must be the rat. They tied him to a tree and put thirteen bullets in his body."

Detective Palazzotto's undercover investigation demonstrated not only the vast scale of the Colombian operation but also the relatively small scale of the New York Police Department's resources for dealing with such big-time criminals. At one point, Palazzotto and his partner, pretending to be coke dealers, got tight with the local leader of the gang, Mario Rodriguez. After making a few buys, one day they told Rodriguez: "Mario, next time we come back, we wanna buy *four kilos* off you." The answer was short and simple: "Anything you want, Vinnie!" When the cops got back to headquarters, they realized that this phase of the investigation had ended. The New York Police Department *did not have $150,000 in cash* for a buy-and-bust operation. "From that time on," remarked Palazzotto glumly, "we had to stop playing dealers and go to surveillance." The Colombians had called the cops' bluff.

The arrest and imprisonment of the Colombians did not put the Bravo family out of business. Colombian law does not permit the extradition of Colombian nationals for drug offenses. A handful of operatives went to prison; the bosses remained unscathed, continuing to use their furniture export business as a front for large-scale smuggling operations.

8. *The Guajiros:* The final piece in the puzzle of the Colombian dope trade is the racial or ethnic component. Just as *La Costa* is distanced from the authority of Bogotá by a great stretch

of history, culture, topography and local autonomy, so by a far greater extension of these distancing factors is La Guajira, the greatest smuggling center, separated from *La Costa*. Colombia's remotest and most primitive province is not even populated by people of the same race as those who dwell in other parts of the country. The Guajiros are a special breed of Indians, who boast that in all their history they have never been conquered.

The special status enjoyed by the Guajira in the world of smuggling—not just dope but guns, gold, emeralds, pearls, sugar, whiskey, coffee, cars and electronic appliances—is explained in the first place by the region's unique geographic location. Thrust into the Caribbean like a giant hitchhiker's thumb, the Guajira is land's end, a remote and sparsely populated region with a long and indented coastline, including a number of sheltered bays where deep-draft ships can anchor close to shore. One side of the peninsula belongs to Colombia, the other to Venezuela; but in practice, both sides belong to the Guajiros, who constantly cross and recross the borders with scant regard for the niceties of international commerce.

Though smuggling was always a common practice in the Guajira (the German traveler Alexander von Humboldt remarked in the nineteenth century, "Nowhere else has illicit commerce with foreigners been more difficult to check"), it does not appear to have deeply affected the Indians' life-style until recent times. Papillon lived with a Guajiro pearl-fishing tribe in the Thirties; his account reads like a description of Gauguin's idyllic Tahitians. During World War II, the smuggling business was interrupted by the German U-boats until one day a canny Guajiro chieftain sat down with a German agent. The result was that fuel-starved submarines with swastikas on their conning towers began to slip into Portete Bay, where near-naked Indians swarmed over their hulls with drums of diesel fuel trucked across the border from Maracaibo.

After the war, the Guajiros bought a fleet of old PT-boats and resumed their trade in contraband. It was not until the early Seventies, when the DEA and the Jamaican government combined to shut down the *ganja* trade, that the Guajiros discovered gold: Santa Marta Gold. From that moment, Colombia was overrun by a new race of freebooters and pirates. Commencing with suitcases of weed shoved aboard little one-engine planes at Santa Marta's Simón Bolívar Airport, the Game mushroomed until it became the region's leading industry.

Like a tape that runs out before the tune has finished playing, the information I collected at the library on Colombia didn't tell me anything about what I would find in Santa Marta today. I went over to the Colombian government tourist office and picked up some brochures. Santa Marta was described as "a placid town of 200,000 easygoing, joyous people, redolent with history." Now, does that sound bad? I also quizzed my maid, Gladys, who is from Bogotá. When I told her I was going to Santa Marta, she exclaimed: "Ah, *La Costa!* Those people are very happy! You have a good Christmas. Lots of fun!" Having made arrangements with an agency in New York to be met at the airport in Barranquilla by a college student who would act as my driver, guide and interpreter, I took off for Colombia around Christmas, 1975.

THE LAND OF VIOLENCE AND HEAVY VIBES

Barranquilla International Airport looks like the freight hangars at JFK. Raw concrete walls, corrugated iron roofs, stairs and passageways like cattle runs. Descending to the customs checkpoint, I felt my heart sinking with every step. There's something about arriving in a strange city in a strange country after dark that is always depressing. You can't look around you and get the lay of the land. You can't project your next move forward in your imagination. You're flying blind. If you don't know the language, if you don't have a hotel room, if you can't get a cab, you can get so gloomy that you want to turn around and go right back where you come from. That was how I felt that night. When I got down to the inspection benches, I stared at the plate-glass doors out of the airport. All I could see was a sea of arms, faces and frantic gestures mutely beckoning.

Just as I was getting the wave from the customs man, I heard a voice say, "Meester Goldmann?" Looking around, I saw a very young, monkey-faced kid with an Afro hairdo. He was my guide. He told me his name was César Pequeño. I was delighted to see him. I followed him out of the airport and around the corner to the Hertz Rent-a-Car establishment, where we hired a shiny new Renault in tropical white. It was a natural thing to do, an American travel reflex. It didn't cost me a moment's thought. But, as I was soon to learn, renting a car in Colombia is an act second in danger only to making a pact with the devil.

Cars in Colombia are like cows in India. They are regarded as sacred and can never be killed. Even the oldest, most decrepit piece of junk schlepped down from the used-car lots of Perth Amboy or East St. Louis is regarded by Colombians with veneration. A Colombian will exist on a diet of rice and beans, live in a shack fit only for pigs, starve his children and beat his wife, but when it comes to his car—ah! then, *señor*, he is a lover, a father, a believer and even an artist. Cars in Colombia are adorned like totems. Every inch of the car's surface is decorated like the skin of a Maori warrior. On a ground of red or blue or yellow—some strong primary color—is built up a visual design comprising lines, ovals, squiggles and striking representational motifs. Leaping jaguars, voluptuous women, thrusting, penile aeronautic shapes alternate with cozy domestic features like draped and tasseled curtains on the windows or draped and tasseled curtains *painted* on the windows! The windshield always sports a fringe of jiggle balls and tassels, the hood a couple of fake sports car air intakes, the fenders various embossed ornaments and designs. The whole vehicle becomes a pop art sculpture of the most naïve coloring-book provenance. Naturally, this vehicle is spotlessly clean, even though its driver may not have bathed in a week. Anything that can be done to increase its beauty or improve its efficiency is done, even though the owner is desperately in need of basic medical attention. You get the idea. So, in undertaking to rent a shiny new Renault 4, I was making a deal whose terms I did not fully comprehend. I thought I was laying out a lot of bread for a little white-enamel kiddie car; Hertz Rent-a-Car Barranquilla saw the transaction as practically a blood bond.

César was very excited at the prospect of driving the car, as well he might have been, considering that this was only the second or third time in his life that he had been behind the wheel of a motor vehicle. When he started off with a screech and a jolt, I attributed his lack of finesse to unfamiliarity with the machine. After he had nearly run us into a series of other vehicles, I began to realize that I was on a trial run. His job wasn't made any easier by the road on which we were traveling. The Trans-Caribbean Highway is a perfect symbol of the half-assed country that built it.

The highway can never make up its mind whether it's a modern high-speed express artery or a 1930s two-lane blacktop or just a plain dirt road out of the rustic past. Basically, it's a free-for-all. Every sort of vehicle from an elaborately decorated bus to a dirty farm truck to a broken-down jalopy is out there blasting through the hot tropical night with its accelerator down to the floorboards. Like the house of horrors in the amusement park, the ride is punctuated with catapult stops, shrieking turns and sudden roadside flashes. One moment you're streaking by a garishly lighted *bodega*, its front removed, its stacks of pots and pans and beer bottles glaring out as if caught in a limelight. The next moment, you're flitting by a dim Asian silkscreen of floating houses standing on sticks, like the habitations of primordial lake dwellers. Finally, after a couple of harrowing hours, I landed on a hill overlooking a valley in which twinkle a thousand lights.

César had explained in his clothespin-on-the-nose English that we would arrive too late to get a hotel room. We would stay the first night in a house that belonged to his relatives. When we arrived, we found a group of people gathered on the porch of a bungalow talking and drinking like suburbanites at a cocktail party. I didn't understand a word that was spoken. All I could do was smile and smirk like a monkey. The first clear impression I got was when somebody shoved a bottle of Johnnie Walker Black Label under my nose and poured a shot that would put most men into cardiac arrest. Just pure booze, no effeminate frills like water or ice.

After a scrappy meal of chicken and rice consumed standing up while the dead chicken's brothers and sisters strutted past our feet pecking at the bits of food that dropped from our plates, the party ended, the guests departed. I stepped into the bathroom. I was in Funkyville. The toilet was squat and filthy and not furnished with a seat. On the sink there was no hot-water tap. The tub was a fifty-five-gallon oil drum. When I glanced into the adjoining room, I saw two naked black children lying sound asleep on a bed.

Through a dense fog of exhaustion, I heard César telling me that this was the height of the Christmas vacation season; it was impossible to get a room in Santa Marta. "That's great!" I growled as I threw myself down fully clothed upon a dirty bed. Shoving my shoulder bag under my head to serve as a pillow, I fell sound asleep.

Next morning, I got up early, eager to enjoy the tropical sunrise. Last night Santa Marta was a thousand twinkling lights. What would it be this morning? A quaint old fishing port? A slick new tropicana resort? I strolled out on the porch and cast my eyes down the valley. "Jesus Christ! Where am I?" I exclaimed as I stared in disbelief at the disgusting scene that lay at my feet. Strewn down a dusty, stony slope without a blade of grass were the tin roofs, crumbly walls and water-can-toting waifs of a typical South American slum.

When I recovered myself, I started shouting for César. He appeared with a goony grin on his face. "Let's get the hell out of here!" I barked. We hopped in the car and left the slum in a cloud of dust. Reaching the main road, we swung down a wickedly serpentine mountain highway toward Santa Marta, in one of whose worst *barrios*, Machu Picchu, I had spent my first night in Colombia.

Santa Marta is your classic South American banana port. An arm of volcanic mountain slung around a couple of rusty old freighters, a palm-dotted esplanade trying hard to look like Copacabaña, a statue of Simón Bolívar on horseback, a waterfront tonk strip, siesta sleepy during the long hot day but at night—*Panama Hattie!* This first morning we pulled up before a Humphrey Bogart hotel at the end of the beach and ordered breakfast. We were served *café con leche, arepas* (cornmeal cakes laced with grated cheese) and fried eggs that reeked of rancid oil.

After we finished that disgusting meal, I decided to clue César in to my scheme and see how he reacted to playing dope reporter. The moment I pronounced the magic word "marijuana," a look of mocking comprehension filled his face. The more I explained my needs, the more he grinned, nodding wisely now and giving me some shrewd winks. Suddenly, I got a flash: "Hey, this guy must think that I'm a dope dealer down from the States looking to make a buy. Maybe that's what everybody will think. Ha!"

Now I had been told in New York that nobody would believe my story about being a journalist. Some of the crafty types had told me that I had blundered onto the greatest cover a dope smuggler could ever desire. Unlike the States, where reporters enjoy few privileges and less prestige, in South America and particularly in Colombia, which regards itself as having the best, because the freest, press on the whole continent, reporters are *journalistas*—and *journalistas* are big stuff. By flashing my American press cards and handing out copies of my old magazine articles, I could cut into anybody in sight; and, as a couple of heavies told me, if I wanted to work a deal . . .

Well, I didn't want to work any deals; but it was reassuring to think that for once I might get a warm instead of a cold reception. What's more, if these people insisted on thinking I was in the Game, well, maybe I would just let them think so and see where the trail led. It troubled me that my own interpreter harbored these suspicions, so I labored earnestly to convince him that I had no ulterior intentions. He kept smiling and lisping "*Sí, sí.*"

When I'd finished giving my orientation lecture, I asked César whether he had any ideas where we might begin. He said: "Aih like take you Taganga—plenty *marimberos* there." "*Marimberos?*" I echoed. "What are they?" At this, he really cracked up. Then, recovering himself, he explained, "What you call the marijuana, wee call *marimba*. Thee men who sell thees drog to the Nord Americans, wee call *marimberos*. You like Taganga." It sure sounded hot, like some place in Africa. "O.K.," I said, and we took off in our Renault down the waterfront and through the narrow gridiron of streets till we reached the filthiest and most squalid-looking public market I had ever seen. Even at this hour of the day, men were lying drunk in the street, which was strewn from curb to curb with refuse and filled with loud strident *salsa* music. "Theese very dangerous place," warned César, scowling out the window. "*Muy peligroso!*"

Soon we were clear of the town and climbing a very steep winding road up over a spur of mountain thrown forward to the coast from the great masses of the Sierra Madres, which tower above the town. As we drove, César explained that the fishermen in Taganga were real Indians, descendants of the ancient Taironas, who had been enslaved and butchered by the Spanish. This little tribe had survived, thanks to their isolated location, which until recently could only be approached by sea. After a ten-minute drive, we swung around a curve at the top of the spur and started down the other side toward the Bay of Taganga. At the first glimpse of this spectacular vista, I shouted to César to pull off on the shoulder of the road. Of all the places that I visited on the coast, this little fishing village had the most beautiful setting. A chunk of old nitrate-based Hollywood.

Picture the tropical equivalent of a Norwegian fiord: a deep ocean bay surrounded by precipitous mountains that run down to the stunning blue water like the paws of a huge tawny lion. At the back of the bay lay the village, a cluster of low blocky houses painted in strong but faded blues and reds. Before the village stretched a crescent beach ringed with wind-blown palms. Drawn up on the sands were a score of primitive-looking pirogues painted bright red and yellow. Out in the harbor was a big, powerful-looking shrimper and a graceful sailboat. When we drove down to the beach front, I got out to look at these huge canoes, which were straight out of an old comic strip or a movie about the South Seas. César explained that the smaller ones were called *cayugas* and the larger, *bongos*. They had been hand-hewn from huge tree trunks, the marks of the hatchet still visible on their hulls.

As I stood on the beach looking about me, I picked up the sound of *salsa* music coming from a shack before which a number of men were dancing drunkenly. I assumed they were celebrating the holiday. Looking at them hopping around put me in a good mood. There was a restaurant directly facing the water. I proposed that we go inside and get some cold beer. When we walked inside, we found the walls enclosed a courtyard filled with tables roofed with thatch. You could smell the fish frying. As César ordered up the beer with great authority in a loud commanding voice, I looked at the other guests. One table in particular caught my eye. Around it were seated two very good-looking couples dressed in expensive hippie clothes. They had a sleeping infant beside them. "They *turistas* from the interior," sing-sang César when I pointed them out. "Go over to them and introduce me," I urged him. "Maybe they'll talk to us."

César's guess was right on the money. When I met the people, they turned out to be sons and daughters of wealthy families from Bogotá who were living in Taganga like American hippies. Educated in Europe and America, they spoke perfect French and English. Soon we were deep in conversation, and I was starting to edge toward the topic of weed. Like every Colombian in the area, they were full of stories about the *contrabandistas*. When we had finished eating, they invited me to their house, a series of pueblo-like rooms that had belonged to a fisherman. As soon as we got in the door, they broke out some pale grass, which they called *Mona*. Then they began telling me the sad story of the corruption of the local Indians by the American and Colombian dope smugglers.

They said that the local fishermen were descendants of the ancient Caribs, the first people that Columbus had met in the New World. Though the Indians were ostensibly Christians and worshiped at a church in the middle of the village, they still celebrated their ancient rites, beating drums and playing wooden flutes when the new moon appeared in the skies, signaling the ascent of the gods from the sea. Traditionally, the men had fished for the horse-eye jack, the red snapper and the mullet. They would seine with nets or toss sticks of dynamite off the cliffs to kill the fish in the bay. While they waited for the catch, they would play dominoes in their boats or get drunk on Tornillo Rum. The women were the force that held the community together. To keep their menfolk from squandering everything they earned on booze and whores, the women had established the custom of buying the catch every day from their men and then carting it on their heads over the mountain road to the market of Santa Marta. In this manner they kept the children fed and maintained the community at survival level. Then, the dope smugglers discovered the town, and overnight the traditional civilization began to change as the easy money came pouring in.

Now, two or three times a month, a North American boat would pull into the harbor; immediately, all the men would be called into a conference by the smugglers. Late at night a convoy of trucks would roll down from the mountainside loaded with bales of marijuana. Working fast and silently with tight tribal discipline, the men would load their canoes and ferry the bales out to the yacht or shrimper standing at anchor a few hundred yards offshore. For this one night's work, a fisherman could receive $100: the equivalent of a couple of months' wages. If he worked three nights a month for two months running, he received the equivalent of a year's wages for doing practically nothing. The results were predictable.

Now the men rarely went out fishing. Instead, they gathered in the little *cantinas* along the beach, where they got drunk every day, smoked American cigarettes, drank imported whiskey and staggered out on the sand to dance and sing to loud music from a prized phonograph, which some smuggler had given them along with a supply of hot *salsa* records from the States. When they had danced themselves into exhaustion, they would collapse in a drunken stupor and the women would haul them home.

The worst part, my new friends told me, was that every so often the local police would track one of these shipments over the mountain and, while the boats were loading, a couple of truck-loads of federal cops would suddenly come tearing onto the beach, where they opened fire on the fishermen, killing and wounding the men, who often returned the fire, taking their toll of police. Now, it was a very dangerous thing to walk the streets of Taganga after dark. When the shots rang out in the night, everyone ducked for cover and prayed that the men wouldn't be brought home dead. This is what the *marimba* had done for idyllic Taganga.

When we drove back to Santa Marta in the late afternoon, César suggested that we continue up the coast to the next bay, which was the site of Colombia's mini-Miami, *El Rodadero*, the "Beach of the Rolling Sands." Here at a hotel called the Tamaca ("Tomahawk"), I found a pleasant room with a terrace that looked out over the palm trees to the sea. Grateful for a clean bed after the squalor of the night before, I turned in early. When I awoke, I felt like I was on vacation. The hotel dining room was cheerful; the menu offered pleasant things, like tropical fruits and *huevos rancheros*. As the white-jacketed waiter bent from the waist with a pitcher in either hand, preparing my *café con leche*, I leaned back in my chair and sighed with satisfaction. This was more like it! At that moment, the door opened and in plodded César with a woebegone expression on his face—and a terrible gash on his forehead.

"What happened to you?" I asked. "Aih crash thee car," he confessed, looking as though he were about to burst into tears. "What!" I exclaimed. Then, with many starts and stops and lapses into Spanish, he sketched the incredible accident that he had just survived. He had been driving down the serpentine highway from the house on the hill when he began to drift into the op-posite lane. He saw a Toyota jeep coming up toward him, but he was slow to steer back into his lane. Closer and closer came the vehicles to each other. At the critical moment, instead of turning the wheel, he froze. The two vehicles collided head-on. How he escaped serious injury was beyond explaining. Even more extraordinary was the behavior of the other driver.

A moment after the collision, he had jumped out of his jeep—which had been damaged only slightly—and thrown his arms up in the air in a gesture of absolute exasperation. Then, without a second's hesitation, he had put his shoulder to the car and started pushing it across the road. Clear across the highway he pushed the heavy jeep until it reached the precipitous shoulder of the road. With one last desperate heave, the driver shoved the jeep clear over the edge into the valley. As it crashed down the slope, he scrambled after it in hot pursuit.

"What the hell does that mean?" I exclaimed. "Drogs," said César matter-of-factly, touching gingerly the cut over his eye. "Drugs?" I echoed. "Sure," explained César. " 'Es contraban-dista. Right? 'Ee know—car crash, tránsito come. 'Ee push car where hard to find. Then 'ee go down, 'ide drog." "Sure," I thought. "It figures. Hit any car in Colombia and it's even money you'll hit a dope jackpot."

Once I got César patched up with my first-aid kit, I asked him about the car. César said that he had reported the accident to the transit police and to Hertz in Barranquilla. I felt reassured—but I shouldn't have. I had failed to list César on the contract as my driver. What's more, the police had lifted his license.

The next day I heard from the hotel clerk that the manager of the Hertz Rent-a-Car agency had come rushing out to Rodadero and had run around the whole day looking for us; the clerk told me that the manager was hopping mad. Not only had we smashed up one of his precious cars, we were treating the matter as if it were of no consequence. "These Americans!" he had ranted. "They think they can come down here and throw cars around like they do in America! I'll show them! I'll teach them a lesson! I'll have them thrown out of the country!" The clerk warned me, "You better take care of this guy. He can make trouble for you." He was right. Ten days later, he stuck me for $1,200 damages. Fenders are expensive in Colombia.

Once I got established at the Tamaca Inn, I began to observe my fellow guests. They fell into three distinct groups. First, there were the Colombians from the interior, prosperous families on

Christmas vacation enjoying the customary life of a beach resort. The most distinctive group was the Jews. They were straight from Grossinger's or from Miami twenty years ago. They spoke a mixture of Yiddish and Spanish. The men sat at a table all afternoon playing cards with their caps on and the women lolled at the beach swathed in elaborate robes while their fat kids ran back and forth from the sands to the surf.

Another group was composed of young Americans, mostly from the Midwest, who had come down to Santa Marta to enjoy a cheap beach holiday and get off on the local dope. They were dope *turistas*, a distinct and growing class of travelers that for obvious reasons cannot be the target of heavy ads in the slick mags or posters on public transport or articles in *Travel & Leisure*, but who already account for a lot of vacation dollars in certain parts of the world. What was so amusing about these dope vacationers was the fact that they were very small-town America. One young woman told me that she couldn't get over how happy her husband was here in Santa Marta. He was a different man, a lot of fun and very romantic. "What explains it?" I asked. "It's the drugs," she said in exactly the same tone of voice that her mother would have said, "It's the salt air!"

The Colombian government estimates that 50 percent of its tourists come to the country intent on buying drugs. The best bargains in the land are certainly marijuana, hashish and cocaine. Santa Marta Gold, which costs sixty dollars an ounce in New York—if you can get it—goes for about six dollars an ounce in Santa Marta. Cocaine that is 89 percent pure—impossible to buy in small quantities in the States—sells for ten dollars a gram. In New York, a gram of what passes for good coke costs $100.

The important thing about all these drugs is not simply their low price or high quality. To an American, accustomed to being hassled, cheated and even arrested and jailed for possession of small amounts of "controlled substances," the thrill of Colombia is being able to walk around the corner, knock on the door, put down your money and pocket your goods. Not that there is no danger of arrest; the narcs are everywhere and the hotel employees may be snitches. Exercising normal precautions, however, nothing is likely to happen. In the event you are busted, a few dollars buys you off.

The third and most interesting class of tourists comprises the "players," the dope dealers in town to make a buy. Sometimes they were easy to spot: three guys sharing a suite and spending a lot of time away from the hotel on "business." Sometimes, the players were indistinguishable from the dope tourists. We met one young couple who were barely out of their teens. They were married, and they came from a little town in Wisconsin. The husband looked like he worked for Sears, Roebuck. Yet this bland little boy was actually a daring do-it-yourself smuggler.

He had arrived in Colombia with $30,000 in cash stuffed in his boots. He had journeyed alone up into the mountains, where he had negotiated without an intermediary to buy an entire field. Then he stood by for several days while the stuff was loaded and hauled to a clandestine airstrip. He had paid off the cops and arranged everything so that when he flew down from Racine, he would have the load waiting at the field. He showed us a picture that he had had taken of himself sitting proudly atop a tractor buried in grass. He had a couple of uniformed, machine-gun-toting cops in front of him and a couple behind. I could see him showing this picture back home: "Hey, fellas, get a load of this Colombian hay ride!"

One of the goals I had set for myself in Colombia was discovering and interviewing a real red-dirt marijuana farmer. God knows why this was such an obsession with me. Partly, I suppose, it was the desire to get the real lowdown on the herb. Partly, it was the influence of Carlos Castañeda and his hokey books. The idea of a Don of Dope was entertaining fantasy. In any case, there was nothing I wanted more than to hear the lore of the *yerba* from the lips of some marvelous old man who had devoted his life to growing the high green. Then, unexpectedly, one day I got my chance.

I was sitting with my rich hippie friends shooting the breeze when the subject of dope cultivation came up. "How about it?" I asked them. "Could you help me find an old dirt farmer, *un viejo hombre*, who knows everything about the weed?" One of the men frowned and said: "There's a farmer who works for us sometimes. He grows a little grass—but he's not very old. Not as old as you." (*Oi!* Why did he have to say that?) "Great," I exclaimed. "How do we get in touch with him?" "He's in the next room," replied the man. "Whaaaat?" I exploded. "He's making some shelves for my wife," explained my friend, as he went to fetch the man.

After a few minutes during which I was very busy setting up my tape recorder, in walks the marijuana farmer. After taking one look at him, I practically applauded. He was straight from central casting. Tall, skinny, gawky, with wrists and ankles sticking out of his clothes and a big brown-and-yellow sombrero on his head, he was a real Colombian hayseed. Ah, it was too good to believe! I curled up in my chair like a three-year-old waiting for a bedtime story. The first question I put to the man through César produced instant disillusionment. "How long," I asked, "have you been growing the *marimba?*" The proper answer would have been: "Ever since I was a little child, *señor*, and I received my first seed from my father's hand. It is now forty years since that day." Instead, the dude replies: "Two years." "Two years!" I explode. "What were you doing before that?" More Spanish. More answers. Finally, César explains: "This man, 'ee from the interior, where they don't grow *marimba*. 'Ee come to *La Costa*, look for work. 'Ee just now learns and starts to grow." Hmmmm! That was a downer. But, what the hell! Two years are better than nothing. Next question.

"What is the correct season for planting the marijuana?" I continued. Now this was a goody because I had heard the most contradictory accounts of the growing season: that there were two seasons, that it didn't matter when you planted grass because you could grow it year round and there were always crops coming to maturity. Now, at last, I would get the truth.

The dude's answer was long and complicated, and it involved a lot of hissing through his missing teeth and a lot of smiling. This guy was a real peon; he had learned from generations of his peon ancestors that when you talk to the Man you make nice. You smile, and you speak very softly, very deferentially; and if you could just get down and crawl at the same time, that would be the best. But failing that, you must smile a helluva lot and sort of hiss out your answers like a Jap. Finally, I got impatient with his long-winded answer; I interrupted and asked César for a translation of what had been said so far. "He talks a lot of nonsense," says César. "What!" I exclaimed. "This man is very uneducated," continues César. "He uses too many words to say simple things." Now this, I might add, was always happening with my so-called interpreter. Like any Colombian who has had ten cents worth of education, César felt himself infinitely superior to the common people. When I would have given anything to hear their quaint mind-blowing phrases and authentic nitty-gritty dirt talk, César was always copping out on his job and telling me that the people weren't saying anything I wanted to hear.

Well, I put a stop to that, and bit by bit I started to gather the farmer's views on raising grass. He said that in Colombia there were two seasons, the spring season, which began after the rains ended in December, and the regular season, which began in July or August. The grass grown in the spring was not especially good and sometimes turned black as "bullshit." The best grass was planted about a month before the rains began in September; then the plants grew to maturity during the four-month rainy season. By mid-December when the rains stopped, the plants were well advanced. After a month's intense sun, they could be harvested in the middle of January, cured for a week and then baled for transport. That meant that we were just about two weeks from the peak of the harvest.

Delighted to hear that my timing had been perfect, I pushed on with the questioning. I asked about the best soils, the best altitudes, the kind of seed, fertilizer and cultivation. The farmer told me that it didn't matter where you planted grass, the stuff was a weed, it would grow in any place where there was sufficient water. "But doesn't the best grass grow in the high sierras, where the sunshine is most powerful?" I pleaded, harkening back to the Maven's rap about "high-altitude" grass. "No." The farmer laughed. "The only reason we grow in the mountains is to avoid the police. The grass would grow even better in a good rich valley, but it would be hard to hide it there."

At this point I whipped out a joint of some grass we had bought the night before and said: "Tell him I'd like to get his opinion of this stuff. Ask what he thinks of it." As we all looked on, the farmer took the smoldering joint and put it to his lips. Instead of taking a deep soul-satisfying toke, he started tooting on it like my eighty-year-old mother does when she smokes a cigarette. *Toot, toot, toot, tweet, tweet, tweet*—he took a whole series of little baby puffs. Then, he smacked his lips repeatedly, as if he were tasting a wine. Finally, he said something in Spanish. "What did he say?" I asked, brought to the edge of my seat by this great moment. "He says it tastes a little flat." "Flat!" I cried out, casting looks of exasperation at my friends.

The fact is that by and large Colombians don't smoke grass. They grow it, smuggle it, die for it—but they don't smoke it. And why not, you ask? The answer, to a Colombian, is simple. They believe that when a man smokes not the first or the second but the *third* puff of the *marimba*, he goes crazy and becomes a killer. He could kill his brother, his mother, his own children. That's why they call it "killer weed."

So, no one will do business in Colombia with a man who smokes. No one will respect a man who smokes. The only people who smoke in Colombia are kids who have been corrupted by American culture and certain kinds of peasants who come into contact with grass by growing it or smuggling it. The typical Colombian drug is alcohol. Among the Indians and the upper classes, it is cocaine. (I was told by my upper-class friends that high officials of the Colombian government receive as one of their prime perqs a special discount on cocaine. This is provided so that they won't go out into the open market and upset the price structure by bidding against the regular consumers.)

LA GUAJIRA

The longer I stayed in Colombia, the more I heard about La Guajira, the Klondike of the new Gold Rush. Though there was plenty of smuggling going on at every point along the coast, no region could compare with this wild and arid peninsula, with its population of primitive and nomadic Indians. The Guajira today is simply a giant dope plantation; 250,000 acres are under cultivation. Ten thousand families are said to make their living at the Game. These once-poor herdsmen, farmers and fishermen have struck it rich. Instead of scratching out a bare subsistence from parched soil or wandering endlessly in search of water or risking their lives in dugout canoes fishing for lobsters, turtles and pearls, the Guajiros have become *marimberos*. As the newspapers reported, the farmers have converted their yucca, sesame and banana plots into marijuana plantations. The herders and drovers—who possess an intimate knowledge of the hundreds of trails that have been threaded through the mountains and out across the wastelands over the centuries—have become either walkie-talkie-toting lookouts or truck drivers who push their hulking Mercedes along dry riverbeds or upland paths that would appear impassable to strangers. The fishermen have become lightermen. Even the taxi drivers have developed clandestine trades. The local Brink's or Wells Fargo, they carry the dope bosses out to the *fincas*, where they pay off in cash. These hack drivers also maintain a spy network that reports on the activities of the police, the military and the American dealers. The upshot of this universal activity is a gold-rush economy that has the peasants lining up outside the bank in Riohacha at four in the morning, waiting patiently to exchange their American dollars for pesos at a rate of exchange well below the official figure.

The ugly side of dope prosperity is the endless series of murders, kidnapings and mysterious disappearances that fill the local press. Here are some typical stories:

Four men from the interior were murdered outside Tigreras three months ago. They were blown up along with the camper in which they were traveling by a volley of grenades. According to investigators, one of the victims was Jairo Serra. He was liquidated along with his brothers-in-law while impersonating FA-2 [federal police] agents. The men were going about extorting money from marijuana growers.

Three policemen and a civilian were surrounded in Matitas by one of the syndicates. They were killed by machine guns and grenades, mutilated and partially burned. Their bodies were thrown out on the highway a few kilometers from Riohacha.

Councilman Juan Blanco was kidnaped shortly before reaching his home in Riohacha. He has not been seen since. Investigators have information indicating that Blanco owed 60,000 pesos [$2,000] to a syndicate member.

In mid-December, a sailboat was washed ashore. Inside was the mutilated, burned body of a U.S. citizen. A few weeks later the body of another U.S. citizen was found floating a few meters out from shore. The only thing that was found on the body was a crank from a motor that was tied around the victim's neck.

The Guajira combines the worst features of the Wild West and Al Capone's Chicago. It is the story of Taganga all over again but on a grand scale.

What fascinated a college boy like César about the Guajira was less the crime than the fantastic lifestyle of the Guajiros: a bizarre blend of the primitive and the futuristic. Most of the Indians speak only Arawak and adhere to ancient tribal customs like polygamy, bride purchase and blood feuds. At the same time, they furnish their thatched and stilted huts with color TV sets and Betamaxes. A Guajiro warrior may still wear his mysteriously knotted *guayuco* (a G-string with a broad, brightly colored, finely crocheted belt from which hangs a gaily tasseled, crocheted money bag), but when he rolls out of his brilliantly dyed hammock he will shove a nickel-plated .357 Magnum inside his waistband and get behind the wheel of a Ford Ranger camper that is unavailable in Bogotá. Then, he will drive his women—dressed in beautiful, flowing, floral-patterned mu-mus—to do their shopping in the greatest smuggling town in the Western hemisphere, the real-life counterpart of Mos Eisley in *Star Wars:* Maicao.

Maicao is the name of the Game. I couldn't wait to get there. Unfortunately, César had developed a great need to go back to Barranquilla to see his girl friend. So one brilliant morning, I got a local cab driver and started out along the coastal road with a map in my hand that marked the places of interest for a dope tourist.

The two-lane highway ran parallel to the coast, which it sometimes revealed and sometimes lost as it traced its way over hill and dale, with the mass of the Sierra Madres on the right subsiding, slowing into the coastal plain. At first the ground was thick with palms and jungly in texture. It is in these hills, especially around Palomina, that the best grass is grown. The Guajira itself is a desert, but the adjacent regions catch the water fall from the mountains, which descends in rivers that are rushing torrents in the rainy season and shallow streams during the droughts. Every so often, we'd hit a check point, where the soldiers in the striped guardhouses would peer intently inside the cab, looking for signs of illicit activity. A couple of times, we stopped by wayside stores, where mountain Indians in heavy woven costumes would squat on the ground drinking rum and begging money from us. They were little, stunted men, drunkenly aggressive and abusive. The women were dark and attractive, with great solemn eyes and long braids of glistening black hair.

Forty miles into the Guajira, you pass the last foothills and drive out across the great plain. Here an airstrip can be laid down practically anywhere. The ideal spot is along the coast, where a plane can slip in at low altitude and be on the ground before anyone can spot it. Some of these strips receive so many planes, they are virtually airports. The week before I arrived, the Colombians had busted one of the most notorious strips, the Finca las Mercedes, near Dibulla.

According to the papers, when the police hit the place, they caught three planes on the ground. They all bore American registration numbers. With the aid of two Fiat bulldozers, also found on the scene, the police opened up some recently covered excavations near the strip. They found buried beneath the red dirt a DC-4 with its engines intact. They also unearthed portions of several other planes that had been burned and buried. All of the planes had damaged landing gear. A little later, they went back. This time they seized in Dibulla *160,335 pounds of marijuana*— till then the largest dope bust on record.

When we reached Riohacha, the capital of the province, we drove up to the waterfront, where there was a great sweeping wooden quay extending from a palm-studded beach. The town itself was an ancient settlement, its buildings pastel-colored colonial structures opening on squares where statues of Spanish admirals stood with telescopes, cutlasses and cocked hats. Herds of primly uniformed schoolgirls trotted down the narrow streets, ogled by loungers who stood at every corner gossiping or making purchases from the heavily shuttered stores. Riohacha was a bit of old Spain in the New World.

As it was lunchtime, I asked the cab driver if he knew a good place to eat. He took me to a little restaurant on the beach, where we ordered fried fish and beer. As we talked, he told me that he was a native of this town. I asked him if he knew anything about the *marimba*. He snorted mockingly and said: "Who doesn't know about the *marimba?* Half the families in this town have connections with the business. Do you see all these expensive cars parked here in the streets? Where do you think these people get the money to buy cars? The first thing a man does when he becomes a *marimbero* is to buy a luxury car and a gun. Every day people disappear and the families run to the police. Then, a few days later the body is found with thirty holes in it. Many times, the body is never found. It is buried in the hills. Now many people leave the city. There is no order here. Years ago, this was a peaceful place. I remember the carnivals. They were happy times. Now the only talk is about money and killing."

I had heard that cab drivers were often active in the Game. I asked him if he had ever taken a hand. "No, *señor,* I have not done this. But I have thought to do it many times. Who knows? I may still do it. It is very dangerous work, but how else can a poor man make money and buy a house? I have relatives who change at the bank in one day a thousand dollars American money. I wait for them to ask me."

When we drove out of the town toward the Venezuelan border, for the first time I caught the flavor of the real Guajira. The parched land was cracked and scored with dry gulches. Little herds of cattle cropped the sparse vegetation. The last few miles into Maicao, the highway was littered with the refuse of a weekly road market. Finally, we pulled into the town and drove to the heart of the real-life Mos Eisley.

Picture now a dusty, congested gridiron of unpaved streets and shoulder-to-shoulder, cast-concrete one- and two-story buildings dropped onto the wasteland where the new two-lane highway from Riohacha to Maracaibo approaches the Venezuelan border. The town square edges a street that is a cross between the main drag in some Texas frontier town and Orchard Street on the Lower East Side of New York. The sidewalks are lined with stands and pushcarts jammed with shoes, sheets, shaving supplies, LP records and flamboyantly colored underpants pinned up like huge butterflies. Along the store side is an endless succession of open-fronted shops whose merchandise is piled up as it would be in a warehouse.

Amassed inside the concrete hovels of this desert trading post, as in Ali Baba's cave, is a treasure trove of the finest merchandise produced by the most advanced industrial nations in the world. TVs from Japan, cameras from Germany, hi-fi gear from the U.S., Rolex watches from Switzerland, Black Label Scotch from Kilmarnock, Chanel perfumes from Paris and Bavarian porcelain from Munich. The shock of discovering such chic merchandise in this primitive setting is nothing, however, compared to the effect experienced when the buyer asks, "How much?" The shopkeepers, many of whom speak excellent English, quote you prices that are one-half what these coveted items would cost in discount-crazy New York. A fifth of Black Label costs $5, a nineteen-inch Sony color TV costs $150, a pound of grass costs $40, seventy-five-year-old brandy costs $10 a bottle, an Olympus OM-2 camera with a 1.4 lens costs $275, a young boy or girl costs $8 per day. How can they do it? How can they give the goods away? The answer is simple. All this merchandise is bootlegged; and some of it is "hot."

As city planners, the *contrabandistas* don't deserve good grades. Maicao doesn't have one paved street, the water supply is undependable and every block must be guarded by a tough-looking dude who patrols the sidewalk with his automatic shotgun at the ready. Yet the city does boast a thirteen-story Holiday Inn–style hotel with a marble-lined lobby and a swimming pool on the roof. The Hotel Juan is the ultimate smuggler's hotel in the ultimate smuggler's town. Erected with ill-gotten gains and dedicated to the making of deals and the cutting up of jackpots, this caravansary is as much a monument to the Game as it is a necessary facility.

On this first trip, I didn't get beyond the facade of legitimate business conducted in the streets and stores. Later, I would learn exactly how the serious business was conducted between the foreign dope buyers who drove in from Venezuela and sat down with the representatives of the big clans like the Cardenez and the Val de Blancos. These Indian clans had just begun to battle each other at that time and to wage war with the government, which was threatening to send in units from the Rondon Battalion, bivouacked on the outskirts of Santa Marta. On my first day in the Guajira, everything bore a peaceful appearance. Later, this region would erupt in a series of guerrillalike battles between the Guajiros and the Colombian army.

MAKING A CONNECTION

Just before New Year's, I was sitting in the hotel dining room one morning enjoying breakfast when an extraordinarily costumed figure appeared beside my table. He was an Indian whose brown oriental face was delicately lined with a sparse mustache and Charlie Chan beard. He was wearing a pumpkin-colored Ecuadorian shirt embroidered down the center with tropical fruits and leaves. His blue jeans were belted with an Indian sash, and on his feet were bright red-and-white sneakers with red polka-dot laces. His head was crowned by an American baseball cap. The most interesting thing about his appearance was his costly pre-Colombian jewelry. Around his neck hung a string of big stone marbles interspersed with animal amulets. His left wrist was swathed with at least thirty strands of fire-red Peruvian beads. Flashing a big smile, he introduced himself as a salesman of Indian artifacts—or what we would call a grave robber. I invited him to sit down and have some coffee.

I couldn't afford any pre-Colombian gold, but I figured that a hustler like this would know his way around town. I told him about my mission. He said he could introduce me to some interesting people. After breakfast, we drove away from the waterfront toward the back of town, where we came upon a new *barrio* called Hollywood, a checkerboard of little pastel-tinted bungalows with lawns and carports. Like everything that Colombia is trying to become, this neighborhood is a parody of the U.S. as it was twenty years ago, in the age of ranch houses, two-car garages and "I Love Lucy." Television hasn't reached most homes in Santa Marta: the place in the living room that will someday be occupied by the sacred set is filled at this moment by a stereo with a baffling brand name. These stereos are to be found in every prosperous home, but I never heard one that played through both speakers.

Looking about one brick-and-stucco dollhouse, I observe that the furniture is all Castro Convertible Spanish colonial. The kitchen sink has but one tap, hot water being unknown in Santa Marta and water of any kind in short supply, subject to rationing, district by district, at different times of day. (The tap water is full of amoebas, so the sophisticated people, the people who are visiting the coast from Bogotá, install in their kitchens huge ten-gallon jugs of spring water on tipping stands. The local hustlers collect the empty jugs and fill them up with polluted water, which they sell as pure.) Generally speaking, the houses don't look right for men who are making millions of pesos in the smuggling game. But then you have to reckon with the fact that most dope dealers like to maintain a low profile—and a very large supply of ready cash.

The man we had come to see was named Manolo. He was a real Colombian Connection but not a big man by local standards. Getting an introduction to a big connection is like getting an introduction to a big banker; it isn't something that can be arranged through a street hustler. In fact, the only way you can do it is to have the recommendation of one of the connection's other customers, a favor that will cost you plenty. As usual, I was starting at the bottom, but I figured that a little connection was better than none.

To understand what the connection does, you must have a mental picture of the supply end of the Game. Back in 1975, most of the dope that was coming out of Colombia was grown on small plantations in the foothills of the Sierra Madres farmed by dudes like the peasant I had interviewed. Each farm grows only so much weed, and the quality varies according to the seed and the farmer's skill. The first thing the connection has to master is the business of getting the best weed at the lowest prices in the quantities that his customers desire. Colombia produces far more marijuana than it can export; consequently, scoring weed is no problem. Sometimes you can see whole bales of the stuff rotting beside the country roads where it has been dumped because the rains got to it. Quality is another matter entirely. Because the Colombians don't smoke, their quality consciousness is badly developed. They'll always try to sell you stuff that in the States would be rated "commercial." To get the good stuff, you have to know where to go; that's the connection's number one skill.

Once the weed has been collected and baled, the connection has to organize the hauling and loading operation: engaging the crews and renting the trucks, tractors and trailers. Next, he has to rent the airstrip and prepare it for landing, furnishing it with whatever the pilot requires: a wind sock, a radio, gasoline, food, whiskey, cocaine. He has to be able to bring in a boat at night with blinker signals or provide a pilot familiar with the shore. Most important, he has to be completely at home in the labyrinthine network of police corruption, which extends beyond the local to the federal police and entails not only bribery to look away from the crime, but, as in the case of my friend from Racine, bribery to ride shotgun on the load and protect it against hijackers. Above all, the connection has to be so well-connected that he is aware of everything that is going on in the community that could interfere with smuggling operations. He has to have advance word when the central government is sending down the army to make a sweep, when customs has decreed that somebody must take a bust to make things look good in Bogotá and so forth. If the connection is doing his job, he's worth every penny of the fifty dollars over cost that he's charging the American smuggler for every pound of grass that passes through his hands. The connection's theme song is the *Largo al Factotum*.

When we inquire after Manolo, we are informed that he had been up late the night before at the cockfights, but he would be waking soon. Won't we just step out to the carport and join his men, who are having a few drinks. The carport proves to be much nicer than the house. It has been decorated like an arbor with vines and wicker cages filled with chattering tropical birds. You can see the sky but are shielded from the sun. A cool breeze is blowing.

The owner of the house is Gonzago, Manolo's father, a smiling old man who sits in a rocking chair supporting on his lap a pretty little girl with big brown eyes whose stubby hand is constantly grubbing about in a box of cookies. This charming picture of domesticity is violated the moment the old boy opens his mouth. He speaks English, but he's obviously senile or drunk or both, because all that comes out of his mouth are sing-song nonsense phrases and scraps of old English music-hall songs from forty years ago.

Then I'm presented to Carlos and Lucas, who are mulatto hit men from the Guajira. These two guys have ramrod backs, monkey hindquarters, dark complexions, big brown eyes, very curly short hair, huge hands and that type of posture so common among a certain type of American black that suggests that there is a hinge across the man's back at the hips which makes it natural for him to constantly bend from the waist without rounding his back. There is also a white man who looks like Walter Matthau. He introduces himself as an agronomist.

As soon as we are seated, the better-looking of the two hit men, Carlos, begins to do the honors of the house. Holding the bottle of Johnnie Walker Black Label in one hand, he pours whiskey into a glass held in the other hand and shoves it into my face. The style of drinking in Colombia is crude, joyless and compulsive. It's like a game of spin the bottle. First the host pours; then he looks about him for the most likely candidate; then he shoves the drink into your hand. You are supposed to throw back, like a man, an amount equivalent to four shots. If you protest that you don't want the whiskey, one of two things will happen. Either your protest will be interpreted as a demand for some other kind of alcohol, in which case the other two standard drinks will be broken out: wonderful and costly Napoleon brandy or—can you believe this?—Manischewitz wine! If your refusal is not interpreted as a request for another kind of booze, if, God forbid, the host gets the idea that you're reluctant to drink, that you're being coy or hard to get, this steel-muscled jaguar, this pistol-packing killer who would just as soon blow your head off as look at you, will suddenly adopt the simpering manner and enticing posture of an old-fashioned B girl. He'll hold his bottle and his glass up in the air, shake his ass and then, with a killing look from his beautiful soulful Latin brown eyes, he'll plant himself right in your lap and feed you the drink the way a mother feeds a baby.

By ten-thirty in the morning everybody is half loaded. Grandpa is drooling with senile dementia. The grim Guajirons are starting to leak a little mirth. The agronomist is talking about disc harrows. Just then, the star of the show makes his entrance, looking sleepy and befuddled. Manolo has that spoiled Spanish look that comes from having been the pampered boy child in a macho society. He's sensual looking and fat, his face puffed out with starch and alcohol. He looks ten years older than his real age, thirty-four. When he sees us, he smiles with great charm and explains that he was up till dawn. After taking one look at his father, who has now passed out in his chair, with the little girl still seated on his lap consuming her cookies, Manolo indicates that we should leave the house and go elsewhere to discuss our business.

We get in our cars and drive back into town. My Indian friend tells me that we are going to collect Manolo's partner, Don Evandro, who runs a farm-supply store. The Don, I learn, is an older man who comes from a distinguished local family. He had served for years as a judge and was destined to become the governor of the province, but just before his appointment, he was kicked off the bench due to a scandal. He had passed a lot of bad checks to cover his gambling debts. The family wanted him to ease their disgrace by exiling him to the States. Don Evandro was too old to make a fresh start. He swallowed the most bitter pill an upper-class South American can stomach: he went into trade. He had no talent for business, however, so he elected finally to play the Game. Now he runs an airstrip in the banana-growing region west of Santa Marta. Not a very brave smuggler, he is called by all the street boys, *Topogigot* or "Bugs Bunny."

When we step into the store, we are introduced to a small, elegant, aristocratic-looking old dude who appears sadly out of place surrounded by coils of rope, sacks of seed and piles of shiny new plow points. There is some problem about where we should hold our conference. Finally, César suggests that we go up to his relatives' house in Machu Picchu, where no one will be at home but the servants.

We get in our cars and drive up on the hill. Colombians like to conduct business in comfortable circumstances. Instead of hunkering down on the first thing that offers, as an American would do, they busy themselves to make this slum shack into Slumberland. Manolo produces a flamboyantly colored hammock and rigs it with practiced skill, holding the rope between his teeth like a sailor. When he's strung it up, he invites me to lie down inside this soft, clinging body snood. Meanwhile, the others have dragged out chairs and inflated an air mattress and prepared themselves as Americans might for a sunbath or an evening of chitchat on the veranda. When the preparations are at last complete, the men have arranged themselves in a line, with me recumbent in my hammock at one end and Manolo stretched out on the air mattress at the other end and, between us, Don Evandro ensconced in a comfortable rocking chair, the guy who looks like Walter Matthau beside him in a side chair and the Guajirans prowling about the porch like big silent cats. I have no inkling of what will happen. I'm going to let my Indian grave robber do the talking.

At first the conversation is perfectly innocent. There is a lot of talk about the things the Colombians would like to buy from the States. Every South American walks around with a fat catalogue in his head illustrated with all the latest and finest things that are produced in America, from electric gadgets for the house to expensive sporting equipment to the ultimate fantasies of big cars and custom-built yachts. I promise to see what I can do when I get back to New York to help these dudes acquire their favorite goodies. Then, imperceptibly, the talk drifts around to the topic of the *marimba*.

They tell me that if I could just get a boat or a plane and bring it down here, they could load me with any amount of Santa Marta Gold. When I ask them what they charge for this service, they explain that owing to the increase in demand and the problems created by the police, they must have forty dollars a pound. This strikes me as a ridiculously low figure, but I pretend that I'm shocked by such extravagant demands. I tell them that most smugglers pay less. Immediately, they counter by offering to "front" the grass—sell it on credit—for ten dollars a pound. If the load gets through, the balance falls due; if something goes wrong, the debt is canceled and a new load can be arranged on the same terms. Later I learned that this practice was so common that it had received a special name: *gorranado*, which comes from *de gorro*, literally, "without paying." Even at ten dollars a pound, I was told, the connection still makes money because he pays the farmer half that price.

After receiving this generous offer, I say that we shall have to meet and talk again, that I've just arrived in town and I intend to talk to a number of people. This triggers a long series of warnings about the dangers I run from the unscrupulous merchants who abound in these parts. They tell me that I should be especially careful in the streets and even at the hotel because there are so many bandits who prey on American visitors. I'd heard this warning before and knew that it was well founded. I promise to be cautious. What is really on my mind at this moment, however, are not the dangers I am running with thieves but the rather uncomfortable position I am getting into with these dudes. Though I had told them that I was an American journalist, I could see that they were convinced that I was in the Game. Why else would I come all the way down here and enter the company of dope dealers and expose myself to the risks of wandering around out in the Guajira if I weren't looking to get rich?

The funny part was that, as I soon realized, they assumed I *was* rich. The safari suit I was wearing, the Tiffany watch on my wrist, my car, my driver, all the things that signified nothing to me were clear indications to them that I was a wealthy *gringo*. If you don't care about money, people assume you've got money. This is especially true if you're middle-aged and responsible looking. Most smugglers are rugged young boys clearly on the make or hardened old criminals. The only men of my age and appearance who turn up in Colombia talking dope are big shots who play the backfield while the more desperate types run the ball. Preposterous as it sounds, these none-too-experienced locals, Manolo and Don Evandro, were titillating themselves with the thought that they might have lucked into one of these rich and powerful godfathers. Before we left the house that day, they showered me with invitations to their homes, offers of help in every direction and countless expressions of extreme good will. They even suggested that I might find it agreeable to purchase some land and build a home with a fine view of the sea and the mountains—and a nice long private dock. Never anywhere had I received such a warm welcome.

After my meeting with Manolo and Don Evandro, I began to wonder how far I could go if I chose to play the role of the Big American Dope Dealer down from the States and hot to make a buy. At this point, I didn't know enough to play the part convincingly; but as the Colombians were so eager to do business, it struck me that just by meeting the right people and letting them draw their own conclusions I might learn a great deal. Manolo was not a man to trick. I had heard that he had to flee the city a few years before because he shot and killed a man in a barroom brawl. Don Evandro, on the other hand, was a real gentleman. I decided that I would drop into his store and have a little chat with him in private.

The next day I turned up in the afternoon and received a very cordial welcome. We went into his office and talked about the weather for a while. Then I told him that the people I knew in the States were not interested in airplane smuggling, that they always moved their goods by boat. Did he know any connections who were boat loaders? At first he tried to convince me that planes were much better to use because they were fast and safe. As I rehearsed a lot of stuff I had heard about airplane crashes and radar nets, he gradually began to concede that there was a great advantage in doing one big load in a boat rather than making a dozen runs in a small plane. Finally, he told me that for a certain consideration he might arrange for me to meet a big connection whose specialty was exporting marijuana and hashish by boat. What he had in mind was the usual finder's fee. I assured him—as I could do in good conscience—that if anything developed, he would get his share.

The next evening, he picked me up at the hotel and took me to a very modernistic high-rise apartment building along the coast. We stepped into an expensively decorated flat with a stunning panoramic view of the bay. The family, who were obviously upper-class Colombians, were just rising from the supper table. After making some formal introductions, he led me out onto the terrace, where he presented me to a young man who looked like a miniaturized version of Victor Mature. The man spoke good English, but very slowly and drowsily, as if he were loaded on downs. After the usual pleasantries, Don Evandro told him that I was interested in "shipping."

At this point, our host reached across to a table near his chair and opened a drawer. He removed a very fat joint and lit it. After he had taken a couple of slow, deliberate drags, he looked hesitantly at me. Then he made as if to offer me a toke. Without a moment's hesitation, I reached over and took the joint out of his hand. When I had inhaled deeply a couple of times, he looked at me fixedly with his big, dark bedroom eyes and said, "You must excuse me for not offering you some at once. You see, in our country it is very unusual for a man of your age to smoke."

Then, having gotten his head, he leaned back and in his slow, deliberate English, he began to give me the Game. "If you want some hashish, we could make an arrangement. Would you like the blond, the black, the brown or the gray?" I hadn't the faintest idea what the differences were, but I've always been hot for blondes, so I opted for the first. "Good," he said unempathically. "I can get you this material, but the trouble is that this is a very busy time of the year. I don't know in the next month if we could get a boat." Then he gave me a bemused glance and sighed. "You know, our people are interested only in money. Whoever pays the most has the people. I think a captain at this time of year would cost you $35,000. The first mate has to get ten. Each crew has to get $5,000. If you have this kind of money, something could be arranged." I said, "What would the arrangement be?" "We would take the boat," he drawled, "and bring it two, three miles off the Florida coast. Then you would take it in." I said, "What would this cost?" With a heavy-lidded blink, he murmured, "It would cost about eighty dollars a pound." "Christ!" I thought, "he's going to drop hash that sells for $750 a pound at my back door for eighty dollars a pound! What a bargain!"

At this point, I felt I was getting beyond my depth. So I appeared to be lost in thought for a moment; then I said that I would think about it seriously. He smiled dreamily and nodded without saying a word. Don Evandro, who had been sitting back in his chair contemplating the view during this exchange, spoke up and took the conversation off to another, less serious topic. In a few minutes he rose and said that we must leave. Our host appeared to have trouble rising. When I stood up, I felt very light-headed. The grass we had smoked had been the strongest weed I had encountered in Colombia. I slept very soundly that night.

IN WITH THE NEW YEAR—AND OUT WITH MY LIFE!

The climax of my Colombian experience came on New Year's Eve. This holiday is big stuff in *La Costa*. Every girl gets a new dress (generally in a shade of bright red), all the kids get loud fireworks and the new middle-class families that have sprung up in Santa Marta's brand-new residential *barrios* hold parties in their homes with singing, dancing, drinking and eating, all to the accompaniment of a quaint sailor's music, made with a squeeze box and a guitar, that sounds like a Caribbean polka. I had received several invitations for the evening from my newly acquired Colombian friends. I decided to accept them all and spend the evening party hopping with César.

The night began with a preposterously middle-class supper party at the home of an official of the Grancolombiana shipping line whom I had met the week before. He had just built a raw new house, decorated in Holiday Inn Spanish Missionary, of which he was extremely proud. When we arrived he had the stereo playing through one speaker, and in honor of the occasion he served champagne that tasted like fermented pineapple juice.

When it was time for supper, we were ushered downstairs into a tiny dining room. The men, the honored guests, were seated around the table, with the host at one end and myself at the other. The women of the house were confined to the kitchen, from which they would sally forth occasionally to comment on the meal and watch our progress. The cook had made a special effort to please the *gringo*. With a smile she presented the *pièce de résistance:* lasagna made with chicken instead of beef, one of the blandest and most inedible lumps I have ever been served. When the meal was over, our host, who had suffered all the pains of a young husband in Great Neck twenty years ago entertaining the relatives on Friday night, smiled wanly and wished us *Feliz Anos.* We jumped in our car and drove swiftly to the next stop on our Colombian social calendar: the house of Maria, Don Evandro's mistress.

At Maria's there were the usual smiles and salutations, the usual bullshit good will, and, as usual, nothing was happening. While Maria's predatory girl friend Lucinda dragged poor old Don Evandro out of his chair and made him partner her through an erotic Spanish dance, I took a walk down the block with César. The tiny little bungalows of identical design were filled with parties of identical design. Everywhere you saw young women, children and old folks trying to have a merry old time without their men. "Where are the men?" I asked. "They're out dreenking with each other. Later they go see their weemen."

Finally, as the midnight hour approached, we drove over to Manolo's house. When we arrived, the father was already dead drunk and the wife was walking around scowling. Manolo arrived soon after us and with eloquent gestures explained that it had been an exhausting evening of family responsibilities, one compulsory visit after another, all of them accompanied by much "blah, blah, blah." I laughed at his English and sympathized with his plight—which was my own.

As a hoarse foghorn blew, signaling the end of the old year and the beginning of the new, the mood brightened perceptibly on Manolo's patio. The Black Label Scotch appeared to drown out the bad champagne. Our host got up to dance with his wife, putting one hand before his chest, palm forward, in a coy and wonderfully Latin rumba gesture. For one moment it looked as if we might have a party. But no. We were in Colombia, the Land of Violence and Heavy Vibes. While Manolo was dancing I had reached inside my shoulder bag and switched on the portable tape recorder I always carried. It was a stupid thing to do, but I was fearful that if I didn't record one of our conversations, I would never be able to reproduce the way these men talked. What they talked 90 percent of the time was Latin bullshit, but it was their style that interested me. When Manolo came over after the dance and sat down next to me, he launched into his usual rap, offering florid advertisements for himself and derogating the other people with whom he feared I was thinking of doing business. Every one of his self-serving banalities was being soaked up by my little Sony. I could hardly wait to get home and play the tape. As it turned out, I was lucky to get home at all. For when the cassette reeled off, instead of the button snapping up, the machine made a persistent buzzing sound. It had jammed.

Then, in the middle of the platitudes, the self-serving remarks, the smoky Scotch and the distant sound of fireworks, I suddenly woke up to the fact that my life was in danger. Before my astounded eyes, I saw Manolo reach over and pluck from my shoulder bag the tape recorder. I was paralyzed. César leaped up and started to explain the machine's operation, taking care to turn it off as he quoted its price. For one second it appeared that his explanations might be acceptable. But, no—Manolo's stare turned black as he glared at the sinister-looking little box in his hand. He spoke rapidly, angrily. "What's he saying?" I barked at César. " 'Ee says for thees, 'ee could 'ave you *keeled!*" Imagine! Having your life threatened through an interpreter! There was nothing to say. I was caught red-handed.

Glancing about me, I noticed that all the women and the servants had fled. Manolo was struggling now to express his rage in English. "You theenk aihm stuupeed! You theenk aihm a fool! Aihm very smaaht! Aih know something wrong when you always make theese pictures—even whan aih count my *maahnee!* Why always theese *fleek, fleek, fleek?*" "Jesus Christ," I thought, "what if this nut starts thinking that I'm some sort of offbeat narc? He'll pull that gun he's always packin' and shoot me down on the spot!"

Now he was back to rummaging in my bag again. This time he pulled out my camera by the strap and held it out before him like a deadly snake. Finally, he turned and confronted me. "Aihm going to take theese equipments," he announced. "Aihm going to show them to my exphairt. Theese will take a day, two days, three days—aih don't know. When 'ee tells mee what is inside theese machines, aih weel know what to do!" With that threatening remark, he marched inside the house holding aloft the evidence of my crime like a couple of dead rats swinging from their tails.

"What the hell do we do now?" I snapped at César. "Wee must go at once," whispered César, "before 'ee call 'ees men." At that moment Manolo reappeared. I rose and said that I was profoundly sorry for my innocent mistake, but we must now depart. "No, dohn't go yet," said Manolo. Instantly, I flashed with fear. Was he detaining us for a reason? Had he formed some plan when he stepped in the house? Was he waiting for help? My mind was racing wildly, throwing up one paranoid image after another. Finally, I decided to change the subject. Instinctively grabbing for the first thing that came to mind, I said: "Well, if we're not going to leave, then for Chrissake, let's *eat!*"

The moment I pronounced the magic word "eat," the whole mood changed. Suddenly, everybody brightened. The women came fluttering back. The lights went up, the music got louder and soon the servants brought forth the chicken and rice, which had been prepared long before this last supper. We managed to swallow a few dry mouthfuls; then we left quietly, apprehensively, each of us withdrawn into his own thoughts.

As we drove home along the dark road, we seemed to congeal into a single glob of human flesh. César announced that he had no intention of sleeping that night at the house. I was glad to have company in my room at the hotel. Now that I was out of Manolo's house, my mind, which had felt during the meal like a stuffed-up nose, suddenly cleared. It teemed with images of danger. Could he have dispatched a car filled with gunmen to follow us and shoot us down along the road? Would he wait a few days and then order our execution? "From now on," said César threateningly, "everywhere wee go, wee'll have a couple of Guajiros on our tail."

That night I went to sleep in one bed, while César lay down in the other. I was surprised that I didn't feel more fear. Actually, what I felt was a sense of resignation. *Que será, será.* It helps to have lived most of your life and done what was most important to you. Then when you face the end, you don't suffer the pathos of "Not yet! For God's sake, give me one more chance!"

The morning after this fiasco, I awoke from a sound sleep and went down alone to the breakfast room. The moment I stepped off the elevator, I spotted a tough, primitive-looking dude planted on a sofa in the lobby staring straight at the elevator door. When I stepped forth, he glared at me, and I stared back at him grimly. "Ah," I thought, "they don't lose much time, these guys. Already we have our tail." Once I was seated at a table in the dining room, I cast a glance through the room's glass doors. The man had moved his seat so as to better be able to observe me.

After breakfast, I went upstairs and found César lying in bed, with his Afro at half mast. "You got mee in beeg trouble now," he whined. "Stop complaining," I snapped. "They aren't going to do anything to you. I'm the one that's fucked!" "Eef they don't do nothing today, aih don't theenk they do it," he said wistfully. I didn't find this thought the least bit reassuring. Pacing back and forth in the room, I felt a powerful compulsion to *do* something and not sit around waiting for these pricks to do me in.

As I obsessed over my predicament, everything around me began to assume a strange and gloomy coloring. The hotel room, which had always been so bright and beachy, with its big terrace facing the coconut palms and rubber trees, had become a dark cave of paranoid ponderings and plots. The curtains were drawn, the doors were locked, the shower was running, creating an acoustic obstruction to eavesdroppers. Every minute a new threat, a new danger suggested itself. What if Manolo sent his men up to search the room while we were away? They would seize all my tapes. They would take them back to the house, they would play them, they would be alarmed by even such recordings as that with the *campesino*. They would assume that I had taped every word they spoke to me. "We've got to get rid of these goddamn tapes," I told César. "They're just too incriminating."

The only way you can erase a tape, if you don't have a bulk eraser—an electric gadget designed to erase the entire tape with one shot of electricity—is to press down the "record" button and allow the entire tape to reel off at precisely the same speed as it does when you're recording. If the tape is a ninety-minute tape, it takes ninety minutes to erase. If you've got a whole handful of ninety-minute tapes, it takes a whole day to erase them. Meanwhile, as they're being erased the machine can pick up any fresh conversation which is being conducted within its range. So it not only takes a long time to wipe out the evidence; you've got to shield the machine so that it does not record a fresh and even more incriminating conversation.

I took the first tape, slipped it in the Sony, pressed down the red "record" button and the black "forward" button. Then I set the little black box directly opposite the bathroom shower, where it would wipe out the record of our conversations and replace them with the innocent sounds of falling water.

Worrying about incriminating evidence was actually just a substitute for the real worry: the fear that I'd be killed. Frankly, there was no reason in the world why I shouldn't be killed. I had betrayed Manolo's confidence. I had compiled evidence of his dope dealing. Most important, I had made him look like a fool and stunned his macho sense of honor and respect. Human life is cheap in Colombia. For a couple of hundred dollars you could have anybody wiped out. Killing a foreigner or a social inferior isn't even regarded as a very serious crime. There would be a routine inquiry. It would immediately become apparent that I had been talking to dope merchants. The Colombian government would figure it was just another drug-associated assassination. The papers were full of such crimes.

This last volley of thoughts triggered off a chain reaction in my mind. When I'm threatened I get angry; when I get angry, I get hard and cruel; when I get hard and cruel, I want to kill. Or as King Lear put it so well: "Kill, kill, kill, kill, kill!" So I, the nice scholar pussycat, suggested suddenly that we buy a couple of guns and get ready to shoot it out with our assassins. César looked at me with horror. Then, just as abruptly, I said that we should pack our bags and head for Barranquilla. We could lie low there for a day, then jump aboard a plane for the States. "They find you queek and keel you in Barranquilla," he blithered. "They weel think you go to the DAS" (the Colombian FBI). Then I thought about the tales I had heard of wild shoot-outs at the Barranquilla Airport and conceded that he was right.

Suddenly, I had an inspiration. "Listen, César, why don't we try to *pacify* these guys? They're uptight because we taped them and snapped their pictures, right? Well, suppose we go to them and say: 'Look, we know you guys are upset with us. We didn't mean any harm. Just to show you we're on the level, here's all our undeveloped film. You take the film, we don't need it. That way you'll feel more secure, and you'll see we don't mean any harm.'" "Ah, *bueno!*" exclaimed César, brightening for the first time. "Aih go now and geeve them theese theengs."

With that, he was out the door and off to the lion's den. For the next couple of hours, I walked around the hotel as restless as a cat. I couldn't sit down and I couldn't take my mind off our situation. If anything happened to César, I knew the game was up. I could never deal with these dudes on my own. If they grabbed César, I was as good as dead.

Finally, at suppertime, César returned. He wasn't bringing the answer I wanted, but he did have good news. He had taken the film to Manolo's but had found Manolo out. Then he had gone over to Maria's. There he discovered Don Evandro. He had told him the whole story. Don Evandro professed to be amused by it. He had taken the film to give to Manolo. He had promised also to act as our intermediary and make peace. He wasn't concerned, so why should we be? Well, that was making light of the situation. But the mood of doom was now lifting fast. We were beginning to walk erect and think straight and act like ourselves. Suddenly I was filled with a wave of fresh energy. I said, "C'mon, let's get out of here and get a breath of fresh air!"

We strolled down the promenade, looking at the bathers and the people in the cafés. I felt no connection with anything around me. It was as though everything I saw were under glass. In a few minutes, we ran into my Indian friend, who, as usual, was out hustling. When he saw me, he said: "Ah, I look for you everywhere. Come in here, you will meet another American." We stepped into a little bar, and he introduced me to a very tall, rangy kid who looked like the all-American boy. He said his name was Woody. As we started to drink, I told him and the Indian about my adventure of the night before. Neither of them showed any signs of alarm. Woody, who spoke with a twangy Southern accent, said that he knew Manolo well. He had worked with him many times, and though he was capable of violence, especially when he was drunk, this didn't sound like something that deeply affected his honor, which was the only thing to fear. If Manolo thought I was a valuable business contact, he would get over his anger. Then he began to relate some of the scrapes that he had gotten into in Colombia. One story led to another, and pretty soon I invited him back to the hotel to continue the conversation.

By now it was late in the evening. The kid was rapping compulsively. He was all wound up and obviously dying for a chance to unburden his mind. When he sat down in my room, he reached inside his boot and pulled out a long thin plastic bag filled with cocaine. It was excellent oil-based pure cocaine. The kid explained that he was just coming down off a five-day run on this coke. That's why he was so wired up. He'd probably been involved in a very dangerous smuggling operation during those five days, which is why he had kept himself jacked up so high. Now the danger had passed, but the wheels inside his head were still spinning.

As the night wore on, the conversation became more explicit. At first he spoke only in that language of euphemism which smugglers adopt when they're talking to strangers. "I had to go up in the hills and meet these people because we were gonna do a thing and my people weren't too sure that their people were okay." Then, as the coke got to him and the rapport between us improved, he began to level. I started asking him questions about the technique of smuggling. How the planes came in and how they were loaded. Who did the flying and what were the costs. César got drowsy and finally stretched out on the bed to sleep. Now I seized my chance.

I didn't give a damn about anything at this point. I had been in Colombia two weeks; I had wasted days and days sitting around waiting for people to show who never turned up or who sat around talking bullshit. I had spent my money, spent my time, damn near spent my life. Now I was going to learn the truth before the last opportunity blew away. My questions grew ever more pointed, ever more keen. The kid didn't flinch. He wasn't going to give up any information that would threaten his operations, but he didn't mind telling me all the moves on the board. He knew them well enough because he had been playing the Game for years. Though he looked young and innocent, he had started early and played hard. He said he had made $4 million. I believed him. As the hours went by and the conversation grew ever more revealing, for the first time in all the many months I had been researching the marijuana story, I began to get a precise picture of how grass is smuggled into the States.

Next day, the kid came back and we talked again. This time he told me that it was foolish to sit around in this hotel, with the whole area crawling with cops and narcs and hit men. If I wanted to really know how the Game was played, I should leave with him the next day and go out into the bush to a protected *finca*, where we could speak in perfect privacy and where our safety would be guaranteed by well-armed bodyguards. The idea appealed to me. Ever since our scene on New Year's Eve, I had been waiting for the axe to fall. Nothing had happened, but who could say what would occur if we sat around here much longer?

In the next few days I learned more about the Dope Game in Colombia than I ever thought possible. I looked at maps where the secret airfields were marked, nautical charts where the smuggling courses were laid out with compass bearings and fathom soundings. I heard incredible and yet totally convincing eyewitness tales of shoot-outs with the police, treacherous dealings with the Colombians, suicidal parachute jumps and horrible ordeals by sickness, exhaustion and danger as the smugglers abandoned their wrecked planes and headed back through the jungles, the army squads, the customs agents and the narcotics police to the refuge of the coast. It was like seeing a movie that was all cut up into bits and pieces, extremely vivid but so fragmentary that always you were confused, disoriented, eager to stop and ask questions but fearful that if you stopped the headlong course of the screening, the pictures might black out and never come back on again.

The kid was obsessed and haunted by his adventures. He had come to a crisis in his life. He desperately needed a trusted confidant. He gambled on me and I gambled on him. I recognized the possibility that he was just some sort of complicated moocher who instead of coming right to the point and asking for money felt he had to earn it by inventing a thousand and one nights of smuggler stories. I had learned, however, that there was no other way to play this game except to take chances. Now I was taking my big chance. I was lucky. It paid off. I found the key to the Colombian Connection. The rest of the job was just a matter of filling in the ragged, coke-crazed outline.

6 Smuggling, Step by Step

Dope smuggling is a classic example of organized crime. The weed you hold in your hand every time you get high has passed already through dozens of other hands all the way from the hand that planted the seed to the hand that cultivated the plant to the hands that harvested the grass, baled it, hauled it, loaded it, flew it or sailed it across the Caribbean and then passed it to that other network of hands that off-loaded it, trucked it, wholesaled it and finally closed on your cash. When you consider the length and complexity of this chain of supply and distribution, with its demands for skilled operatives, expensive equipment, international communications and sophisticated banking and legal accessories, the natural inference is that dope smuggling must be controlled ultimately by criminal syndicates like the Mafia. The truth is precisely the opposite.

Though there are, perhaps, twenty big syndicates, like the Colombian ring that was busted in New York, the typical players in the Dope Game are loosely knit teams of young men who have no prior experience in crime and who are in most respects indistinguishable from thousands of other young men fresh out of college. The banality of these boys, apart from a handful of specially endowed leaders, is perhaps their most striking characteristic. Being in so many ways just like everybody else, they suggest what a thin line divides the ordinary citizen today from the successful criminal. Apart from courage, the only thing required to become a dope smuggler is a certain amount of capital. Even that is easily acquired, thanks to the extraordinarily favorable economics of the Game.

Generally speaking, smugglers are former dealers. As we've seen already, dealers are found in every school in the country. Several years ago, a government report estimated that the number of people dealing dope was approximately 175,000. Most of this staggering number were kids, either in public schools or colleges. Now suppose a kid buys a pound of high-quality weed for $350. He breaks it down into sixteen ounces at $45 an ounce. He clears $350. If he can get himself ten pounds a month, in six months he's got $20,000, enough to buy a seat in the Game. Or suppose he gets a job running dope in cars from the Mexican border or Florida. He goes down to a ranch in Texas and picks up a rental car. He fills the trunk with 200 or 300 pounds of weed and drives it to Atlanta, Chicago or New York. At $2,500 a run, doing two trips a month, in just four months he's got his $20,000 stake. At this point, he either starts buying in bigger quantities and getting other people to run for him or he takes a share in a smuggling operation. If he makes one move, one run, he'll quadruple his money. If he goes one more time, he could come back with a couple hundred thousand dollars. It scales up very steeply.

Meantime, he's learning the Game. He's become a member of a crime family. Some smuggling gangs are real families, especially in the South. You find the brother, the sister, the brother-in-law—even the mother! They're all in it. Like John David Steele, the former mayor of Hallandale, Florida, who was busted in 1976 bringing in seventeen tons with his twenty-one-year-old son. The family that tokes together totes together. The typical smuggling family, however, is not a real family. It's a bunch of guys who have been pals since they were in high school. They have known each other for years, played games together, drunk together, partied together, all close bonding relationships. Then, bit by bit, they drift into the Dope Game.

The steps from getting together with your friends to buy a pound to going out to bring in a ton are many and small—but they follow naturally. It doesn't take a life of crime to get you out on a boat or up in a little plane with a load of contraband. People do it every day. They get an idea and pretty soon the idea has got them. Or maybe smuggling is an idea whose time has come. An idea that doesn't take a lot of telling or selling.

Now suppose you decide to take a small two-engine plane and run down to Colombia. Assuming a crew of two men, one pilot and one smuggler, you'll have a maximum load capacity of 1,000 pounds. A thousand pounds of marijuana, even if it's good quality weed, is only worth, tops, $350 a pound. Three hundred fifty thousand dollars sounds like a lot of bread, but if you have to buy a plane that costs $150,000 and pay a pilot $30,000 to make the run and then you have to buy the merchandise for $10,000 in front and $70,000 more when you score, your expenses for this little operation are $260,000 just for basics. This doesn't include the off-loading crew ($10,000 per man) or all the costs of getting the deal together, like the thousands you're going to drop in Colombia trying to find your connection.

So the smuggler who stops and thinks, or the one who runs and breaks even begins to wonder if it wouldn't be better to put some more valuable merchandise on his little plane. The next step up from grass is hash. Colombian hash is not a quality product. It's not resin hash, like the Lebanese produce, but herbal hash, which is simply ground up and tightly compressed whole plant substance. It looks like great big two-pound chocolate bars. This stuff is cheap in Colombia, but in the hash-starved States, especially in the South and Southwest, where nobody ever sees any Middle Eastern hash (particularly now that constant warfare is disrupting the traffic from Lebanon), you can get $750 a pound for it. Now your load has doubled in value, and your costs haven't escalated by much, because the cost of the material is always the smallest item in a smuggling budget.

So long as you're doing the job, however, there is no reason in the world why you shouldn't make a lot more money if you have the balls to throw on top of your load a little garbage bag full of cocaine. Colombian hash is an inferior product, clobbered together by the local Syrians, who appear to have forgotten their ancestors' techniques. Colombian coke is another story entirely.

Colombia produces excellent coke of its own, and it lies directly athwart the main supply line running up from those coke utopias, Bolivia, Peru and Ecuador. For $18,000 in Colombia you can buy a kilo of coke that is worth $40,000 wholesale in the States. ("Stepped on," or cut, twice, this same key, swollen to three keys, is worth nearly $120,000 on the street.) Assuming you've got a good connection who is not going to burn you with a big cut in Colombia, ten keys of coke can make your trip a bonanza. You've still got your profit of anything from $50,000 to $300,000 on the grass or hash. At the same time, you've now acquired a nice little bonus of $120,000 in powder money.

It's true, of course, that cocaine is now the number one target of American narcs, who like to nail the heavy drugs but don't like to catch the bullets that come flying back from an H bust. Still, what have you got to fear in a little plane flying 5,000 feet above the earth? If things get really tough, you can always throw the stuff in the sea. You don't even have to land with it. You can drop it to the off-loading crew in a flight bag and let it worry about whether there's any heat in the woods that night. So grass smuggling in small planes is rarely purely a marijuana operation.

The best thing you can say for plane smuggling is that it's very fast and very safe. Or perhaps I should say safe from the law. In 1976 about sixty smuggling planes were known to have crashed. Probably a great many others were lost without a trace. The problem with the planes is not the police or the radar networks or the interdiction forces of foreign militaries. Pilot error or mechanical failure, plus the standard practice of overloading the planes by 50 percent or more, produced most of these crashes. So the bottom line of airplane smuggling is the pilot's skill, the condition of his machine and the smuggler's greed level.

Now, let's look at the other route: the sea. Sailing is obviously the most sensible way to ship a low-density, big-bulk product like hay. Ships are designed to take large loads long ways at low cost. They're vulnerable, tedious and emotionally explosive because after thirty days of living without privacy in a space the size of a couple of king-sized beds with a load that can put you in prison for five years you tend to get cranky.

Still, sailing is one of modern America's most cherished experiences. Nor is there any reason why it shouldn't pay for itself. Let's take the classic beginner's luck scenario. You buy a Morgan 41-foot, two-mast motor sailboat for $50,000 new or $25,000 used. You strip it down for smuggling, install your Loran and take off with a piratical little crew of three fiercely determined people. You sail down for two weeks; you sail back for two weeks. You bring home about 7,000 pounds of weed at a fraction of the cost of running it in an airplane. If you're a sail freak, you'll have the experience of a lifetime, because nobody but a smuggler—or a wealthy nut!—can afford to take a month off in February to sail all the way from Florida to the north coast of Colombia. Your basic problem is not the sailing, which isn't all that hard in the halcyon seas of the prime Caribbean vacation season. Nor do you have to worry about the Colombian end of the operation. If you've done your preparatory work right, you'll get loaded. The biggest problem is that some Coast Guard cutter will come up on you in the middle of the night, throw a searchlight on you and tell you to heave to.

The answer to this little nightmare is to fly a foreign flag—not a fake, but a real honest-to-god Union Jack earned by registering your boat in the Bahamas or the Cayman Islands or some place in the British Commonwealth. That puts the Coast Guard off like Off puts away mosquitoes. The rest is just a matter of being shrewd about when and where you come in. Very few people die at sea; the only hang-up is that after thirty days of Errol Flynn or *Kon Tiki* they get busted in some asshole Southern town.

Now let's take the attitude of people who are really keen on *doing it*. Let's ask all the questions, raise all the objections, expose all our phobias and act like "I gotta be shown." Let's go back to the planes and trace a typical operation from the ground up.

First, you have to pick your plane. The ideal plane for Colombia would be a battered old aerial tramp steamer, with a cargo capacity measured in tons, range enough to bring the load up into the American heartland and the kind of giant tires and piston shock absorbers that make landing feasible on even the roughest strip. There are plenty of such planes on the market at prices that are astonishingly low. Their names comprise a catalogue of smuggling ships. The Lockheed Lodestar is the plane that the late Kenny Burnstine, king of aerial smugglers, made famous—and infamous. A small, two-engine airliner of the Forties, the Lodestar is available also in a souped-up version called the Learstar that can do 300 miles an hour. The Howard 500 is another classic of the Game, a hopped-up version of the World War II Ventura patrol bomber that can carry a payload of five tons for 1,200 miles at a speed of up to 350 miles per hour. The B-25 was the star of

Thirty Seconds over Tokyo; one of them stands like a war monument on the edge of the airport at Santa Marta where it was discovered one morning, abandoned by its crew. The Curtis C-46
won fame hauling cargo over the "Hump" from Burma to China
in World War II. In its bulbous fuselage, this familiar Caribbean
cargo craft will pack away up to nine tons of weed, making it a
colossal flying cigar. Even the DC-3, the Old Faithful of commercial flying, can make the run if fitted with range-extending fuel
tanks.

All of these wonderful old tramps are great for hauling dope,
but they all suffer from the same crippling disability. As aircraft,
they are oddballs, eye grabbers, attention getters. They are so
well suited to the job of dope smuggling that everybody who
looks at them entertains the same suspicion. As the best policy in
any illegal activity is to maintain a low profile, most smugglers,
especially beginners, commence their careers by buying a standard, mass-produced, executive-type plane. A dozen considerations ranging from economy to availability to inconspicuousness
to matching the capability to the task dictate that we choose as
our classic light-aircraft smuggling vehicle the Cessna 310. There
are a dozen other two-engine planes that could make this run, but
it would be foolish to bother about them. The Cessna is the neat-
est, nicest little knife for cutting this particular cake.

The first question is, if you are a smuggler, how do you go
about buying a Cessna 310? Basically, this problem divides into
two sections: do you want it new or used? If you want a used
plane, which need not cost more than $50,000, your first move is
obvious. You pick up at your local we-carry-everything newsstand
a copy of *Trade-a-Plane,* the yellow-leafed tabloid-sized thrice-a-
month bible of the used plane business. It's seventy-five pages of
ads for used planes and odd parts and strange things that you just
can't imagine a pilot buying—like a hydraulic baling press. This
little trade mag is fascinating. It attests to the incredible private
aviation boom: the 5,000 airstrips in Texas and the 150,000 private planes in Florida. One of the reasons why smuggling can't be
stopped in America is that the quantity of apparatus and the
number of people capable of making the moves is so great that
nothing short of the combined forces of the Army, Navy and Air
Force could ever hold it in check.

Now let's assume that our smuggler has picked his plane and

got his money together to make a buy. What does he do next? Well, he sure as hell can't walk into the local office of Cessna and throw $150,000 down on the desk for a new ship. He's got to be cool and cagey. He's got to have an intermediary. Ideally, he ought to have himself a nice legitimate businessman who can demonstrate a plausible need for a private plane. Today, this is no problem because the number of businesses that operate their own aircraft is enormous. There's been an incredible growth in business aviation recently for a host of reasons, ranging from the competitiveness of the economy to the cutback in airline service to the elimination of low-traffic air routes to the lowering of the speed limit to fifty-five miles per hour. Everything has conspired in the last few years to make businessmen say, "Hell, why don't we buy our own plane?"

So you get a nice corrupt businessman, and you tell him: "Look, I have this little thing going. I need access to a plane from time to time. I don't need it all the time. Generally, I'd need it for a two-day shot. The rest of the time, you've got it. I'll inform you a week in advance that I need the aircraft Thursday or Friday or whenever. At that time, you'll put it at my disposal. Naturally, I'll pay for the whole thing." Well, Jack, you don't have to be Simon LeGreed to go for that sweet deal. It's a score! What's more, if anything goes wrong, if the plane crashes or it's caught or it gets hot, you've got your cop-out. You're gonna say: "Gee, officer, I can't understand it. We parked it like we always do. Next morning Jimmy went out there. When he didn't see anything, he called me up and I said. . . ." Nobody is going to get hurt, you dig?

We have the plane. The next thing is to get the connection in Colombia. As the story of my first trip shows, you simply have to be a good shopper. Go around and use your wits and try to separate the phonies from the real people. Shrewdness is the smuggler's most basic gift. If he isn't canny, if he can't read the signs, he better pack up and go home. So far as quality goes, you've just got to stick to your guns. Don't take the first thing they offer you. Insist on the good stuff. Say you're going to look elsewhere. Act like you're in a used-car lot. It's no different than doing business anywhere.

Remember, too, that once you've established yourself in Colombia by doing a deal, most of the supply problems disappear.

Instead of stumbling around like a novice getting ripped off in hotels and propositioned by people who may not be able to deliver, you become a regular customer entitled to all the normal business courtesies and considerations. The dope industry in Colombia is so well organized today that when a well-connected foreign buyer arrives, his shopping trip is conducted no differently than a buying trip to the garment industry in New York or the stockyards of Tulsa.

The buyer is met at the airport by a charming Colombian who speaks perfect English because he was educated in the States. Ushered into a late-model white Renault, the customer is whisked to a towering apartment building in Barranquilla, Cartagena or Santa Marta, where he will be secure from the armed robberies so common in the hotels. (He will also be watched carefully to make sure that he doesn't try to do business with a rival connection.) After his wishes have been understood, he will be passed through a series of carefully guarded checkpoints until one afternoon, after a long and tortuous ride over the lunar landscape of the Guajira, he finds himself inside a big canvas-covered lean-to in the wilderness. Inside this dope warehouse, he will examine 30,000 or 40,000 pounds of weed that has been collected from a score of local plantations. The buyer opens sacks, examines buds, rolls up grass and smokes it. Gradually, he picks out whatever he wants, or he insists upon being shown better merchandise trucked in from other plantations.

Until recently, the grass in this warehouse would have come from disguised little plantings in the Sierra Madres. Today, with worldwide demand for dope booming and the Game so highly organized in La Guajira, the old system of surreptitious cultivation is being abandoned. In the summer of 1977, the biggest marijuana plantation in the world was discovered smack in the middle of the Guajira. First reports marveled at the extent of the planting and the scientific technique of cultivation. Laid out with a surveyor's transit and fertilized with chemicals, 3,600 acres spread lush and green across a plain that is normally arable only during the brief rainy season. The *marimberos* had installed diesel-driven pumps at the Tapias River and were irrigating the area—just as the United Fruit Company had taught them to do at the banana plantations in the neighboring state of Magdalena. Eventually, it was estimated that when this bust went down, a *million* pounds of pot was just two months from harvest. The Colombians are still trying to figure out how to destroy all this weed.

Once the buyer has picked out his merchandise, he gives the baling order. Marijuana is shipped either loose, pressed or semi-pressed. The latter is the preferred pack because it preserves the buds entire, giving the product a high cosmetic appeal and preserving the resin and pollen, which can be destroyed in high-compression baling. If space is a primary consideration, as in small-airplane smuggling, the marijuana can be squeezed into bricks that are almost as hard and dense as clay. The size and shape of the bricks or bales can also be stipulated by the buyer. As one connection told me: "We'll press it any way you want it—even in hearts!"

The typical Colombian pack is a two-by-two foot block weighing approximately thirty pounds. This little bale is taken out of a trash compressor and wrapped with newspaper. Then it is encased with as many as six layers of plastic garbage bags, which are taped down firmly to exclude air. (Fresh marijuana is full of moisture, which determines largely its weight. If the grass is not carefully sealed, it loses weight rapidly, perhaps as much as one percent a week, which in turn reduces its profitability.) Another common practice is to take two of these newspaper-swathed cubes and wrap them in the same garbage bag to make a two-by-four *bulto*, which is then cinched about the middle with burlap for ease of handling. Yet another standard practice is to insert the whole pack inside a sugar sack or burlap bag to protect the easily torn plastic. Once grass has been prepared for shipment, it is stored on log platforms to protect it from ground damp and rodents.

Now we're set to make our move. We have the cash and the crew. We have a connection who will provide all the goods and the loading. We have the plane. The only thing lacking is a means for disposing of the merchandise. Smugglers are importers, not wholesalers or retailers. Generally, they make a deal with somebody who will be standing by with cash in hand when the goods come ashore. This guy buys the whole load and moves it with his trucks to his stash pad. The money changes hands, and each crew takes off in its own direction.

In order to make more money, groups that are not doing a

lot of smuggling will split up the dope when they get back and sell it off themselves. If you're a dealer at heart, selling the dope is not a burden. In fact, it's the thing you enjoy most: sitting there, being charming, cutting it up and talking about it, giving people samples and tastes and bullshitting. But there is another type of guy who can't stand dealing. It's so fuckin' mercantile, it makes him puke. This kinda guy just likes to risk his life. If he isn't doing that, he's bored.

Now, let's go to the move itself. The basic plan is to fly down, pick up the load and fly back. According to regulations, if you're leaving the country, you should file a flight plan; and as you're coming back into the country, you should radio that you're arriving, where you're arriving from, what kind of aircraft you're flying and the nature of your load, if any. Smugglers don't necessarily ignore these rules, because there's no need to really ignore them. For example, if you're going to fly down to Colombia and you're taking off from Miami, there's no reason why you shouldn't file a flight plan. There is no great danger in the procedure and much to be gained.

When you file a flight plan, you leave and enter the country legitimately. This takes the heat off you, and it does not restrict your movements. There are large areas in the Caribbean which are marked in gray on flight maps and labeled "uncontrolled area." This means that the electronic beacon and communications equipment in these zones is so inadequate that the FAA fences them off as lying outside its area of responsibility. As it happens, some of these areas lie directly along the flight paths to Colombia. So it is possible to file for one of these spots and then to disappear for hours or even days without anything suspicious appearing in the FAA's control rooms. Let's consider a typical flight plan from Miami to the north coast of Colombia and back.

The pilot calls up the control center in the morning and files for Port-au-Prince in Haiti. He's leaving the country with nothing heavier than a couple of handguns; so there is no reason why he shouldn't act as if he were on a routine business or pleasure flight. Haiti is one of the smugglers' favorite countries because it maintains no air defenses or radar and handles the traffic in and out of its airport at the capital city very loosely. When the pilot lands four hours later in the kingdom of "Little Doc," he can fill up his gas tanks and stretch his legs. Then he takes off for the north coast of Colombia. Four hours later, he slips into a clandestine airstrip out along the Guajira or in the Cienega district near Barranquilla. With his tanks still half full, he can load and get off the ground in half an hour. In that short space of time, it is virtually impossible that the police can seize him.

Once he's airborne, he heads for the next spot for which he filed: the Caicos Islands. This cluster of black-populated isles just north and east of the Windward Passage is almost exactly at the midway point between Colombia and southern Florida. The islands are an "uncontrolled area" and therefore a perfect place to land and refuel. The local customs agents are corrupt as hell; if they offer to search the plane, a few hundred dollars buys them off.

If the thought of landing on a Caribbean island with your plane stuffed to bursting with contraband gives you palpitations, you can arrange to refuel at the airstrip in Colombia. When you go down there on your shopping trip, you tell the connection: "Hey, Jaime, when you bring the *marimba* to the strip, have the men bring four fifty-five-gallon tanks of aviation gas and a motor-driven pump." The Colombians will do anything for money. If they're going to load you with grass, why shouldn't they load you with gas? You had better make sure, however, that the gas hasn't been watered, a typical, cheapo Colombian trick that is practiced at the local filling stations.

The way to avoid this and any other problems at the strip is to send an advance man on a commercial flight a few days before you plan to make your move. The advance man can go out to the strip, make sure the merchandise is what you ordered, check out the fuel, verify that the cops have been *schmeered*, get the Colombians to patch up the holes in the ground and generally take care of business.

The day before you make the move, you call the advance man in Barranquilla or Santa Marta and you discuss your vacation plans: "Hey, Babe! How's the weather down there? I'm thinkin' of knockin' off work and comin' fishin'. I hope it's not too *hot!* Ha, ha, ha!" The call is monitored by the Colombians, of course, but what can they make of this dumb *gringo* tourist conversation? When the job is done and the load has been dispatched, the advance man flies home on a commercial flight. Sometimes, he even beats the smuggler back.

The flight to Colombia is over 1,000 miles, a long way for a little two-engine Cessna. If you put into the plane all the extra gas tanks that it was designed to hold, you have just enough fuel to make the trip; but you don't have enough to make it safely. Nightmare stories of running out of gas and being forced down in all sorts of hot spots are the standard barroom talk of airplane smugglers. One dude told me recently about a flight he made with an inexperienced pilot that almost cost both of them a stretch in a Colombian prison. They took off from the States and flew down to an area near Barranquilla. A strong east-to-west wind blows always off the coast of Colombia. On this particular day it was a tremendous gale. When the pilot started to turn west to make his landing approach, he caught such a blast of air in the tail that he was blown clear past the strip, past the Barranquilla area—damn near to Panama! When he finally got the plane turned around, he had to bore through the same wind to get back to the strip.

Now he was so low on fuel that he had to keep jerking up the nose of the plane every minute to make the last bit of gas in his tanks slosh into the feed pipes. Eventually, they were forced to land at Barranquilla International Airport—without a flight plan! The Colombians assume, quite reasonably, that any light plane landing in this fashion is engaged in smuggling. They clapped the two dudes into jail and started threatening them with the customary nine-year sentence. Finally, the boys were able to contact their boss in the States, who arranged for a couple of smart Colombian lawyers to buy them out of prison. So ended Operation Ill Wind.

The solutions to the gas problem range from loading the plane with plastic jiffy bottles of fuel to building in an extra tank at the back of the cabin or even carrying a collapsible rubber tank that can be ditched when it's empty. Theoretically, it is possible to carry enough fuel in the cabin as freight to refuel the plane on the ground from its own resources. Making your plane into a tanker is dangerous. The rubber tank may spring a leak, with the result that soon you're flying in a plane that is awash in highly combustible fuel!

When a smuggler returns to the States on a flight plan, he has to find some way to discharge his cargo without alerting the military radar operators or the civilian flight controllers to his real purpose. Many scams have been invented to solve this problem, ranging from the simple expedient of dropping the load while maintaining a normal flight pattern to flying in close formation with another plane so that both planes merge on the radar screen as a single blip, which continues its course even when the first plane drops to the ground to make an illegal landing. The problem with all these devices is not that they fail, but that they keep the smugglers sweating to stay inside the constricting guidelines of legal aviation. Many smugglers believe that with air traffic so heavy and the computerized surveillance of announced flights so keen, they run less risk if they simply take off whenever the moment is ripe and "haul ass." Let's proceed now on the assumption that we're operating in that great old Southern tradition of the blockade runner. Let's fly the trip again without a flight plan.

The flight to Colombia starts out like any trip. At 3:00 A.M. you get your weather report at the airport and take off. Depending on winds and weather, it can take anywhere from six to seven hours to fly nonstop from Florida to the Santa Marta area. The pilots follow the standard flight paths or vectors that are laid out around the world like aerial highways. They pick their way from one radio beacon to another as they move south over the Caribbean islands. The most direct flight path would be to fly over Cuba, but that is not advisable because the Cubans are pretty touchy about foreigners violating their air space. What's more, the U.S. still maintains its big naval base at Guantanamo Bay, and Gitmo sends out a powerful radio-radar beam that swings in an arc of 160 miles. This means that the pilots have to fly over the Windward Passage, holding to the eastern side of the passage about twenty miles off the coast of Haiti. They could fly over Haiti—and sometimes do—but the mountains there reach elevations of 10,000 feet.

Once you've cleared the island barriers and are cruising south over the Caribbean, you pick up the radio beacon from either Barranquilla or Riohacha out in the Guajira. When you're less than 100 miles off the coast, you begin to get the first sublime vision of the Sierra Madres, glittering at their peaks with year-round ice and snow. Everyone who has made the flight recollects with awe the majestic appearance of those mighty mountains. By the time the coast is clearly in view, the aircraft is coming down low over the waves to run into the strip as inconspicuously as possible.

By this time, contact has been established between the plane and the advance man at the strip. He's got a Narco, King or Collins VHF radio that can reach hundreds of miles out to sea. He signals the pilot that everything is cool on the ground. Then he talks the plane in by indicating the landmarks or by giving course directions in degrees. Ideally, the pilot should have gone down on a commercial flight before the move and looked over the terrain. Ideally, he should have rented a small plane and actually flown over the area. The ideal is seldom realized in smuggling operations. Often the pilots fly down the first time by the seat of their pants.

When you get down to the north coast of Colombia, there are a hundred places to come in. In the Guajira, there are areas with a landing strip every half mile. There are so many strips that sometimes the biggest problem is coming down on the right one. Landing anywhere in the world but Colombia is a routine matter. You line up the plane, crank down your flaps, reduce your air speed, point the plane at the ground and come on in. In Colombia, you can't count on happy landings. During the dry season, things aren't bad. The dirt strips are rough and pitted, but you bang and bounce your way to a stop without much trouble. In the rainy season, the whole style of the Game changes. Now you're talking about Russian Roulette. How many times can you come into a rutted, cratered strip that has been soaked to the consistency of mud without getting knocked on your ass? Even if you land safely, you may bend a prop or damage the landing gear so badly that you can't take off. Even the simplest repairs are difficult to obtain in such circumstances. While you sit on a hot strip in a hot plane, you watch the Colombians come apart at the seams. Their behavior may swing from extortion to desertion to murderous rage. After all, if they knock you off, they still have the load, the front money and your quarter-million-dollar plane. It never pays to hang around at the scene of the crime.

What does a clandestine airstrip in Colombia look like? Let's go back to the Finca las Mercedes. Though the strip is only five miles from the coastal highway, it is totally screened by the configuration of the land and by plantings of yucca. When you drive by, you may see workers plowing peacefully with a tractor. They do a little farming just to keep up appearances. Back inside the property, there's a lot of work of a much different character.

The main strip is 7,200 feet of red dirt running at a right angle to the coast, two miles distant. Days before the plane arrives, big trucks—or during the rainy season, tractors—haul the grass by night from the neighboring hills down to the strip. The grass is baled on the premises and then piled up on platforms screened from aerial observation by a stand of trees. When a plane is expected, a wind sock is rigged and the loading crew stands by to go into action. The moment the plane lands, the Indians start to hustle. It's the only time in their lives that they move fast. Before the plane's propellers have stopped spinning, the load is going into the cabin and the gas into the tanks. The charges for this valuable service are ridiculously low. A two-engine plane can land and load for $1,200.

Finca las Mercedes has been busted many times; but it's back in business again and doing nicely, thank you. A bust in Colombia is like a hurricane elsewhere: it knocks things down, kills a couple of people and stops business cold for a few months. Soon life resumes its normal course and all the damage is repaired. After all, what would the cops gain if they really succeeded in putting down the smuggling trade? A Colombian cop makes about sixty dollars a month. Most busts of this sort occur because some wise-ass refuses to pay off. With dozens of flights going in and out of the region every day, the Colombians always think that they can sneak one by. Though the *schmeer* may be just a few hundred dollars, peanuts to an American, the Colombians are such poor ignorant people that they try to play it cheap. Then the local *jefe* gets pissed off and orders a raid to teach his countrymen a lesson. That's about the extent of law enforcement in Colombia. But it does get people jailed and killed. There are several dozen Americans rotting away in Colombian dungeons because they got busted in a country without law and order.

Recently, under heavy prodding from the Carter administration, the Colombian government has stepped up its antismuggling operations by instituting overflights and even staging a few spectacular airborne assaults on the landing strips. Because all the local police units have been corrupted by the smugglers, these attacks have proceeded directly from Bogotá. On January 25, 1978, at the height of the smuggling season, a military helicopter appeared suddenly above a strip near Dibulla where an American Piper Navaho was being loaded under a camouflage net. When the smugglers opened fire on the plane, the fire was returned from the air. The helicopter landed near the site, where it was soon reinforced by another helicopter. A pitched battle ensued that ended with the special attack force that had been dispatched from the Colombian attorney general's office defeating the smugglers and seizing the plane, its two American pilots, ten Colombians, ten vehicles and 336,000 pounds of dope stacked under a tarpaulin.

Once the Guajiros realized that their operations were being threatened by aerial attacks, they concluded a fast deal with the Venezuelan terrorists and obtained some hand-held heat-seeking missiles. Now government pilots are being warned to use extreme precautions in flying over the Guarjira.

Taking off on the return flight is the most dangerous moment of the trip. The plane, stuffed with hay and gasoline, is like a giant incendiary bomb. If the runway is too wet or too short or if the takeoff is made after dark—with the strip barely visible in the headlights of a jeep or a row of coconut shells filled with flaming oil—the pilot may crash without ever getting off the ground. Even if he does get airborne, the enormous strain on the overloaded engines may produce a momentary malfunction that flips the plane out of control. The next moment, the finely engineered aircraft is reduced to a jumble of flaming and exploding wreckage. Every Colombian connection recalls such disasters. Sometimes he also recalls that the takeoff was preceded by violent arguments or much drinking and coke snorting. The pilot, his nerves ajangle and his reflexes numbed by alcohol and fatigue, may have been in no condition to make the split-second decisions that could have saved his life. Then it's time to call for the bulldozers. Sometimes the charred fuselage is buried with the shriveled corpses of the crew still inside it.

Returning from Colombia on an illegal flight is just like flying down—with one important difference: you've got to run the gauntlet of NORAD, North American Air Defense Command. NORAD extends the U.S. out to sea to a distance of 200 miles with a line-of-sight radar beam. Owing to the curvature of the earth, the farther this beam projects from the shore, the farther off the sea it flies. When you're 200 miles out to sea, you can fly a few hundred feet above the water and not appear on the controller's radar screen. As you get closer to shore, you've got to get down lower, lower, lower, until you're practically skimming the waves, which is what the Entebbe raiders had to do for the entire length of the Red Sea. This is called flying on the "deck," and it shouldn't create any problems if the pilot is in good shape. Exhausted from flying sixteen hours straight and mesmerized by the waves, he could make a mistake and ram the plane into rock-hard water at 200 miles an hour. Or, coming in at night without lights or moon, even a fresh pilot can make an error.

Strictly speaking, it shouldn't be necessary to fly on the deck because the radar alert applies only to planes flying more than 180 knots an hour. On the other hand, Customs agents have begun recently to man the radar networks intermittently in the course of their interdiction operations. In October 1975, as part of Operation Star Trek, a coordinated crackdown on smuggling in the Gulf of Mexico and across the border, Customs agents manned the coastal radar from Tampa to El Paso. They also put up a number of radar scout planes and used portable radars to monitor the holes that occur here and there in the coastal radar nets. Whenever a plane was spotted coming in low without a flight plan, a Customs plane was alerted to check it out. The result was the seizure in fifty-one days of seventeen aircraft. Considering the enormity of the illicit air traffic across the Mexican border, this catch did not make a dent in the Game. It did add, however, yet another note of anxiety to the war of nerves. Most smugglers flying in without a flight plan these days are getting way down on the deck.

When the smugglers arrive at the end of their runs, they have a great many ways of discharging their cargo. They can land on a small field which shuts down every evening but keeps on its lights. They can land in a housing subdivision along the southwest coast of Florida, where many projects once begun were abandoned during the recent recession, leaving behind miles of unused roads and leveled construction sites. They can come in on a farmer's field or a dry lake bed. There are lots of places where you can put down a light plane if you know the country. Another technique is to parcel out the load into six big packages and attach them to cargo chutes. Either these chutes can be opened by a lanyard attached to the plane, or they can be triggered by barometric devices that open them automatically at a given altitude, say, 1,000 feet. When the load lands, it is sometimes lost, especially if it is dropped in woods or swamp. To assure recovery, smugglers may attach electronic beepers to the bales and locate them with little radio finders.

Dropping loads can produce bizarre consequences, as in the case of the Florida wildlife officer who was sitting one night on a boat in a swamp keeping watch for alligator poachers. He heard a small plane approaching at treetop level. Instinctively, he aimed his flashlight up at the plane. The next instant a sixty-pound bale of marijuana hit the boat, knocking out its bottom. The officer not only came close to getting killed; he had to wade back to shore past the alligators he was guarding.

Once the cargo hits the ground, the off-loading crews go into action. Four-wheel drive vehicles, campers, vans scramble so fast and efficiently that minutes after the plane has landed or passed overhead the load is riding out of the area as fast as the speed laws allow. Once the vehicles hit the highway system, they disperse in every direction and the chances of making a bust are nil. People living penned up in the big cities fail to realize how much of America is still wide-open land. Down in central Florida, for example, there are miles and miles of farms, pastures, woods and swamps where planes can land and trucks can run and anything can come to earth unnoticed.

If you're an ambitious smuggler, you graduate one day from executive-type planes to big transports. Buying such a ship is surprisingly easy. The Lockheed Lodestar, for example, was used extensively by the military as a medium bomber. This means that loads of Lodestars are stashed away at the government's giant aircraft storage facility at Davis-Monphan Field in Arizona. It also means that periodically the surplus sales division of the Defense Supply Agency holds an auction at the field and gives away these old planes for a song. You can buy a Lodestar for as little as $20,000. The Lodestar is slow, at 230 miles per hour top speed; and it is not a plane with a great cruising range: 800 miles with full tanks. But it is a load carrier. It can carry a payload of up to 4,000 pounds. This made it perfect for the old Jamaica run from Florida. For the Colombian game, a much better aircraft is the DC-4, called the C-54 in its military cargo configuration.

C-54s can be bought for as little as $15,000 at government auction; but, then, you spend a fortune patching them up. One of the four engines or a whole chunk of the control console may be missing. Apart from the time and money entailed in running around finding spare parts that were last manufactured thirty years ago, there is the problem of disguising the plane's ownership when it is so well documented. There is an obscure regulation, for example, that stipulates that any plane that was ever in government service must file to obtain a "sojourner" every time it leaves the country. If an FAA radar controller picks up a big blip on his scope that is flying without a flight plan, it could be an automatic bust and confiscation—even if the plane is not carrying a load of contraband. Nevertheless, some of the most daring smugglers of recent years have worked with C-54s that were either rebuilt by their own mechanics or picked out of the pages of *Trade-a-Plane*, where they are advertised in airworthy condition—cheap—at $80,000.

The C-54 has a cruising speed of about 240 miles per hour, a range of 3,500 miles and a lifting capacity of 14,000 pounds. It cannot carry more than 5,000 pounds of pot, however, because grass is such a bulky product that it fills the plane's hold without matching its carrying capacity. The great advantage of the aircraft is that it can fly down to Colombia and back without requiring any refueling operation. What's more, it can fly far up into the heart of the U.S., into the Midwest, for example, where nobody is on guard against smuggling planes.

Generally speaking, the future of the Dope Game lies in the North and the Midwest. Too much heat is building up around Florida and the Mexican Border states to allow the Game to go on forever in its traditional pattern. Even the primary source of supply in Colombia could be shut down someday if the American government finds some way to put enough pressure on the Colombians. Were that to happen, the Game would have to go even farther afield: to Brazil or Africa or some distant point that could be reached only by long-range aircraft.

The great disadvantage of large airplanes is that they are far too conspicuous. A classic case in point was provided in August of 1975 when a C-54 was busted atop a mountain in Georgia. The pilot performed an almost impossible feat in bringing the big bird in on a crudely improvised strip lighted with a string of 100-watt bulbs. He landed in a space of 1,000 feet, *one-fifth the length specified by the flight manual.* Thirty-two hundred pounds of pot and eighty-five kilos of hash were taken off in a truck and a van. The smugglers would have gotten away had it not been for the fact that every resident of the area was on the phone calling the local police and reporting the crash of a big four-engine airplane into the mountaintop. When the police arrived to investigate the air disaster, they ran head-on into the smugglers, crashing out of the woods with their vehicles coated with mud and trailing honeysuckle vines. As it turned out, the flight was profitable in one sense. When the flier, a former carrier pilot named Robert Eby, surrendered himself to the authorities a week later, he was approached by a man who wanted to make a movie of the incident. Unlike so many film projects, this one actually came off. It is now showing in drive-ins around the country as *The Polk County Pot Plane.*

Smuggling by sea is a very different game than smuggling by air. Apart from all the practical differences between flying and sailing, there are important emotional distinctions. Temperament is a crucial element in any sort of outlawry. The temperament of a sky-boy who can jump into a plane with an unknown pilot and take off for a one-day flight into God knows what is not the temperament of a sailor, accustomed to the regular rotation of watches and the long, steady pull it takes to get somewhere on the sea. What's more, in our society sailors far outnumber fliers. Thousands of young men and women can crew on a sailboat but would be unable to perform even the simplest chores in an aircraft cockpit. When you put all these factors together—the economic, the emotional and the question of skill—it is not surprising that most people think of making a dope run in a boat. Indeed, nothing is more characteristic of the fantasy life of America in the mid-Seventies than the dream of standing stripped to the waist behind a wonderfully knurled and spoked yacht wheel with your old lady at your side as you cast a keen eye to windward and bring on home that big load of gold that is gonna put you on Easy Street!

I've talked to a lot of people who have sailed dope in from Mexico, Morocco and Colombia. They all recollect the experience as being the greatest moment of their lives. Even if they had trouble or got busted or even served time in prison for the adventure, the look of bliss on their faces as they tell you how it feels to be way the hell out in the ocean on this marvelous old 1939, British-built, solid-teak, forty-four-foot, canoe-sterned, sloop-rigged mother is something you don't ignore if you measure things by their happiness quotient.

One of the first people with whom I discussed yacht smuggling is a boat broker down in Savannah. He told me that in recent years a sizable number of his customers had been smugglers. In fact, he got very friendly with one smuggling group and obtained a clear impression of how they were conducting their business. As this chap is a natural-born talker, let him tell you about yacht smuggling:

"What these smuggler boys are lookin' for is a boat that will carry a heavy load—that's more a consideration than a fast boat. At one time, people would get these big wooden tubs and sail down to Colombia and get what they needed and haul ass back. Then Customs started pickin' up on that kinda boat. Now your trend is toward a newer, more expensive yachtin' type boat that maybe wouldn't be so conspicuous.

"I knew one instance—this guy, the first time he did it, this is the identical boat that he used. [Holding out a sales brochure] That's a fiberglass forty-one-foot sailboat, a Morgan. What they did was take out everything easily removable: the dinette, the steps going up the companionway. Then they piled up the bales in the main saloon area to within a couple of feet of the overhead. Jest enough crawl space so they could lay down and sleep on top of the dope. Then after these people made the run, they came back to me and bought another boat, a fifty-seven-foot motor sailer with a steel hull. The Morgan cost about $50,000. The fifty-seven-footer cost $125,000. I don't know what they did with the Morgan. Maybe they sank it. Those kinda people don't like to use the same boat more than once or twice because somebody sees it and reports it and then they get on the Coast Guard's lookout list.

"If you were a smuggler and wanted to buy, let's say, a $150,000 boat, basically what ya gotta do is . . . Well, I can tell ya 'cause I've been through it one time. You decide on the boat you wanna buy and then go take a look at it. This particular boat happened to be in Fort Lauderdale. I had gotten a listin' on it for these guys 'cause I knew exactly what they were lookin' for. I got 'em a bunch of listin's, and we narrowed it down to 'bout three boats. They looked at the three boats and said, "This is the one we want!" Then they went back and talked to their banker and made sure everythin' was all set. They wanted to do the deal in the Cayman Islands 'cause down there they could reregister the boat with British papers and that way stay clear of the U.S. Coast Guard and the whole paperwork thing here in the States."

The Caymans are a British Crown colony comprising three tiny islands south of Cuba with a total population of 13,500. The Switzerland of the Caribbean, Grand Cayman, is the best place in the Western Hemisphere to deposit money with no questions, to do business behind a fake front or avoid most forms of taxation. The most impressive feature of Grand Cayman is the incredible array of imposing concrete-and-glass banks slotted into the old streets with their quaint dry-goods stores. First National City Bank, Bank of Nova Scotia and Bank of Montreal are some of the major institutions, but there are dozens of others less well known. All told, there are more than 170 banks and trust companies—one bank for every eighty Caymians!

The boat broker continued: "Now, originally, when they came to me to buy the boat, they wanted to put cash on me. But I couldn't see tryin' to get back into this country with $125,000 in cash. So I told 'em I wasn't gonna do it. So, for about 5,000 bucks they hired a lawyer and set themselves up a corporation, and I flew down to Grand Cayman with a bill of sale. The attorney handled the paperwork, and the banker—I don't know whether he knew what was goin' on or not, but he forked over to me a cashier's check for $125,000.

"The boat was documented with the U.S. Coast Guard, which is an international type of registry. I had a Coast Guard bill of sale. I gave the bill of sale to the attorney in Cayman, who was a British guy, and he in turn took it to the minister of shipping. They made out a bill of sale from the ministry of shipping. Now the boat was legitimately in British registry."

Six months after the yacht broker told me about the smuggling ring that had bought the fifty-seven-foot Morgan, I persuaded him to introduce me to a member of the crew. This young man continued the story by relating what happened when they took the new boat down to Colombia. My first question was how he felt starting off on such a risky venture. His answer was surprising:

"Frankly, I was amazed at my lack of concern. I had been constantly dropping hints to my friends in the Game—very broad hints—that I would like to go out as a crew member. Then, one day I got a phone call. That was it! I quit everything, including a job I had held for two years. It was just like enlisting in the Army. You just drop everything and go!

"Getting ready for the trip was a great pleasure. Who doesn't enjoy going into a sailing store and spending $800 on line and foul-weather gear? Or going into a grocery and buying six carts full of food? I had six grocery carts jammed up at the check-out counter. It took two taxicabs to haul all the stuff to the dock. You don't want to do anything unusual when you're smuggling, but it's not unusual to outfit a boat for an ocean cruise. It's just a helluva lot of fun!

"Now, when you equip a boat to go on a run like this, you want the best electronics you can have because electronics *can save your ass!* We installed an expensive Loran and depth finder, but we didn't bother with radar. All radar does is pick up masses. Most radars on pleasure boats are good for about ten or fifteen miles. The only time you use them is in fog or rain, when you're going through a channel and you can't see anything. Radar shows you the buoys on the screen. Loran is what you really want for ocean sailing. It measures the time difference from one beacon signal to another in microseconds and gives you your position, accurate within a few miles. Of course, you better have somebody aboard who can shoot the stars with a sextant because if your power fails, your Loran is useless.

"When it was getting time to take off, we moved out of our port in Florida and sailed to the Bahamas. Florida is actually the closest place to Colombia you could leave from, and lots of people say that if you're going down clean, why not act clean and just split? You don't have to file any papers or give notice when you leave the States. The smart boys know different. They know that the marinas and docks of Florida are crawling with guys either in or out of uniform who keep tabs on every suspicious-looking boat that enters or leaves the basin. They come right up to the boat sometimes and say, 'Hey, where you boys fixin' to sail?' They act real friendly. Meanwhile, they're checking you out real good. So when we were getting to the takeoff point, we shifted to the Bahamas. Checked into Bahamas customs at West End, the first island you get to. Then, we just tied up and relaxed. Did a little busy work on the boat—there's always something to do—and sat back waiting for the word. We were already provisioned and fueled—you don't want to do those things in the Bahamas. We were just waiting for 'O.K. boys. It's set. Go!'

"We left from a remote Bahamian island, San Salvador. Our plan was to sail down, load off the coast of Colombia, sail back to Florida, unload very fast and then check in officially at the Bahamas. We made sure plenty of people saw us in the Bahamas. The records would prove we had been there. So if it ever came to an issue, how could we be fucking around in Colombia if we were sailing around the Bahamas?

"Going down to Colombia, you've got a quartering wind from the northeast. That's the trade winds. They blow really steady and make the trip easy. When you get into the Windward, you've got a current that's also helping you. Once you get into the Caribbean, however, that wind starts to swing more from the east than the northeast so the last leg you got to run your motor pretty steady or waste a lotta time tacking. You got to remember that these motor sailers don't sail as well as a pure sailboat. They're designed to be big and roomy—comfortable.

"The weather is always a big consideration sailing. That time of year, February, March, around in there, you got beautiful vacation-style weather. The hurricanes are mostly in August and September. The Northers end in January. The weather should be perfect. Just a beautiful sail!

"It took us about a week to sail down there. During that time we ran a tight ship. You usually have two people on watch for three hours; after three hours, one guy goes off and another guy comes on. Each man stands six hours on and three hours off. You try and set things up so the change of watch comes around meal-time. The off watch can fix breakfast or lunch and the other watch can eat while they're on duty.

"When you're not on duty, you sleep or fish or work on the boat. Or listen to music or get stoned. If you have two men on watch, you don't have to be super-alert. The men can take turns steering, and the guy who's got nothin' to do can lie down on the deck and grab some shut-eye. You trim the sails from time to time. Night is just like day. It's all routine.

"Things will go wrong, of course. Typically, what happens is that you're experiencing perfect sailing, you're high, the stereo's playing on deck, you've got piña coladas mixed—and you love everybody in the world! Suddenly, your jib halyard has snapped, a steel cable. Your jib is half out in the ocean. The shit has hit the fan! Then everybody has to turn to and work like crazy! It's moments like this when you experience that tremendous sense of camaraderie. You've hauled your buddy up the mast in a bosun's chair; and even if that boat is rocking just slightly, when you get to the top of that mast, the swing from side to side is like a nightmare. You look at that poor guy up there slapping against that mast, with the shrouds tearing at his skin, and you have to grit your teeth not to feel it. When he finally gets the job done and comes down again, the feeling you have for him is religious.

"Most people don't realize how salt, stress and sun breaks things down on a boat. You don't need heavy weather to have things go to pieces. When you're running dope, you can't go into port for every little repair. You've got to improvise. We had a guy on our crew that we called Rigger. This guy was a genius with chewing gum and tape. One time, the check valve broke and water was coming into the generator through the exhaust pipe. So Rigger takes a potato and carves a perfect plug for the pipe. Every time we shut off the generator, we start yelling, 'Somebody's got to change the potato—who's gonna do the potato?'

"When we got down off the coast of the Guajira, it was a righteous sight. These mountains towering up there and that strange sand haze hovering above the beach. We figured we'd hang there for a couple days and then slip in at night to load. The first morning we get down there, our man on shore calls us on the radio and says: 'Come on in!' 'It's daylight, man!' we answer. 'Don't worry about it!' he says. He was right! Everybody knows what's going on down in Colombia. All those American pleasure boats cruising offshore and those big trawlers from Galveston, Texas—who do they think they're kidding?

"So after weeks and weeks of fucking around, it finally gets very real. Out from the shore comes a whole fleet of these red *cayugas*, all decorated and painted up like something out of *Mutiny on the Bounty*. They've got these little one-cylinder putt-putt motors and they're loaded down with bales of dope. When they get close, you get a good look at the guys, and they're sure-enough Indians. They got these Iggy Pop haircuts and head-bands—and they're wearing G-strings! They come banging up against the side of our boat on both sides and start tossing bales at us like crazy. They're freaked out because they could get caught in the act, so they want to get unloaded as fast as possible. It was all we could do to make a human chain and stash that dope in the saloon fast as they threw it on deck. Fortunately, we knew exactly how we were going to stash. Our decks were cleared for action.

"Same time as these guys are loading you, they're ripping off everything they can get their hands on. If they can score even a simple kitchen knife, they've had a big day. A five-dollar bill makes the guy who gets it a man with a price on his head. You've never seen such pure greed. So the whole thing happens in a blur. *Cayugas* are banging against both sides of your boat, other *cayugas* are standing off waiting to come in, your contact man is down there in one boat yelling orders at these guys. Everything is happening at once. Right in the middle of the dope bales, you start catching sacks of coffee, great big stems of bananas and fifty-five-gallon drums of fuel! It all comes flying on deck like a shit blizzard.

"When we got that sucker loaded, we were ready to explode! So far as we were concerned, we had done the job, We got so crazy, we turned the stereo all the way up and started dancing around on deck. Just at that moment, we heard a plane engine. I looked up. Swooping up straight over us was this two-engine transport with LAOS written across the wings. I freaked! I fig-ured it was a CIA plane on loan to the DEA. I figured they spot-ted us and we were in for trouble. Later, I realized, it was proba-bly just a smuggling plane doing the same gig that we were doing.

"You do get paranoid once you're loaded. You can't hide the stuff, and the boat reeks so bad that anybody could smell the load from a hundred yards away. You never forget that odor. Other-wise, it's funny how indifferent you become to all that dope. Every day you climb over bales and stare at bales and open bales to take little samples. After a while you could be hauling sugar or coffee or cotton. It's just a load. One of the things you do get into is trying to crack the code on the bales.

Every load has stuff that is of different grades. When the

balers sew the dope up, the man in charge marks the bales so he can find the good stuff and maybe take his piece out of the best. Our operation was highly compartmentalized. We were the sailing crew. It was just like in the service: the tank crews don't know anything about the infantry. So we would think, 'Gee, I wonder if all the bales with circle 1 are the best stuff?' Then, we'd cut a little hole in the bale and smoke some of that stuff. Our biggest problem was that I mislaid the rolling papers. We had to use newspaper, calendars, any- and everything to smoke all that dope.

"Coming back we ran into terrible weather. Storms, gales, water spouts a mile high. There were only three of us and we really needed four men. So each man had to work to make up for that missing man. I forgot all about sleeping. I got into an energy stream that was so powerful, I felt like Superman. Then, when we got north of Cuba, in the fishing channel there, we hit a calm and didn't move for a day and a half. You can imagine how that felt— sitting there with 13,000 pounds of dope. We did some motor sailing; but with that weight, we were crawling. One great advantage we had was our captain. He was a master of his craft. He had spent years on the water. He knew everything and had complete authority. When you're sailing, somebody has got to make those decisions and make them fast, because vacillating can be more dangerous then just making the wrong move. Once it's no longer smooth sailing, the crew starts to get anxious. Even a boat on the horizon that you can't make out yet—the crew is flashing: 'What is this? What do we do?'

"The other side of the trip home is all the thinking you do. When you're standing your watch at night and all that phosphorescent sea is around you and it's just the stars and the thrust of the boat and you at the wheel, your thoughts turn to so many different things. 'What am I going to do with this money?' That's a big thought. Or 'Gee, I'd love to get home and see my old lady!' It's amazing how guys will sit down in that cabin and write a letter to a woman they're always complaining about when they're home with her.

"I can't tell you much about how we brought the dope in—we may want to use that spot again. I'll tell you one thing: we off-loaded those bales one every few seconds in an unceasing beat. Then we cleaned that boat cleaner than any boat has ever been cleaned. We had covered every crack and cranny with tape so that the seeds couldn't get down in the crevices and give us away. When we got back to the Bahamas, you'd have thought that boat was right out of the yard.

"Looking back, I'd say it's hard not to be romantic about what we did. Bringing pot back is a good thing, a noble thing. It may be against the law, but all through history there have been laws that proved to be unrealistic and unjust. So this is one of those moments in history when the people with the courage go out there and break those unjust laws and feel the pride of being pioneers. I won't deny that you're also inspired by the thought that you're going to make a lot of money, but when you've got those big, thick stacks of green, wadded together with rubber bands in your hands—the effect is pure anticlimax. It's not the money, important as that is for opening doors and giving you new opportunities. The real thing is the *trip*, the adventure.

"The things you worried about when you left home no longer seem so important. You've had more important things to worry about. You really had your ass out there on the line. What's more, you learned to cope with those much heavier worries. You thought: 'What if a Coast Guard cutter comes up on us in the Straits of Florida.' Finally, you thought: 'Oh, fuck it! I'll get out of it somehow.' You lose the fear of being busted. You know that if you've come this far, you can go further. You've stepped into a stream of energy. The adrenaline is filling your veins and arteries. It's pumping and pulsing through your body. There's no other high like it. You can fuck all day long—and that's great! This is something else. Smuggling is the ultimate *rush!*"

Off-loading a shipment of smuggled goods is the moment of truth, the D Day that even veteran smugglers anticipate with a lump in their throats. Those who have organized the operation and brought it this far have a lot to lose—maybe even their lives. The odds *against* getting nabbed don't quell the quick churning in the guts that begins when the whole unloading scene starts to reel off like a movie.

The best picture I obtained of an off-loading was provided by Robert Perkins, director of the Charleston Patrol, an armed and specially trained unit of U.S. Customs charged with interdicting dope smuggling into Georgia and the Carolinas. In August of 1975, Perkins received word from an informer that a big load of dope was coming into a place called Sutherland's Bluff, down near Sapelo Island, one of the most remote and thinly inhabited sections of the Georgia coast. (Customs will pay any informant a "moiety:" half the value of the seized merchandise up to a maximum of $25,000.) Marshaling all his people into a convoy of trucks and cars, he took off on a suffocating Saturday afternoon for Savannah. There he briefed them on the operation. Then the CPOs piled into their vehicles again and rolled down I-95 until they were in the vicinity of Shellman's Bluff, a popular Saturday-night drinking spot about a mile from the smuggling site.

It was very important that Perkins get his men into the area before the smugglers began unloading, but he was afraid to invest the area with a big posse lest some spy spot them. He could not contact the local police because lots of redneck sheriffs are into the smuggling game just as their daddies were into bootlegging. So he ordered his people to pull off the highway into a rest area, where no one would ever think to look for them. Then he dispatched four specially trained scouts to slip up to the smuggling site and spy out the operation. These men had gone to Navy frogman school. They were trained to cross rough country, to swim for miles underwater, to get close to a criminal operation without being seen. Their orders were to wait until they saw the dope coming off the ship. Then, they were to signal the rest of the officers with the code word "Eyeball."

The area the smugglers had picked to land their load was a classic bit of Southern coastal scenery. Sutherland's Bluff is a stretch of twenty-foot-high bank along the Sapelo River, which winds down to the ocean through a landscape of gnarled live oaks streaming with Spanish moss. On this hot, humid night, the moon, a smuggler's moon, rose like a giant orange ball from the swamp. When it got higher, it turned into a silver disc beaming down like a floodlight on the narrow, sandy riverbank.

Around ten o'clock the patrol scouts were scoping out the position. They reported that there were many police in the area: both the local sheriff and his deputies and some Georgia highway patrolmen. As some of the Customs men were undercover agents wearing civilian clothes, the presence of the police posed the distinct possibility that in the confusion of the raid some of the "good guys" might be shot as "bad guys." Perkins ordered all his people to take out white rags and tie them around their right arms.

Then the scouts got up to the riverbank and began reporting the scene there. About twenty smugglers were scrambling all over the bluff. They had nine campers and vans. They had moored a houseboat at right angles to the beach to act as a floating dock.

Now a big shrimp trawler was seen coming up the river, being led by a little pilot boat. The shrimper was the *Hazel B,* her port of registration Savannah. She was coming to anchor adjacent to the houseboat. The smugglers were swarming out to meet her. The cargo was coming off. The word was *"Eyeball!"*

Perkins ground out his last cigarette and gave the order to attack. The whole convoy dashed across the highway and down the local road until it hit the narrow, sandy track that leads to Sutherland's Bluff. Suddenly, Perkins stared through the windshield in disbelief. There, blocking the road squarely, was a Georgia highway patrol car. Its occupants were standing on the side of the road looking straight at the oncoming Customs men. Shrieking to a halt, the lead car of the Customs caravan disgorged a very angry Customs man.

"Robert Perkins, director, Charleston Patrol, U.S. Customs," snapped Perkins, flipping open his leather ID wallet with its gold-and-blue badge. The sergeant who had been driving the car looked perplexed. He explained that there was no way he could get his vehicle out of the road. "Well," growled Perkins, who was now beginning to have his suspicions about this inopportune roadblock, "if she's not gonna go that way," jerking his thumb backwards, "she's damn well gonna go *that* way," jerking it forward, "or *you're under arrest for obstructing a federal officer in the performance of his duty!*" The astonished highway patrolman stared for a moment; then, without saying a word, he jumped behind the wheel and drove the car furiously down the rough country lane, tearing off bumpers, fenders, scraping and smashing the undercarriage, until by the time the car reached the creek bank, it had been totaled.

Meanwhile, many of the CPOs had jumped out of their vehicles and run on foot toward the river. Firing broke out at once. One smuggler rolled out of a van with his pistol blazing. A CPO got off three fast rounds from the hip with a shotgun. The local sheriff, who claimed to be leading a raid on the smugglers, was caught out in the river in a small boat. Spouts of water erupted around him. When he stumbled ashore, he found out Perkins and accosted him. "Your goddamned bastards been shootin' at me!" he snarled. Perkins laughed. "Sheriff," he replied, "if my 'bastards' been shootin' at you, you wouldn't be standin' here talkin' to me." The sheriff promptly disappeared.

After a few minutes of violent scuffling, half the smugglers surrendered; the others tried to make getaways. They raced off into the bushes and stole boats and got onto Sapelo Island. There they spent a dreadful night contending with mosquitoes, bobcats, rattlesnakes, bears and a million seed ticks. One or two escaped; the rest gave themselves up the following day.

When the final tally was made, Perkins had bagged twenty-one men, a sixty-five-foot shrimp boat (whose real name was *Gemini II*), nine motor vehicles, a houseboat, a 25-foot launch, $11,000 in cash and eighteen tons of marijuana worth about $10 million. It was the biggest dope bust, up to that time, in the history of the Southeast.

GETTING BUSTED—AND GETTING OFF

Supposing that worse comes to worst and the smuggler gets busted, does it follow that he will wind up in prison? Certainly not! American law is written and applied in a manner that makes it extremely difficult for the authorities to make dope charges stick. For every guy who is imprisoned, there are dozens who get busted and get off. In fact, I have often heard smugglers say that given the proper quality of legal representation, there is no longer any reason why anybody busted for marijuana the first time should serve time.

Curious to know how this was possible, how every day people are caught red-handed with huge amounts of narcotics and escape conviction, I went down one afternoon to New York's legal and administrative quarter around City Hall to speak with one of the top dope lawyers in the United States: Michael Kennedy. I met a youthful, good-looking, lithely athletic man with the cool intellectual manner and ready command of perfectly formed sentences characteristic of a college English professor. He knew exactly what was on my mind, and he had the ability to lay out the whole legal game so perfectly that I decided to simply transcribe his presentation and offer it to the reader as a textbook statement of the case. Let's kick back now in Kennedy's cheerful, spacious, memento-bedecked office on Broadway and hear how the guilty are proven innocent.

"The basic defense in narcotics cases," began Professor Kennedy, "is the prohibition of unreasonable search and seizure that comes from the Fourth Amendment to the United States Constitution and which has been incorporated in all state constitutions in accordance with the Fourteenth Amendment. The concept of the Fourth Amendment is that individuals have certain rights of privacy within the confines of their homes or, as the Supreme Court phrases it, their 'zone of privacy.' A zone of privacy is your automobile, a motel room, a men's room, anyplace where you think you might reasonably expect that no one will interfere with you. So long as you are within that zone of privacy, the state can penetrate it only when it has *probable cause* to believe that a crime is being committed.

"If the police violate the zone of privacy without a search warrant, the burden of proving that there was probable cause rests upon them. Therefore, the best way for the police to pierce the zone is to obtain a warrant from a magistrate. The police officer is obliged to sit down and write out the facts—not his suspicions but articulable facts—that cause him to believe that a crime is being committed. If he has received his information from an informant, this informant must have proven his reliability on previous occasions. *An anonymous call from a tipster is not probable cause.* Information purchased from some street cat is not probable cause either—unless this particular informant has been employed before and found to be reliable. When the officer completes his affidavit, he goes before a judge and swears that the information is correct. This provides some protection for the zone of privacy; for if it can be proven that the policeman has lied, he becomes liable to a perjury indictment.

"The magistrate examines the facts and decides independently whether or not there is probable cause. What he does in effect is ask himself: 'Is the action described in this affidavit consistent with innocent activity or is it inconsistent with innocent activity, implying that the activity is criminal?' He asks further: 'If there is a crime afoot, is there probable cause to believe that a particular person is responsible and do we know who this person is?' If the judge is persuaded there is probable cause, he issues the warrant. The warrant is very specific. It stipulates that the police may go to X apartment or house between certain hours. When the police officer serves the warrant, he must follow a clearly defined procedure. He must identify himself as a police officer; he must say, 'I have a search warrant'; he must display the warrant, conduct a search, prepare a detailed inventory of things seized and return the inventory with the warrant to the magistrate, who files it with the court documents where it can be examined by the defendant and his counsel.

"There are four or five exceptions that allow searches without a warrant. One is consent. Now, very few people who are hiding contraband are willing to consent to a police search; yet it's remarkable how many consent cases you encounter in the courts. The cops lie about consent because they figure their word will prevail over the word of this drug-crazed hippie.

"Another exception is 'exigent circumstances,' that is, a situation in which action must be taken at once or the suspects will escape. This exception connects with the doctrine of 'plain view,' the notion that anything that is in plain view is outside the zone of privacy. If you and I were sitting in a car, waiting for a light to change, for example, with a lot of big marijuana plants in the back seat, a cop could bust us without a warrant. Yet he could not come up to our car and demand to look inside the trunk. The cops have figured out how to leverage this concept into a greater exception. A dope lawyer is always running into cases where the police allege that when they accosted the defendant, he suddenly reached into his pocket and took out all this contraband and threw it on the ground or into the bushes, where it was in plain view. Plain view may also entail the use of binoculars, telescopes or what have you. It cannot be the justification for phone taps or the use of transponders, which are radio devices that can be put secretly aboard planes suspected of smuggling to track their flights. Wire taps and transponders require warrants.

"Another exception to the demand for a search warrant is border crossings. There is an implied assumption that we consent to Customs examining everything on our persons or in our possession when we pass over the border. This privilege derives from the government's right to levy tariffs on imports. Dope smugglers often avoid the borders by flying up into the middle of the country. To deal with that type of situation, the law developed the concept of the 'functional equivalent' of the border. If the government can prove by the use of, say, a transponder that you flew nonstop from Santa Marta to Little Rock, they can bust you in Arkansas without a warrant or probable cause for an unauthorized border crossing.

"Let's take a case that sums up all these principles. The biggest marijuana case I ever handled was a sixteen-ton seizure near Los Angeles in late 1975. The smugglers were caught red-handed. They had been using skip-jacks [very fast speedboats] to run the dope from a freighter into a yacht basin. Once into shore, they would pick up the skip-jack and haul it by road to a warehouse where they would unload the dope. Now let's consider how the authorities proceeded on this case. At first sight it would appear that they had the goods on these men.

"Confidential information was the original source of the investigation. Then direct observation through field binoculars established the identities of two of the men, who proved to have prior marijuana convictions. A check on the boats being used showed that they had been purchased by young people who paid for them in large sums of cash. Further observations showed that the boats would leave the marina riding high in the water and come back riding low, heavily laden. Finally, a police officer went to examine one of the boats and detected a strong odor of marijuana. At that point the men were busted and their warehouse full of dope was opened and the drugs seized. No warrant was deemed necessary.

"The bust was spread all over the front page of the Los Angeles *Times*. A couple of months later, the case hit the papers again. This time the headline read: JUDGE FREES MARIJUANA SMUGGLERS IN 16 TON CASE. The public was bewildered but the verdict was just. We argued at the hearing that there was no probable cause for the search and seizure. The fact that two individuals have been involved once in a marijuana crime does not imply logically that they are doing the same thing again. The fact that boats went out light and came back heavily laden is similarly without criminal implication. The boats could have been loaded with bananas, crabs, water, anything. The fact that the officer smelled marijuana might be a corroborating factor if there was other and valid evidence but in itself it means very little. Odors may be misinterpreted or imagined. The authorities also argued that the marina was the functional equivalent of the border. This the judge denied, pointing out that people were constantly coming in and out of the area in boats. If the authorities could have proven that the boats had gone outside the twelve-mile limit, they might have had a better case; but they were never able to follow the boats' movements once they were out of sight. At the end of the hearing, the prosecutor was screaming in frustration: 'Judge—*sixteen tons!* We caught them red-handed and you're cuttin' them loose!' The judge said: 'That's correct—that's what the Fourth Amendment is all about.' Very courageous judge. Emanuel Real, a former United States attorney, a tough prosecutor but a law man. My clients went scot free.

"The sixteen tons of marijuana in this case were destroyed, presumably; and often destroying the contraband or seizing the suspects, money, boats, vehicles et cetera is really the rationale for a bad bust. Even if the suspects go free, they have suffered heavy losses, which in the case of the hardware and cash are very difficult to recover.

"The primary prosecutional weapon in dope cases is not search and seizure. The favorite device is the snitch—the informer. There are two classes of snitches. One is the undercover operative, the cop in disguise. The other is the individual caught in the act who is 'turned' or told that if he will give up his friend he will be let go free. Turning people is far and away the most popular bust technique employed by the narcs today. The vast majority of the cases result from having busted someone and turned him. Sometimes the cops will bust a whole bunch of people on the edge of an operation—even the women and the children—so that they can get someone who will turn or so the men will turn to release their women and children. Sometimes they will take people and squeeze them hard—terrorize them. They'll take a particularly young and impressionable person and say, 'You're going away for twenty years!' Or they will say, 'You will be denied bail pending appeal. You won't be able to see your lawyer. You won't be able to see your friends.' They threaten to take away the human rights that they are sworn to defend. Finally, the snitch will break down and start to tell them things. He will talk and talk until he sees that glimmer in the narc's eyes, until the snitch feels, 'I'm getting there, getting through to him.'

"I will not represent snitches. I loathe the whole business. I maintain that it is inherently unfair, unjustified and illegal for the government to encourage an individual to solve his criminal problem by laying it on another man's head. Why should a snitch be able to walk out because he gave information against his partners, who did no more than he did? The government is not only subsidizing the criminality of the snitch but placing a premium on betrayal and treachery. They are also putting a premium on perjury, because many people lie to the investigators. The government agent will keep pressing and pressing, saying, "That's not enough. . . . That's not enough,' until the snitch comes out with something that never even happened.

"When you're faced with a snitch on the stand, about all you can do is persuade the jury that the man has such a strong motivation for lying that he should not be believed. Sometimes you can get an 'accomplice instruction.' The judge will tell the jury: 'You may view with suspicion the testimony of this accomplice because he has the motivation to lie; and, if you believe that he is lying, you can disregard the entirety of his testimony.'

"So far as all these threats that they make against people they're trying to turn, they are gross exaggerations. In most cases a marijuana trafficker will be a very good candidate for probation. Even with prior convictions, the amount you will serve will not be very great. If, for example, under the federal system you are sentenced to ten years, there is no way that you will serve more than a third of that time. The raw weight of the sentence bears little relation to the time served. In this day and age, it would be almost unheard of for a second offender to serve more than a year or two for marijuana. The offense is just not that serious anymore."

At this point I asked Michael Kennedy whether it is true that dope lawyers make large sums of money defending their clients. His reply was surprising. "I would make much more money as a corporate lawyer or as a defender of insurance companies or in my original practice, which was litigating accident cases: airline crashes, train wrecks and other cases where people are seriously injured. I found that work both boring and unpleasant. It's not very pleasant trying to turn pain and injury into dollars and cents.

"The reality of dope practice is that the big money belongs to the individuals who don't get caught. When you get caught you have nothing. Your load is gone, your cash is gone. Now you have

to hire a lawyer. As the government knows, a person in that situation has got to hustle. He's probably going to pull another job,
dumber than his last one because now he's more vulnerable. So
there isn't a great deal of money in dope practice unless you want
to participate as a criminal.

"I would not engage in any criminal activity with dope
dealers because it would be too easy for them to give me up in
order to save themselves. What's more, as a lawyer who has often
antagonized the authorities, I must be particularly careful not to
allow myself to be set up on a completely phony offense. Clients
will say to you, 'Take this money under the table.' Then they'll
bust you with the IRS. I don't care if the money is legal, illegal,
laundered or what. I give everybody a receipt and pay taxes on all
of it. Furthermore, when somebody asks me to do something
illegal, like participate in a prospective crime, I assume that person is *wired*. I say: 'No, thank you—that's not my game.' Many
lawyers in the business of representing criminals end up as criminals themselves because they identify too closely with the action.

"I identify with the human situation. There's an extraordinary imbalance between the drug smuggler and the DEA. The
DEA has unlimited resources. They have the ability to buy witnesses, buy any piece of evidence they want, scare a person into
doing anything they want him to do. Correcting that imbalance is
my game. That's the social value of my work."

Though most informers are, as Kennedy remarks, either undercover narcs or smugglers who have been "turned," there is a
third class of informer who is much more interesting and evil.
This is the informer who works a deal whereby he trades information on other smugglers in exchange for protection of his criminal
activities. Such informers can become wealthy very fast because
once they get a license to steal, they are in the most advantageous
position in the Game. At the same time, they are in the most pre-
carious and dangerous position because they are subject to repri-
sals from both sides.

The strength of such men and the secret of their success lies
ultimately in their totally, one might say psychopathically, objec-
tive view of the Game. Instead of seeing the law, for example,
through the enlarging lens of fear or guilt, they see the "heat" simply as men of limited resources and intelligence who are trying to
accomplish a nearly impossible task and eager for any help they

can obtain. Knowing the real weakness of the authorities, the criminal informer can strike remarkable bargains with the law and get away with murder. On the other hand, such informers recognize that the dangers they run from the dealers and smugglers they betray are not so great as they are imagined to be by the ignorant. Why should a betrayed smuggler run the risk of a "murder one" rap just to avenge himself? As the criminal informer never testifies in court but only before secret grand juries, killing him would not even eliminate a witness. So by preying on the weaknesses of both sides, the hard-core criminal informant is able to profit richly, while at the same time fulfilling his deepest desire, which is to rip off everybody.

THE SMUGGLER AS HERO

Undercover narcs, paid informers, co-conspirators who have been "turned"—all these shadowy, or shady, antagonists have been employed to bring down the dope smuggler. Yet, it could be said that the major trafficker's worst enemy is not the fink but that familiar tragic nemesis, *hubris;* or, as we would say today: egomania coupled with a big mouth. The tragic flaw of the classic hero is even more characteristic of the underground hero, for neither in the underground nor the underworld has modesty ever been a virtue. The smuggler, who is the latest hero of both these dark worlds, is simply true to type. Like the celebrated black pimp who boasted on the first page of his biography that he made more money every year than the President—and then was thrown into prison for income-tax evasion—the smuggler is torn between the instincts of self-preservation and self-assertion. What's more, as the media begin to exploit his exploits, the temptation to swagger, to boast, to spill the beans and incriminate himself will increase to the point where every smuggling crew will include a film crew or at least an as-told-to writer with a signed contract and a fat advance in his pocket. (Recently, I was approached indirectly by a major TV network that had budgeted a quarter of a million dollars to film a smuggling operation. When I asked why they were contacting me, the reply was: "We figured you had the connections.")

Meantime, the smuggler hero is surfacing everywhere: in Hollywood films (*Lucky Lady, Star Wars, Midnight Express*); in the nonfiction novel (*Snow Blind*); book-length reportage (*Weed*); pop song (Jimmy Buffett's "A Pirate Looks at 40"); and in countless magazine articles in a range of periodicals stretching all the way from *High Times* to *Time* (cover story, January 1979, "The Colombian Connection") to *The New York Times*. Riding such a wave of adulation, is it any wonder that the smuggler—whose best work so often goes unnoticed—should sometimes take a bow that leads to a bust?

The smuggler's public image is a fusion of the outlaw bravado of the Wild West with the sex-drugs-and-money glamour of the rock star. Like Mike the Marijuana Maven, whom we encountered in the first chapter of this book, who boasted about his "hits" (those successful marketing choices that won public favor) and who worried that "if I fuck up, I may fuck up America," the young and ambitious dope smuggler regards himself often as an extension or rival of the defiant culture heroes of the Sixties. He will brag about his enormous power—"Man, do you realize how many people I reach?" He will tog out in the latest country-and-western threads. He will exhibit that mixture of exhibitionism and paranoia so characteristic of the rock star. In a world where the power of illusion and the illusion of power are so hard to distinguish, the dope smuggler is an exemplary contemporary character.

Let me sketch now the profile (to borrow a favorite term of the DEA) of a typical young smuggler. Like any merchant who believes in his product, the smuggler is a walking advertisement for dope. When he gets up in the morning, he rolls his first joint and he never stops rolling and smoking till he falls to sleep in his chair the following morning. A classic "multiple drug abuser," he doesn't stop with smoke but engorges constantly great quantities of cocaine, hashish, Quāāludes and tequila. When he's under great stress, he soothes his nerves with heroin or charges his battered brain by dissolving his coke in water and injecting it with a syringe.

Like any well-prepared international criminal, the smuggler will have a complete set of forged or illegally obtained identification documents. His passport will carry his picture; but the name and other details will belong to some child who died at the age of two or three, leaving no other documents behind him but a birth certificate, the first item in a "paper trip" or buildup of illegal credentials. Once the smuggler has his passport, he can add an international driver's license, credit cards, voter registration—a whole wallet stuffed with vinyl-coated goodies.

Naturally, the smuggler would never think of using his credit cards because they leave a trail of traceable transactions. The ideal customer, he pays for everything in cash. Professional pride forbids him to touch any denomination smaller than a hundred-dollar bill, his basic medium of exchange. All his bills should be crisp and clean, suitable for rolling up into the straws through which he snorts his cocaine. When he travels on business, his money is carried by his burly, gun-toting bodyguard, who either stuffs the money into his boots and pockets or wraps it about his body in money belts. As a typical transaction may entail hundreds if not thousands of bills, the money may not be counted—it can be *weighed.* Any American bill weighs one gram; hence, reckoning 454 grams to the pound, a pound of hundred-dollar bills is equivalent to $45,400.

Next to his dope and his money, the smuggler's other basic gear is his cassette player and his gun. The former is indispensable for the long empty hours when he is waiting for the connection or riding on top of the bales at the back of the smuggling plane or boat. The latter is basically a macho appurtenance, like the *toga virilis.* (Should any serious danger impend, the preferred weapon is the automatic shotgun or the Israeli submachine gun called the Gallil.)

The smuggler's world is entirely male and macho. The only women that impinge upon it are the smuggler's lady friends, who run to certain types, *viz.:*

Nice girl of good family gone bad: She may be from Miss Twit's Finishing School, or, even better, a South American girl of aristocratic origin corrupted by American culture. She is prized for her femininity, essential goodness and naïveté. Her big drawback is that she isn't wicked enough to be exciting after the first thrill of violation.

The foxy lady: She should be black or at least mulatto. Ideally, she is an exotic, like a black Chinese girl. She's been around and is into girls as well as boys as well as groups. She holds her own with the smuggler's fast life-style and is his mental equal. Her principal disadvantage is that she's cold as ice and manipulative as an octopus.

The good old lady type: She's not a great beauty or especially erotic, but she's warm and friendly and experienced. She's taken a couple of busts and been kicked around in the streets. She does what she's told and takes serious risks on the smuggler's behalf. She's honest, nonexploitative, not too smart and a little masochistic. Nice but dull, she finally gets kicked in the ass again.

The juvenile delicious: This is a crazy little JD of fourteen or fifteen, who ran away from home and immediately began rolling around in the gutter. She not only balls the smuggler but all his friends. She'll do anything for kicks and has dropped as much acid as Tim Leary. She gets ordered around and treated like a dumb kid, but she has a great time getting wasted and listening to all the tall tales of the Game. God knows what will become of her when she grows up. Will she become a madam?

With this brief sketch of the smuggler to guide us, we can now appreciate the stories of three of the most notable smugglers of recent times and understand especially the defects of personality that led to their downfall.

The most celebrated dope smuggler of modern times was a middle-aged man who chose deliberately to abandon a successful career as a stockbroker and real estate speculator in order to enjoy the thrills and glamour of a hero of the counter-culture. The name of this worthy was Kenneth G. Burnstine. His career furnishes a particularly bizarre example of that now-familiar phenomenon: the mid-life crisis of the American male.

Kenny Burnstine was first and foremost a great flier. He commenced his aviation career as a combat pilot for the U.S. Marine Corps in Korea, continued it as a trophy-winning racing pilot, and concluded it as a charred, virtually unidentifiable corpse found amid the wreckage of his P-51 Mustang in the Mojave Desert. In his palmy days, during the early Seventies, the ebullient Burnstine partied it up in a $650,000 mansion in Fort Lauderdale, surrounded by a five-foot wall inside which prowled two Great Dane attack dogs and a caged lion. On the gate was posted a notice that read: TRESPASSERS WILL BE EATEN.

It was in the late Sixties that Burnstine graduated from the then-exciting businesses of stockbroking and real-estate speculation to the vastly more exciting and lucrative racket of drug smuggling. "His original reason for getting into the dope business," recalled one informant, "was the intrigue. He said it got his adrenaline going. Apparently, he was accepted by the community *because* he was a smuggler. He claimed that he went to the best parties in town and rubbed elbows with the best people. They treated him good—better than they had treated him as a businessman." Of course they did! Every schmuck calls himself a businessman, but a *smuggler . . .* ! Well, that's pretty heavy.

By 1972, Burnstine was flying high as the boss of a reputed $50-million-a-year smuggling ring disguised as a rent-a-plane corporation titled Florida Atlantic Airlines (FLAIR). FLAIR's specialty was the Jamaica run: a takeoff after dark in a two-engine Lodestar; a two-hour flight to the *ganja*-growing area near Negril; a half-hour loading with no refueling; then back to southern Florida before daybreak. For a while, the business was spectacularly successful. Then, the evidence of this surreptitious traffic began to literally pile up.

First, a FLAIR Lodestar crashed on an abandoned airfield in Jamaica. Next, Burnstine, who billed himself as "the world's greatest pilot," crashed twice in notorious drop zones off the Florida coast. Then, a Lodestar suffered a "nonsurvival high-speed crash" in eight feet of water about four miles west of Chub Cay in the Bahamas. Investigators found 240 pounds of marijuana in the wreck, plus the body of the copilot. The pilot, who was never found, was Burnstine's chief of operations, Mike Zorovitch. The mystery of his disappearance was deepened by two facts: he had just taken out a huge insurance policy; he was scheduled to be the star witness at the trial of Brooklyn congressman Bertram Podell, who was subsequently convicted and imprisoned for taking a bribe of $41,350 from Burnstine's company to exercise his influence on behalf of the airline, which was seeking to obtain a government contract for mail delivery to the Bahamas. Just three weeks after this sensational crash, a Lodestar flying to Tampa from the Bahamas with Burnstine at the controls made a forced landing on a deserted road. Investigators found track marks indicating that the plane had been met by a number of wheeled vehicles. A week later, Burnstine crashed again in a Catalina flying boat and was picked out of the water by a passing yacht.

The climactic incidents in this bizarre history occurred during the month of January 1974. First, a FLAIR Lodestar crashed into a high-rise apartment building at Pompano Beach, killing the crew of three and strewing 4,000 pounds of marijuana along the sands. A week later, another Lodestar hit some utility lines near Fort Meyers, a major smuggling area on Florida's southwest coast. In the wreckage, the police found 2,000 pounds of weed. Burnstine said that dope smugglers were renting his planes without his knowledge. The boys in the Game said that government agents were sabotaging the planes.

Meantime, the irrepressible Burnstine, a good-looking, virile man in his early forties, was boasting, throwing his money around and sharing his coke and his confidences with those charming Southern girls who have been called the "Mouth of the South." Basically, there are only three ways to lose in the smuggling game. Either you're stupid, unlucky or a show-off. Burnstine wasn't dumb, and his mere physical survival proves his good luck. What destroyed him was his life-style. It isn't easy to elude the narcs if you're a "colorful character." The lawmen are spread so thin that virtually anybody can get by them; but if they get a chance to concentrate on one man, he's doomed.

Burnstine's bust was right out of the DEA's textbook. During 1975, he conspired to bring cocaine and marijuana into the U.S. from Mexico with a group of good ole boys who turned out to be undercover agents. He was tried, convicted and sentenced to serve seven years. To stay out of prison, he turned state's evidence and appeared as the key witness in a number of sensational dope trials. A Florida state representative, a famous gun merchant, a Teamsters' official and many other prominent people became the targets of his accusations.

Out on $100,000 bail, "the world's greatest pilot" continued his racing career. On June 16, 1975, while preparing for the California National Air Races, he took off in his souped-up P-51 Mustang and zoomed over the course. While making a high-speed turn around a pylon, he was heard to exclaim over the radio: "My God! It's stuck!" An instant later, his plane crashed and exploded in a ball of flames. Up in smoke went not only Ken Burnstine but sixty-four indictments. Can anyone believe his death was accidental?

Not so glamorous as Burnstine but equally notorious is Harry "The Rock" Hoffman, who boasted that he was "bigger than Vesco" and who certainly justifies the description on a physical basis. A 276-pound, baby-faced, Buddha-bellied lad with wavy

hair down to his shoulders, the Rock looks like one of those por-
cine country music stars that are all hulk and hair.

At an age when most young men are scuffling to make good
on their first little job, Harry Hoffman—whose first job was dog-
catcher of Muskegon County in Michigan—became a wealthy
man. He bought a private island in the Bahamas and a lavish
mansion once owned by Jack Nicklaus; he bought or bought into
numerous restaurants in the Caribbean and the U.S.; he rode in a
Rolls-Royce, had a helicopter at his beck and call and did his
long-range traveling in chartered Learjets. His smuggling
methods were rough and ready, but they served well enough
until he got his bad break.

The scandal that put Hoffman's name in headlines was not of
his own making. It was all the fault of his lieutenant, a tough-looking, heavily whiskered dude with a thirst for hard liquor and a
drinker's temper: Marvin Flowers a.k.a. Ryan Redford, Robert
O'Neal and "Smooth." In June 1974, Flowers had a sit-down with
some Boston lawyers at the Don César Motel in Saint Petersburg
Beach. His behavior when he left the motel driving his black Lin-
coln Continental makes one wonder how he ever got his nick-
name. Cruising north on U.S. 19, he was passed by a motorist
who cut directly in front of him. Ignited into rage, he trailed the
man to an apartment complex and threatened to beat him up. At
that moment an off-duty waitress arrived home and stopped the
brawl. Flowers followed the waitress or was invited into her
apartment. Her story is that when she came out of the bathroom,
she found Flowers lying on the sofa stark naked. When she refused to ball him, there was a scuffle. Finally, she succeeded in
getting him back in his clothes and out the door. She called the
police and lodged a complaint. The cops took off, looking for a
black Continental.

When they found the car, it was parked beside the highway,
out of gas, with Flowers sound asleep behind the wheel. Beside
him on the seat was a briefcase containing $387,000 *in cash*. A
search of Flowers's wallet produced a note reading: "Georgetown
Sea Buoy. Start looking next Thursday night . . . won't expect
anybody after midnight. Find a place for me to unload plus charts
of the area."

Arraigned before a statewide grand jury impaneled to investigate the narcotics traffic in Florida, Flowers refused to talk. As he told a reporter, the money "wasn't counterfeit; it was legal. It wasn't stolen, and I don't feel I should have to answer questions to anybody about where it came from." The grand jury thought differently. They indicted Flowers for conspiracy to import marijuana. Also named in the indictments were Harry Hoffman, Hoffman's mysterious partner, Gerald "Buddha" Haruki, two of Flowers's brothers and a gaggle of road runners, roustabouts and boat captains—virtually the whole gang.

Almost two years elapsed before the charges were finally adjudicated. During that time, Flowers was arrested in Philadelphia after getting into a fight with a passenger on an airplane, indicted and extradited by his hometown, Muskegon, on charges similar to those in the Florida case and, finally, arrested in December 1975 for crossing the border illegally from Mexico into the U.S. along the old Smuggler's Trail near Brownsville, Texas. In his company at this time was a fat, baby-faced lad named Harry Hoffman.

When the indictments were handed down, Hoffman was beyond reach of the law, residing in his mansion in the Bahamas. For a year he tried to gild his image in the islands, giving, for example, $100,000 to a local health clinic. The authorities adjudged him, nonetheless, an undesirable person and threatened him with deportation. At this point he fled to Costa Rica, then to Panama and Mexico. Finally, he tried to slip across the border with Flowers.

Four months after Hoffman's return, there was a fresh scandal. A former mayoral candidate in Saint Pete was charged with offering a bribe of $55,000 to a local judge; the string attached to the bribe was a demand that Flowers be allowed to "walk away from his pending felony case [and] collect the monies that were seized from him at the time of arrest."

Meantime, one of the unindicted members of Hoffman's gang surfaced and revealed himself as a DEA informant. His name was Vernard Earl Follett. According to his lengthy deposition, Follett had been working both sides of the street for years; but all he got from the narcs were scoldings because his reports came in late, whereas from the smugglers he received generous salary increases that boosted his price from $3,000 for his first job to $25,000 for his last. Follett's fumbling but detailed testimony blew the case wide open. It offers a highly revealing and no less highly entertaining view of the secret workings of a big-time smuggling syndicate. If you enjoyed *The Gang That Couldn't Shoot Straight*, consider the comic possibilities latent in this account of one of the biggest smuggling runs of 1975.

The story commences about a month before the "move," with the ship captain, Jimmy Taylor, a commercial fisherman from Fort Meyers, being given nearly a million dollars in cash to carry down with him to Colombia. When the time comes to bring the stuff in, the Hoffman Gang is holed up in a motel in Atlantic Beach, South Carolina, with dealers from all over the country, who have come to pick up their shares of the load. The day the ship is expected in, some helicopters are spotted in the area. Instantly, the two leaders, the Rock and Buddha, panic. They order their men to burn or sink the off-loading boats. Follett, who is just a flunky, talks them out of it: "I said, 'No! Let's get it in.' I wanted to get *paid*."

The boat is supposed to signal its position by radio, but no message arrives. Finally, the smugglers are reduced to cruising the neighboring waters looking for the mother ship. The day after the helicopter alert, which proves to be a false alarm, one of the gang tells Follett that the boat is in, but he doesn't know where it's docked. The two men drive around a local game preserve until they find the site. The off-loading is already in progress. It isn't a very sophisticated operation: "The boat was just rammed into the shore. We built a raft and used a rope to the boat to pull the raft back and forth." It takes two and a half hours to unload the 48,000-pound cargo. Then, it develops that the dealers from Detroit are too frightened to come out to the landing site to pick up their share of the dope. Again, the lowly Follett has to take the initiative. He drives the Detroiters' truck out to the beach, loads it up and drives it back to the motel. At this point, the job is done and the danger has passed. Just the same, the stupid smugglers manage to get themselves busted.

They leave town in a rented car without bothering to make any payment. A few miles down the road, they're pulled over by a patrolman, who charges them with "larceny after trust." The smugglers are carrying twenty-five pounds of weed for a party and a vial of coke. When the cop opens up the pillow case which they've used to bag the weed, he says: "What's this?" Follett replies: "It's dirty laundry." The cop laughs and says, "O.K." Next day, the smugglers are bailed out by a local attorney. They return to Saint Pete.

A couple of nights later, Flowers calls Follett and tells him they're going to see the lawyers from Boston who have brought down the money to pay the ship captain, Taylor, for his work. Next morning Follett reads in the papers that Flowers has been busted with the cash. The gang flees and Follett goes down to the Bahamas to report to Hoffman.

Follett confesses that he has been working with the DEA. He assures the Rock that everything he told the narcs was lies. Hoffman becomes alarmed. Then, he cools off.

At this point, Hoffman has broken with his partner, Buddha; most of his gang is on the run. A smuggler arrives with a proposition. Hoffman needs a man to receive the load. Who does he choose? Follett. The one-time flunky is now the Man. Follet takes his last five thousand from the boss and goes back to the States.

Eventually, he decides to cooperate with the authorities, who promise him $25,000 for his testimony. Just before the trial, in April 1976, Follett, the state's star witness, disappears. The D.A. is ready to drop the case. "It's too far away from Christmas to hope that anything will happen," he remarks wistfully.

Then, in July, after the case has been blowing hot and cold for two years, the state gets a break. The ship captain, Taylor, and his mate, angry because they have never been paid for their work, agree to testify for the prosecution. Hoffman and Flowers are being defended by the redoubtable F. Lee Bailey. There is a flurry of last-minute plea bargaining. The jury is about to be impaneled. Suddenly, the D.A. announces that the defendants have decided to plead guilty.

A deal had been worked out. Hoffman and Flowers agreed to relinquish claim to a total of $535,000, which had been seized in the course of the investigation. (To the original $387,000 had been added another $148,000—dug out of one of the gang's backyard!) They also agreed to accept a sentence of six months to three years in the state penitentiary. When the plea-bargaining session concluded at the Pinellas County Courthouse, in Orlando, Hoffman, who had gone through the proceedings with a had-it-up-to-here expression on his face, was rushed by the local press. As Bailey hustled his client down a staircase, the cynical smuggler allowed himself just one parting shot. Alluding to a Prudential Life Insurance commercial on TV, he told the eagerly questioning reporters, with a sneer on his face: "I gave them a piece of the Rock!"

The bizarre fallout from the case continued for weeks after its conclusion. The county was obliged to advertise that anyone who had a claim on the money was entitled to step forward and state his case. About twenty-five individuals and organizations tried to get their piece of the Rock. Typical of their claims was the pitch of an actor at the local dinner theater, who argued that since Hoffman and Flowers had done such wicked things with their ill-gotten gains, it would be poetic justice if the county financed a record he was eager to cut, which would bring joy into the lives of thousands of citizens.

Marvin Flowers was paroled in January 1977. Harry Hoffman was locked up in September 1977 and released on parole at the end of June 1978.

7 The War on Drugs Escalates

THE BUST OF THE KAKI

As the seagoing smugglers began to escalate the scale of their operations in the mid-Seventies, the two agencies of the federal government primarily responsible for interdicting this traffic, Customs and the Coast Guard, worked to develop new modus operandi. Their greatest problem was the inviolability of ships in international waters. Their solution was to obtain through high-level diplomatic initiatives the cooperation of those foreign governments under whose flags or through whose waters the smugglers sailed. Eventually, a history-making precedent was established and the War on Drugs went into a new phase. The case that changed the rules of the Game was the bust of the motor vessel *Kaki*, discovered and seized in international waters in March 1976 in a combined Customs, Coast Guard and DEA operation directed from Charleston, South Carolina.

The story commences on a flawless spring day, about sixty miles off Hilton Head, South Carolina. The Coast Guard cutter *Dauntless* is steaming southwest over a sea so calm that it barely ripples. What does a modern Coast Guard cutter look like? If you saw *Lucky Lady*—the campy movie about rum running in the early Thirties—you know that during Prohibition the Coast Guard operated clumsy looking wooden patrol boats with thick-barreled Lewis guns on the bow.

Today's space-age Coast Guard has vessels that were designed by skillful naval architects expressly for the purpose of the Coast Guard. The *Dauntless* is a snubby, dart-shaped vessel with a high foredeck, a steep, three-story pilothouse and a long, low stern unencumbered by smokestacks (because she's got a stern exhaust system). Built for service, not for show, she can cruise 5,000 miles without refueling. She can make up to eighteen knots while giving chase. If things get ugly, she's got a 3.5-inch naval rifle on a revolving platform on her foredeck. It's questionable how many real gunners the Coast Guard can muster; but, theoretically, if a smuggler refuses to lay to and runs away, the *Dauntless* can wham a high-explosive shell into his tail.

The real secret of the *Dauntless*'s potential as a dope catcher is none of these things, however; it's the hulking amphibious helicopter which she totes piggyback on her 70-foot stern flight deck. Twice a day this HH-50 "flying lifeboat" windmills off the cutter's back and disappears over the horizon. There it ogles every vessel within a 25-mile radius. Shimmying right down on a suspect vessel's stern, the chopper can pore over the picture as long as it likes. In fact, if the boat is small and stationary, the helo can land beside it and come aboard for a friendly chat. Armed with eyes such as these, infinitely superior to the traditional sighting devices—the ambiguous blip on the radar screen or the dubious profile in a pair of binoculars—the *Dauntless* is a formidable weapon in the War on Drugs.

This day, however, she's on a much tougher mission than Operation Buccaneer. You don't have to be Sir Francis Drake to catch a galleon laden with Colombian Gold in the narrow straits between Mexico and Cuba or Cuba and Haiti. At certain times of year, the dope boats come through these waters like Operation Sail. Nor is there any problem once the big, powerful cutter has caught the little sailboat with its crew of sun-bleached hippies. Forty-one-foot Morgans don't fight back. What the *Dauntless* is doing on this patrol is a very different story. She is in search of a vessel that some authorities say does not even exist: the dope world's equivalent of the Abominable Snowman or the Loch Ness Monster. The *Dauntless*'s target is the Mother: the ghostly South American freighter that is reputed to bring hundred-thousand-pound loads of dope up from Colombia into the coastal waters of the U.S.

The legend of the Mother had been growing for years before the *Dauntless* left port on its memorable mission. At first the freighter was purely an inference, a hypothetical posit. On many occasions small boats had been seized off the east coast carrying what was unquestionably Colombian dope but evincing no capacity to make the lengthy trip themselves. How did the dope get into the boats? Was it picked up at some dumping ground, like the Bahamas? Or was it picked up at sea—from a mother ship? That was the problem that vexed the authorities until one very determined law enforcement officer decided to stop speculating and act as if the vessel did exist.

It so happens that I was present at the very moment when the idea of busting the Mother popped into the head of the master buster. It was January 12, 1976. I was on my way home to New York from my first trip to Colombia. I stopped off for a few days in Charleston to recuperate. As I often do, I checked in with my friend, Robert Perkins.

I found him fuming this day over a bust that had been reported in the morning paper. The day before, Customs, with the aid of the DEA and some state and local police, had swept down on an isolated fish-processing plant on the Pamlico River in North Carolina and busted a huge 112-foot fishing trawler loaded with fifteen tons of dope. Among those arrested at the site were the former mayor of Hallandale, Florida, John David Steele, and his twenty-one-year-old son. In a nearby warehouse another ten or twelve tons of dope were seized, to say nothing of such ancillary equipment as an airplane, a mobile home and a couple of automobiles. One would have thought that Perkins would have been delighted with the success of the operation—but he was infuriated. His information was that the trawler had picked up its cargo from a hovering steamer that could have had aboard it four or five times the tonnage seized at the fish-processing plant. The failure to go after the mother ship, the big one, was what rankled in Perkins's heart.

During the course of our conversation, I mentioned that when I left Colombia, the peak of the harvest was only one week distant. Allowing a week for curing and a couple of weeks for loading and transporting, the big ships should be in action again very shortly. Perkins listened attentively and finally said, "I'm gonna get me one of those Mothers."

The very next day, he told me later, he wrote up a plan of interdiction, which he dispatched to the headquarters of the Fourth
Customs Region in Miami. The plan revolved around the use of
an S-2 long-range reconnaissance plane: the plane that looks like
it has been captured by a flying saucer. The saucer is a radar
dome that enables the plane to monitor surface or air traffic for a
hundred miles in any direction. Capable of cruising for seven
hours at a stretch, the S-2 could be dispatched twice a day to
wing out across the Atlantic, surveying an area of a couple of
hundred square miles off the coast of the Carolinas. If it detected
a suspicious vessel, it could radio the information into the patrol
headquarters in Charleston and a thirty-two-foot Customs boat
could be dispatched to the spot to maintain surveillance with its
surface radar and catch the smugglers in the act of off-loading
their cargo into a lighter. At that point Customs or the Coast
Guard could seize the mother ship and make the biggest dope
bust in American history.

The only problem with this operation was the legal question
of what evidence was necessary to justify the arrest and seizure of
a vessel flying a foreign flag in international waters. Customs or
the Coast Guard can board any vessel flying the American flag,
but it has no right to challenge vessels under foreign flags
unless it finds them in flagrant violation of American law.

This was an old problem. It went right back to the days of
Prohibition, when the territorial line was only three miles off
shore. The bootleggers used to line up their smuggling vessels off
the coast of Long Island, along what was called "Rum Row."
Standing out in those waters winter and summer, rain or shine,
they ran a seagoing freeport. Every night they would receive fast
launches, so-called contact boats, from New Jersey, Manhattan,
Long Island and Connecticut. These boats would pick up loads of
bootleg whiskey and rush them back to shore through the Coast
Guard blockade. The game of hide-and-seek had gone on for
years until Congress had passed the Hovering Vessel Act. This
law empowered the Coast Guard to seize any vessel hovering off
our shores for the purpose of loading contraband cargo into vessels entering our waters. The only problem with the law was that
it hadn't been invoked in so many years that nobody remembered
how it worked.

When Perkins laid his plan before Customs, the agency had

to call in its legal department to clarify the issues. Customs passed the plan and the buck to the State Department. Eventually, it landed on the desk of Henry Kissinger, chairman of the President's cabinet committee on narcotics. When Kissinger said O.K., the Coast Guard drew up a memorandum which should be tacked up in every smuggler's pilothouse. It sets forth with great precision just what you have to do to get yourself busted on the high seas while flying a foreign flag. As there has been so much confusion about this issue, let me quote from Commandant Instruction 5920.6:

For the protection of the right of freedom of navigation on the high seas, Article Six of the 1958 Convention on the High Seas provides generally that vessels on the high seas are not subject to the jurisdiction of any state other than their flag state. There are, however, several exceptions to this principle of exclusive jurisdiction of the flag state. One of these exceptions recognizes the competence of the coastal states to enforce its applicable laws against a foreign vessel located on the high seas if its actions establish a "constructive presence" within the territorial waters or contiguous zone of the coastal state.

"Constructive presence" is established when a foreign vessel located on the high seas adjacent to the customs waters works as a team with another vessel (e.g., one of its boats or a contact boat from shore using the foreign vessel as a mother ship) to violate the law in the customs waters. Any such violation committed by the contact boat while it is in the customs waters is imputed to its "teammate" as well, thus bringing the foreign vessel constructively within these waters and subjecting it to law enforcement action while it is actually on the high seas adjacent to the customs waters. Constructive presence, therefore, can be said to have three essential elements: (1) *actual* presence of the foreign vessel on the high seas *adjacent* to the customs waters; (2) *actual* presence of the contact boat *in* the customs waters in violation of U.S. law; and (3) good reason to believe that the two vessels are working as a team (or did work as a team) to violate U.S. law. Constructive presence, and the concomitant susceptibility to U.S. law enforcement action, continues only as long as all three of these elements exist. If any one of the three elements ceases to exist, the constructive presence of the foreign vessel ceases, and no law enforcement action can be taken against it thereafter unless hot pursuit was established while constructive presence existed, and such pursuit was maintained uninterrupted until completion of the law enforcement action. The evidence which establishes each of the three elements must be available for subsequent court proceedings.

Perkins's plan was approved in principle, but it was rejected in practice. Headquarters in Miami said that the smuggling traffic was heaviest in its own backyard; it wished to maintain the greatest concentration of personnel and equipment in that area. (Customs had also completed a huge and vastly expensive center in Miami, which they wanted to start paying for itself by showing impressive results in all areas, including drug interdiction.) Perkins protested and asked what he could do with his one thirty-two-foot boat, which was so often out of commission that his men had to work on it during their spare time, his one little airplane, which was so small and slow that any smuggler craft could outrun it, and his little fleet of motor vehicles, which were being driven into the ground. (Once he complained that one of his cars was running on bald tires. Headquarters replied: "Lay the vehicle up.") It was a pathetically small armament to patrol 8,595 miles of intricately indented coastline.

Perkins, who once said to me, "A man won't amount to much in this business unless he's right much of a hunter," felt he had earned the right to try for the Mother. It's easy to imagine his chagrin when headquarters informed him that the operation could not be approved. His chagrin changed to wonderment a month later, however, when he learned that the Coast Guard had picked up his plan and altered it to suit their resources. Instead of a big, electronically sophisticated scout plane, the Coast Guard substituted a big, electronically sophisticated cutter with a plane based upon it. The result was precisely what Perkins had predicted. Within one week of her first patrol, the *Dauntless* discovered the Mother and busted her.

The cruise began routinely with the age-old rotation of watches and just a little more than the usual amount of grumbling because the presence of the chopper aboard the cutter made for much more work among the crew. For recreation the Coast Guard had put aboard the vessel that campy costume-and-prop romance about rum running, *Lucky Lady*. The film makes fools of the Coast Guard and romanticizes the smugglers beyond belief. It must have given the crew a lot of laughs. As for excitement, there was virtually none until one night, when the ship was cruising off the Port of Charleston.

The *Dauntless* picked up on its radar a vessel that was hovering suspiciously close to the coast. It was just the right size for a marijuana mother ship, about 200 feet long. It was positioned just where it had been predicted such a ship would swing into the coast to meet its lighters. What was most suspicious was the fact that it was dead in the water. As the officers on the bridge studied the image on the radar screen, they realized that at this very moment this mysterious vessel could be off-loading a cargo of dope into a fleet of speedboats or cabin cruisers.

Altering course and revving up their engines, they began to close on the suspect vessel. Perhaps they altered their running lights to look less like a cutter and more like a fishing vessel. Perhaps they ran up to the top of their mast a green-over-white fishing-at-night flag. The Coast Guard is chary of revealing its secrets, but these are the stratagems often adopted in such situations.

Speeding along at eighteen knots, the cutter was soon in sight of its prey. Peering through night-vision devices, the officers on the bridge could make out the vessel distinctly. It was big, all right, and absolutely motionless. Closing rapidly with nerves taut, the *Dauntless* suddenly switched on its searchlight and discovered—another Coast Guard vessel! It was the buoy tender *Papaw*, out of Charleston, anchored for the night.

Apart from such false alarms, the week's cruise had yielded no signs of dope traffickers. Every day the cutter would launch its helicopter, once in the morning and once in the afternoon. The chopper would describe every vessel that was moving on the sea. If it identified a vessel that offered any reason for suspicion, the cutter would hail it, stop it and search it, usually on the pretext of document verification or safety check. On the afternoon of the eleventh, however, it was decided to vary slightly the customary procedure. Instead of making the afternoon launch after lunch, the flight was postponed until evening chow was served around five o'clock. When the watch finished supper, preparations commenced for the flight.

Launching a helicopter from the deck of a 210-foot vessel that may be pitching or rolling as much as seven degrees is a tricky operation. It demands not only a skillful pilot but the active cooperation of virtually every officer and seaman on duty. First, the aviation crew has to take the wraps off the chopper and give it a preflight tune-up. Then, about fifteen minutes before launching, the bosun pipes flight quarters. The damage-control parties start slamming shut and securing the watertight doors connecting the after-compartments. The fire-control parties don red vests and bring their hoses and foam extinguishers up to the flight deck. A combat information center is manned below decks. A radioman stands by a ship-to-plane transmitter on the bridge. The launch crew, who wear blue jackets for identification and noise suppression helmets, stand by in nets that are lowered over the side of the flight deck. Up on the bridge the commanding officer heads the ship into the wind and adjusts his speed and bearing so as to minimize pitch and roll.

When the helicopter has been prepared, the flight crew board it. The crew comprises pilot, copilot and two enlisted men, who serve as lookouts. After the instrument check-out, the pilot calls the bridge and gets the last-minute information on the ship's heading and pitch and roll conditions. The actual control of the launch is in the hands of the helicopter executive officer, who acts as intermediary between the bridge and the cockpit. He gives the pilot permission to switch on his engine. He gives permission to take off.

When it's time to fly, the pilot holds up both hands balled into fists with the thumbs erect. When he swings his thumbs outward, the launch crew unsnap the quick-release webbing straps that hold the plane to the deck. Then they jump clear of the flight deck into their safety nets. When the executive officer gives a thumbs-up signal, the pilot lifts the chopper about six feet off the deck. He goes into a momentary hover to test the engine. Then he flies smartly off the side of the cutter. Once clear of the ship, he switches over to forward flight and takes off on his course.

On this cruise, the pilot of the *Dauntless*'s helicopter was Lieutenant Mike Allen, a veteran Coast Guard flier who has flown hundreds of patrol missions and developed an extraordinarily keen eye for appraising vessels from the air. Here is his own account of what happened the afternoon he sighted the Mother:

"It was a perfect day. What we call 'flat-ass calm.' Smooth as a mirror. Not a ripple on the water. Temperature in the seventies. A perfect day.

"The ship was headed south that day, so I decided to run out in front of it for about twenty-five miles and then arc around in a circle. Our altitude was a thousand feet.

"Shortly after takeoff, when we were about ten miles from the ship, I spotted a vessel ten to twelve miles down to the southwest. The only reason I saw it was because the sun was low in the sky, casting a red glare in the west. The boat was a tiny silhouette against that sunset glare. I identified it properly as a coastal freighter or a tanker.

I proceeded toward it, and when we were about two miles off, I noted two smaller vessels to the north—the same direction in which this freighter was sailing. Of the two smaller vessels, the nearest one was maybe two miles off the bigger ship, heading north, as I could see from her wake. The other vessel was maybe another two miles beyond that one, and it didn't appear to be moving at all. I figured I'd come back and check those vessels later. I didn't make any connection between them and the freighter.

"I came up to the freighter off the port quarter, the left rear side, and went into a hover. I looked down and read the name off the stern. On both sides it said KAKI and PANAMA. Now, our procedure when we identify a boat is that we get her name, port of registration, length, color, construction and anything peculiar. Then we spot the ship's position and course. To get the position we use a device on board the plane that picks up an electronic beacon signal from the cutter. We tune it in on our automatic direction-finding equipment and the needle points to our ship. Using that reading we can find out exactly what our position is in relation to the cutter and radio back the position of the vessel over which we're hovering.

"Now as we were getting all this information together, I noticed that the after-cargo hatch was open. I was looking down into it at an angle and it looked pretty much empty. But way down at the bottom I could see some manila-colored plastic bags. Now just a month before, I had seen those same kind of bags floating in Biscayne Bay. That was when we got a bunch of people unloading marijuana in Coral Gables. I had never seen marijuana packed in bags like that before, and that night as we were flying low over the bay, shining lights down in the water, I thought the bags were just some sort of big buoy. When I got down real close, I realized that they were bags of marijuana. Something like that sticks in your memory. When I spotted those same bags in the hold of the *Kaki*, I became very suspicious.

"Now I decreased my altitude and came right over the ship.

Just hovered on top of it. On the right side of the helicopter we have a big door. I made my lookout open that door and look right down on the deck of the freighter. He said, 'Yes, there are plastic bags and burlap bags too.' At that point, I knew we were on to something pretty good.

"So I raised the helicopter up over the horizon so that we could make a good transmission. We didn't talk in code. We just said: '*Dauntless*, this is eighty-two. We have a siting report for you.' They said, 'Go ahead, eighty-two.' Then we gave them the information: 'Power, steel, coastal freighter, 180 feet, *Kaki*, Panama P.R., gray hull, orange king posts, appears to have plastic and burlap bags in the after-hold, which is open.' Then we gave them the position of the *Kaki:* 'One-nine-zero degrees, magnetic eighteen miles.

"While we were sending back the information, I was flying as fast as I could toward one of the two boats we had spotted heading north. She was a sport fisherman, a thirty-five-foot Bertram. When I dropped down to get the name off her stern, I was surprised to see that there wasn't any name. Now if you've ever been in a marina, you know that all the boats have names. This one had none and what's more it looked like something had been painted out. So I swung around to the front to get the registration number. It was hard to read. The numbers were little and the bow was flared. So I put the helicopter practically down on the water right off their starboard bow. By that time, they were dead in the water. Two people were sitting in the back, waving at us. They had their fishing poles out, but it didn't look like they were catching anything. We were sitting just a couple of feet away from them, but even so, we couldn't make out all those numbers. We read MD7774— —but there were a couple of other numbers that we couldn't make out. The one thing that was noteworthy about the boat was that it was riding very low in the bow. We also snapped some pictures of both the *Kaki* and this Bertram, but the battery on the flasher failed and the pictures didn't turn out.

"We climbed up to altitude again, radioed our information back and then took off for the third ship. This turned out to be a shrimper. It was anchored with its stay lines out and its nets drying. Nothing unusual about that, but we radioed the data back to the *Dauntless*. At this point, we got orders to go back to the *Kaki* and keep it under surveillance.

"When I got back overhead, I got a feeling of disorientation.

When I spotted her she was sailing north; now she was sailing east. I looked around and saw a little oil slick that marked the course of the vessel. Sure enough, you could see that just about the time we buzzed her, she had made a ninety-degree turn and taken off for the open sea. Once I saw that, I knew something was amiss. No cargo ship makes a turn like that and suddenly heads out to sea.

"It was getting dark now, so I switched off my lights and cruised the *Kaki* at 2,500 feet. I was hoping they wouldn't notice me at that altitude. Apparently, they were very conscious of me.

"At this point, the *Dauntless* was closing at full speed with the *Kaki* to take up a surveillance position about ten miles from the target ship. The *Dauntless* radioed me that on their radar screen they could see another and much smaller vessel closing also on the *Kaki*. 'Great!' I thought. 'We're going to see an off-loading.' Then it turned out that the mystery vessel was nothing more than a radar ghost from our helicopter. This mistake proved at least one point: that it was the *Kaki* that they had on their radar screen."

As soon as the *Dauntless* received the information from the helicopter, it relayed the data back to headquarters, Seventh District, Miami. There the data was relayed again to the various law enforcement computer banks around the country: to Coast Guard headquarters in Washington, D.C.; to TECS, the Customs brain bank in San Diego; and to EPIC, the DEA information center in El Paso.

Within seconds readouts from these sources began to come back. The shrimp boat was not under suspicion; the Bertram had a Maryland registration and no lookout; but the *Kaki* was a suspect vessel. Back aboard the *Dauntless* the teleprinter chattered abruptly: MAINTAIN COVERT SURVEILLANCE AND STAND BY FOR FURTHER INSTRUCTIONS.

Covert surveillance meant standing off at a distance of ten to twelve miles, just over the curve of the horizon, and keeping the *Kaki* on the radar screen. In such a position the cutter would be invisible. What the *Dauntless* did not realize was that the *Kaki* had its own high-powered radar. All through the long chase to come, the *Kaki* was watching the *Dauntless* on the same round fourteen-inch screen with the perpetually revolving hand and the strangely replicating diagonal lines on which the *Dauntless* was

watching the *Kaki*. Lieutenant Allen had done a great job of scoping out the suspect vessels, but he had missed one thing: that
steadily revolving cylinder on top of the *Kaki's* pilothouse.

The teleprinter aboard the *Dauntless* was not the only place
where the returns from the information banks came popping up.
All over the country printouts were appearing on machines that
were manned or allowed to chatter on in mindless indifference.
At one of these machines at the Coast Guard base at Charleston
stood Ensign James Brueninger, a husky blond lad with a passion
for busting what he calls "dopers." The public information officer
on the base, Ensign Brueninger was accustomed to keeping tabs
on everything that was going on. When he saw that two boats had
been sighted off the shore along with a potential mother ship, he
picked up his phone and called Mr. Perkins.

The man who conceived this whole scheme was home eating
his supper when the story broke. The moment he heard the registration number on the Bertram, he recognized it as a boat which
he had had under surveillance for a couple of months. He not only
knew the boat and its owner; he knew exactly where it was
berthed—and where it was most likely heading at that very moment. It was an amazing coincidence, but not all that surprising
when you understand how thoroughly Mr. Perkins performs his
work. Here is how he got a line on the Bertram nearly two
months before the boat was first used in a smuggling operation:

"Our officers, in the course of their day-to-day patrol, had
gone up into the area around Georgetown to learn the back roads
and the possible off-loading sites. One day, after working through
some swamp and woods, they stumbled on a couple of docking
sites that were right off the Intracoastal Waterway [ICW] but
completely unknown to us. If these men hadn't performed their
scouting duties so well, we would never have guessed those docking sites existed, because they were so tucked away that you
could pass within a couple hundred feet of them on the ICW and
never know they were there. Eventually, we did photograph
them from the air, but you could never see them from a boat or
get close to them by road. They were on private property and the
only roads going in there were little dirt roads secured with
chains and padlocks.

"Anyway, some of our people through the special training
they had received, worked their way in to where you could see

what was going on. At one dock about eight miles north of Georgetown, they found five or six boats of various sizes tied up. Approximately one mile south of this basin was another private dock. Here they found a very suspicious-looking vessel called the *Mr. K.* She was a forty-three-foot fishing vessel with an extra deck on top of the main deck and running back on the same level as the cabin roof. There were no rails on this top deck, only a hatch in the rear that would be the perfect size for dropping through a bale of marijuana. She was brand new and had a powerful radar on her front mast. Now this type of top deck had been noted before on boats that were used to unload from marijuana mother ships out at sea. When you get the deck up that high, it makes loading the boat a lot easier, and it provides much more covered storage space to stash the load. Another boat docked in this same basin was a thirty-five-foot Bertram that had no name but bore the numbers MD7774S. Neither of these boats were listed either with our TECS information bank or with the DEA's EPIC.

"We dug around a little bit and discovered that the property on which these boats were located was owned by a Mr. Carroll Kinsey. He had a construction business up in Maryland, and the *Mr. K.* had been built last year in a Maryland shipyard to his specifications. The Bertram was also a new boat, and its registration was also out of Maryland. Well, the suspicious circumstances of these boats and the fact that a couple of cars we observed on the property were registered to people suspected of drug trafficking put us on guard. We requested that the local office of the DEA install some sensor-operated cameras to record the movements of those boats. These cameras can be set to respond to a variety of triggers: sound, heat or vibrations. Wouldn't you know that the day the cameras arrived was the very day this bust went down."

The terrain the smugglers had chosen in which to prepare their little nest is the most picturesque in the South Carolina low country. In the seventeenth century it was divided by the lords proprietors of the Carolinas into "baronies." In later times it was the region that supplied most of the nation's rice crop. The plantations were ditched and delved for hundreds of years by thousands of black slaves until they assumed the mazy, lush and fertile look of the Mekong Delta. The most prized part of the region is the so-called Waccamaw Neck, the narrow strip of land between the ocean beach and the winding Waccamaw River. Here Bernard Baruch offered lordly hospitality to great men like Roosevelt and Churchill. Here on the old Hagley Plantation, with acres of live oaks, numerous sandy roads and little slip-away inlets, the smugglers had settled in.

Carroll Kinsey had bought his riverside property two years before. He had built a two-story house upon it and spent $50,000 dredging a cut back from the river to a lofty open-sided metal boat shed he erected and provided with docking facilities for several vessels. He had brought his two boats, the *Mr. K.* and the Bertram, down the Intracoastal Waterway from Maryland and hired a local boy, Claude Lee Altman, the nephew of the long-time deputy sheriff, to prepare them for fishing.

When a local DEA agent flew over Mr. Kinsey's property to photograph it from the air, he was startled to discover not 300 yards north of the discreet docking site an old abandoned airstrip, on an adjacent property, that had been gouged from the river-bank straight into a tall stand of pine trees. From the air it looked like giant barber's clippers had been run into a forest. The strip was old, narrow and covered with tall grass, but it would be a simple matter to pull a boat up to the end of the strip and load a small plane and then send it winding out over the river and into the blue. The area was so thinly populated and the trees around the strip made such a good visual and acoustic shield that virtually anything could be done without fear of observation or detection. So when Mr. Perkins got that Maryland registration number, he knew exactly with whom he was dealing.

Jumping into his little blue Datsun, he drove down to the Coast Guard base at the foot of Tradd Street, near Charleston's historic battery. There he closeted himself in an office with Ensign Brueninger and a local DEA agent, Harold Stein. Working quietly and efficiently, the three men kept tabs on the chase for several hours. As there was no vessel available immediately to go after the Bertram, Perkins requested the Coast Guard in Georgetown to keep watch for it at Winyah Bay below the city. Once inside the bay, the Bertram should by rights head north up the Waccamaw River toward its base; but there was just the chance that it might turn south and take the Intracoastal Waterway in the opposite direction.

At the mouth of Winyah Bay, the Coast Guard maintains a tall white conical lighthouse. The guardsmen there have a twenty-one-foot open wooden boat. Perkins asked them to get out into the bay to maintain their lookout. The Coast Guardsmen launched their double-ender and ran out into the bay near the southern entrance to the Intracoastal Waterway. They sat there for hours. Finally, around midnight, they spotted the Bertram running in without lights. They watched it head north up the channel and disappear. Then they ran back to the lighthouse and phoned the word to Perkins. "Fine," he said. "How are you keeping her in sight now?" "We aren't," the astonished Coast Guardsmen replied. "We were told to report which way she went. That's all." "Damn," said Perkins, as he realized too late that his instructions had not been interpreted as sensibly as he had assumed. "Get back in your boat and find her!" The Coast Guardsmen did as they were told, but ten minutes after reembarking, they heard their motor cough. They were out of gas.

Perkins wasn't counting on them any longer. He had radioed his patrol officers to take positions along the channel running north, one man on the bridge at Georgetown, another further upstream. The first officer reported shortly. He said it was too dark to make a positive identification, but judging from the sound of the engines, the Bertram had just passed under the cast concrete highway bridge that spans the Waccamaw above Georgetown. Now Perkins awaited anxiously a report from his second scout, who was positioned a couple of miles upstream. The minutes ticked by. The portable VHF at Perkins's side uttered not a word. Once or twice Perkins called his man. He had nothing to report. Finally around 1:00 A.M., it was obvious that something had gone wrong. The Bertram had vanished.

To understand the boat's sudden disappearance, you have to reel back to the moment when the helicopter buzzed the Bertram. At that time it was running into shore with a cargo of 5,000 pounds of marijuana. Two young men were operating the boat. One was Claude Lee Altman. The other was a short, powerfully built Italian boy from Brooklyn with an Afro haircut and Roman eyes, Joseph Paul Terri. These two lads had taken out the Bertram that afternoon to make the first of a series of two or three off-loading rendezvous with the *Kaki*. They had communicated with the vessel by means of radios with matching crystals. They had taken aboard their load swiftly and efficiently: seventy-eight plastic-wrapped burlap bags, each containing sixty pounds of dope. They had stashed most of the grass in the cabin of the boat, where it would not be visible. Then they had taken off for their home base. When they saw the helicopter buzzing the *Kaki*, they realized their danger instantly and took measures to disguise themselves. All the dope that was not in the bow cabin, they stashed quickly. Then they shut off their engines and stuck out their fishing poles. The only thing that bugged them was the appearance of their boat. When they turned off the engines and stopped the forward planing movement, their bow dipped into the water like a duck with its bill under the surface. Then the helicopter came right down on top of them. They were alarmed. The damn thing could have landed beside them and busted them on the spot. Or one of those great big blades could have hit the boat—or even cut their heads off! It was a scary moment. But they played the scene for all it was worth, waving their hands and making like goofy fishermen.

When the chopper finally took off into the gathering dusk, the boys decided to make a little change in their plans. Instead of running right into the bay, where they might be spotted, they took off up the coast to the north. There they cruised around for several hours until, around midnight, when they came down from the north on the reverse course from that on which they had been reported. They made for the mouth of the bay and got a few miles up the river. Then they ran out of gas. All that evasive action in the ocean had burned up their fuel supply.

Now they were dead in the water in the middle of the night in a hot boat with 5,000 pounds of dope in the cabin. Quickly they got on their radio and called another member of the team who had stayed at home. He was a tall red-faced fisherman from Charlotte, North Carolina, named Thomas McKay Gaede. This dude had been scheduled to go out to make the off-loading that day, but he had developed a toothache so excruciating that he could not stand the strain of the trip. He had remained back at the base and sent Terri instead. When he got the message that the Bertram was out of gas, he went out and got into the cab of a pickup truck to which was attached a little outboard-powered skiff mounted on a truck trailer. He drove out onto the highway and headed for the only gas station open at that hour in Georgetown.

By this time it was 1:00 A.M. Perkins was leaving the Coast

Guard base with Agent Stein. Eager to get close to the action, he raced up Route 17 toward Georgetown, an hour away. On the highway he picked up the cryptic half-coded messages from his men on stakeout. Nobody had a clue to what had happened to the Bertram.

Finally, it was 3:00 A.M. and everything was totally SNAFU. Men had been roused from sleep in the middle of the night. Machines had been summoned into action. A crew with a high-speed Cigarette racing boat were barreling down the highway from the Customs substation at Wilmington, North Carolina. A giant S-2 reconnaissance plane was poised to take off at the crack of dawn from Miami. DEA, Customs and Coast Guard personnel were either in the field or standing by awaiting orders to move. It was a big deal, all right, but there was just one problem: they had lost the smugglers.

Then, Perkins's car radio crackled with a very interesting message. A CPO driving through Georgetown had noticed some unexpected activity at the local filling station. A pickup truck hauling a small boat with an outboard motor had been observed standing in the station. When the patrol officer investigated, he discovered that the owner of the truck was filling four five-gallon cans with diesel fuel. The kind of fuel used for boats. When the cans were full, the man, a tall, red-faced chap in his late twenties or early thirties, had gotten back in his truck and headed through the city to the bridge across the river. Headed across the bridge and north again. Headed finally for a road adjacent to Mr. K.'s property that went right down to the river and ended in a boat launching ramp. The CPO watched from a distance as the man launched his boat into the Waccamaw River and took off into the night—heading south.

Not thirty minutes later, the Bertram was picked up again— for the first time in over three hours—heading north along the river.

Now everybody began to converge on Hagley Plantation. Patrol officers were posted on all the roads leading out of the area, with orders to stop anybody coming out but not to attract at-tention to themselves or stop anybody going in. Perkins and DEA agent Stein got as close to the plantation as they could, creeping around on the sandy roads near the river. Using night-vision devices, optical instruments that concentrate light thousands of times, enabling a man to literally see in the dark, they watched as the Bertram pushed past its normal docking site and rendez-voused with the *Mr. K.* The meeting point was just up the river from the two docking sites. For an hour before dawn, they saw the two vessels huddled together. There was activity, but there was no way of knowing precisely what was going on. Then the vessels parted. The Bertram came down and put into the upriver docking site. The *Mr. K* came down further and tied up at Mr. Kinsey's dock. Then all was quiet. The load had been landed—or at least the boats were back where they belonged.

Now was the time to close in and make the bust. But the light was bad. The moon was down and the sun not even dimly felt on the horizon. As they say in the Low Country, it was "black night." Perkins reflected on the situation and decided to wait. The whole area was tightly tied down. No one could escape on the roads or along the river. The only danger was that the smugglers might flee into the woods and hide out until they could escape. It was better to wait until dawn, when the fugitives could be seen and pursued.

The last hour before the bust passed slowly. Radio silence was maintained. Perkins wondered what was happening to the *Kaki* far out at sea. He wondered whether there were other small boats loading off it that night and running into shore. He had sta-tioned his own Customs boat in Winyah Bay, where it could in-tercept any other boats running in. And those two young Coast Guardsmen? They had refueled and were way up the river now, blockading the channel.

The real question was: where was the load? Had it been stashed along the marshy or woody shores of the Waccamaw River during the several hours when contact had been lost? Was it on Mr. Kinsey's property? Pretty soon they'd have the answers. Or would they?

For one hour, Perkins murmured instructions into his radio and watched the luminescent hands on his watch crawl around the dial. Finally, it was 6:00 A.M. The sun was glimmering over the marshes. Everything was in readiness for a move. Perkins put out his last cigarette and pressed down the button on his radio. He said, "Let's hit 'em!"

"We went in two cars," recalls Perkins. "We busted a chain across the private road. We skidded up. A real heavy dew that morning. You could leave footprints. In that dim light you couldn't see real good. But we knew that nothing come out of there. We could see the Bertram tied up next to the side of a boat that was tied up to the dock. Even standing on the dock and looking across the other boats, you could see marijuana residue. You could scoop it up off the dock by the handful. When we saw that, we went on and hit the thing. We found only one man aboard. He was sacked out, sound asleep. This guy, Terri, from New York. We woke him and put cuffs on him. We left two men to guard him and went on down the road a mile to where the *Mr. K.* was tied up.

"Now we figured we'd get the grass and the rest of the people, 'cause that's where the houses were. We boarded the *Mr. K.* and found the fish-hold hatch locked. We tore that lock off. We went down in the hold and sure enough! There was the grass!

"As soon as we found the grass, we went up to Mr. Kinsey's house. I knocked on the door. Couldn't get any response at all. So I took my gun and banged on the side of the house with my gun barrel. When the wife pulled the curtain aside on the front door, first thing she saw was me standin' there in uniform with a .38 in my hand. Scared her to death. I guess it's a frightening thing jes to see someone there in uniform. But she let us in.

"Harold and I went straight into the house. Meantime, he had come out of the bedroom in just his shorts and undershirt. Nice-lookin' elderly man. We identified ourselves and told him briefly what was goin' on. He said, 'Lemme go back in the bedroom and get some clothes on.' Now I seen too many instances where somebody does that and comes out shootin'. So I told Harold to go in with him. Be sure he didn't come out with a gun.

"When he came out, pullin' his pants on, we sat down and explained the whole thing to him. He acted very, very surprised that these illegal things were being done with his boats. I suppose what we have to assume at this point is that he was completely innocent because nothing has been proven against him. But he's a far wiser man now than he was then.

"Shortly after we got into the Kinsey home, the two officers remaining with the Bertram radioed that the pickup truck seen earlier in Georgetown hauling the skiff was approaching the dock area. It was Altman and Gaede comin' back to pick up Terri. We grabbed them and that ended our part in the bust.

"Then we got the radio and called the Coast Guard base, where I had left another radio. We told them that we had the stuff and that the word was 'Go!' "

When the Coast Guard learned that the Bertram was actually carrying a load of marijuana, it flashed the information to Washington, where a call was placed immediately to the State Department. The first man to handle the call was a young economist named David Wagner. He was told that the Coast Guard had a Panamanian vessel under surveillance, that it was carrying marijuana and that the Panamanian government should be contacted to obtain a "statement of no objection" to a search and seizure of the vessel. Wagner took the request to his boss, Edward Nadeau, a deputy country director. Together they then informed Ambassador at Large Cyrus R. Vance of what was happening. He told them that he would give his permission for the bust. Vance called the Coast Guard himself and assured them that they had the permission of the Panamanian government. Then he ordered Wagner to contact the American embassy in Panama and ask them to get the formal statement of no objection.

When Wagner contacted the embassy, they were puzzled by the request. "What is a statement of no objection?" they asked. Wagner explained the situation. Eventually the embassy's minister-counselor, Raymond E. Gonzalez, called His Excellency, Acting Minister of Foreign Relations Carlos Ozores and obtained that official's permission to "stop the *Kaki* in international waters, to board it, to search it and, if contraband were found, to seize the ship and arrest the crew."

All this diplomatic wheeling and dealing consumed the better part of Friday. By the time the boarding order was dispatched to the *Dauntless*, it was late Friday afternoon. The two vessels were now 200 miles off the coast of the U.S. at about the latitude of Fort Lauderdale. Finally, the message came through. As the teleprinter chattered, the radiomen read:

"Board *Kaki* and if contraband located, seize vessel under authority of 19 USC [United States Code] and 15:86. If required arrest master and POB [persons on board] under authority of 21 USC. Proceed to Coast Guard Base Charleston with seized vessel."

This was the word the crew of the *Dauntless* had been hoping for during the past twenty-four hours. The mood aboard the ship changed instantly. From the sternly repressed feelings of the long chase now there bubbled to the surface the enthusiasm of a team charging out on the field. The engines began to roar as the cutter worked up to its maximum speed. The officers on the bridge began to consult about their procedure. The crewmen awaited the signal to take action.

By 5:30 P.M. the *Kaki* was in view. It was a stubby, miniaturized looking vessel plowing along in seas that had worked up during the night until they were rolling with eight-foot waves. As the cutter approached the *Kaki* on its port side, a series of flags were hoisted from the bridge signaling: "You should stop or heave to. I am going to send a boat." The signals were ignored. At the same time, the cutter's radio operator radioed the same message—with no results. Finally, at a range of no more than 100 yards, a Puerto Rican seaman with a bullhorn in his hand hailed the *Kaki* and shouted the message in both English and Spanish. The only response was a flag, a Panamanian flag, which came fluttering up the *Kaki*'s taffrail.

A crewman appeared on the deck of the *Kaki* holding a megaphone in his hand. He hollered back in Spanish that they were in international waters and were under the Panamanian flag. The Puerto Rican seaman shouted back that permission had been granted by the Panamanian government to board the vessel. Again, the *Kaki* crewman explained that they would not stop in international waters. After ten minutes of this futile parley, the cutter hoisted another set of signals: "You should stop and heave to. I am going to board you." More words were exchanged between the two vessels until, finally, a third and more menacing set of flags fluttered up the mast. This last message read: "You should stop or heave to. Otherwise I am going to fire on you." At this point, recognizing the futility of further signaling, the *Dauntless* radioed back to Miami:

"*Dauntless* closed subject vessel at a distance of 100 yards of subject vessel. *Dauntless* hailed subject vessel. . . . Subject vessel continued to claim she was in international waters and would not heave to."

Ten minutes later the teletype machine chattered the reply: "Regarding M/V *Kaki*. Use whatever force necessary to board vessel."

As soon as he read this "hard copy," Commander Iken ordered general quarters sounded. He spoke over the public address system. "Now all hands—man your general quarters battle stations. *This is not a drill!*"

A low siren sounded as the crew scrambled to their stations. Men donned life jackets and steel helmets. The ship's phones switched over from electric to voice-operated circuits. The fire and demolition crews broke out their equipment. The ship buzzed with excitement.

Aboard the *Kaki*, only a football field distant, all these preparations for combat were clearly visible. Most menacing were the preparations to use the *Dauntless*'s guns. On the bow, a gun crew stripped off the tarpaulin protecting the 3.5-inch rifle, which was swung around on its revolving platform until it pointed directly at the *Kaki*. On the wing bridges, the .50-caliber machine guns were manned and loaded and deployed in the same direction. At this point, in the gathering gloom, the *Kaki* switched on its running lights. But it did not slacken speed or alter its course. Finally, the word came crackling through the intercom: "Fire three bursts across her bow." A gunner's mate standing on the wing bridge behind the long-barreled .50-caliber fired three well-spaced bursts across the freighter's bow. Instantly, the *Kaki* disengaged its engine and began to lose sea room.

At this point, a well-armed boarding party gathered on the port side of the *Dauntless*, where a twenty-one-foot open boat was being readied for launching. As soon as the *Kaki* hove to, the boat was lowered from its davits and the party clambered down ladders into it. Commanded by the cutter's executive officer, Lieutenant Commander Wilkins, the boarding party consisted of one other officer, five seamen and a Charleston patrol officer who had boarded the vessel in Miami. All were armed with .45s. A couple of men had shotguns. They pulled away and were guided to the *Kaki* by a bosun's mate, who had to steer the open boat through big eight-foot waves that sent it standing on its beam ends.

A Jacobs ladder had been dropped from the side of the *Kaki*. The men came aboard. They ordered the crew into the wheelhouse. There they seized the vessel's papers, charts and log. Next, a party went to search the hold. It reeked of marijuana but there were no bales of grass. *Fifty-five thousand pounds of weed had been thrown overboard during the course of the night.* All that was visible in the hold were dozens of sacks of what appeared to be sand but was in fact gypsum. Down between the sacks could be seen marijuana residue. The CPO took some of the spilled grass and put it inside his narcotics test kit. Tossed inside a plastic bag and doused with a reagent, it instantly registered a deep red: a sign that it was high-potency grass. The word was transmitted to the *Dauntless*, which in turn radioed it to Miami. Immediately the message came back to arrest the crew and bring back the ship.

The vessel itself was a disgusting and unseaworthy old tub. Rusty, greasy, filthy, badly maintained, it was like a pirate ship, with its crew of ignorant sullen sailors and its angry vituperative skipper. In the cavernous hold, a tiny bilge pump struggled in vain to hold down the rising water. In the galley, the cook had a goat tied to the stove and a couple of chickens running loose. (They were killed and eaten before the vessel made port.) The crews' cabins were stacked with filthy mattresses, and the walls plastered with pictures of voluptuous blonde nudes. The whole outfit was clearly expendable.

During the course of the trip back to Charleston, one of the crewmen was discovered trying to throw something overboard. It proved to be a Florida driver's license with the name Louis Gordon Wendler. When the CPO aboard *Kaki* ran a make on Wendler, who had been speaking Spanish and trying to pass as one of the Colombian crew, he turned out to have a three-page narcotics record. He was in fact the connecting link between the big American syndicate that was running the boat and the Colombians who were manning it.

It is customary in the Colombian dope trade to send one American along on every smuggling vessel to serve the same function aboard ship that the piece of cardboard serves in the freshly laundered shirt: to be the stiffener. Colombians are notoriously prone to cop out when the going gets hard and to fail to make their rendezvous. They do not respond to radio messages from shore, they stand too far out to sea to be reached by the lighters and they sometimes turn tail and bring their loads all the way back to Colombia. That was probably why Wendler was aboard. He was the stiffener.

When the ship finally dragged into Charleston the following Sunday afternoon, it was met at the dock by a team of U.S.

marshals. In a drizzling rain, the manacled Colombians, stoic and uncomplaining, were herded into a bus and hauled to the county jail. At their arraignment the next day, there were language problems. Charleston has very few Spanish-speaking citizens. A few translators were rounded up from the local college, and through these people's efforts the necessary legalities were gotten through. Then the long wait commenced. For three months, the maximum time allowed under the law, the trial was stalled. Meanwhile, a lot of wheeling and dealing was going on behind the scenes.

The Colombians were charged with four separate crimes: conspiracy to import a Schedule 1 controlled substance; importing such a substance; possession of such a substance; distribution of the substance. Each of these crimes carries a maximum penalty of five years in prison and/or a $5,000 fine.

On June 14, 1976, the trial of the *Kaki* commenced in the federal courthouse in Charleston. The trial chamber was a magnificent antique interior, with red walls and rich wooden wainscoting. Portraits of eminent local jurists stared down on the proceedings. At one end of the room on a handsomely carved dais sat the black-robed judge. At the other end of the room before the visitors' gallery was a double row of temporary chairs, each equipped with a headphone so that the Colombian defendants could follow the proceedings through a simultaneous translation. It looked like the setting for the Nuremberg Trials.

The judge, Sol Blatt, Jr., was the son of the South's most successful Jewish politician: the man who had been for thirty-five years the speaker of the South Carolina House of Representatives. A small, bald, owlish man in heavy horn-rimmed glasses, extremely soft-spoken and gentle in manner, he distinguished himself by the concern he showed for the defendants' rights and by his charmingly rural pronunciation of the word "mar-ree-wana."

The first two defendants to appear before the bench were Altman and Gaede. Altman, twenty-six years old, short, broad, blond with thinning hair, wearing a short-sleeved sport shirt, looked like hundreds of the local yeomanry. Gaede, thirty-three, was taller, thinner, older, shock-haired and long of nose, dressed uncomfortably in a tan suit. His thin white-haired uptight mother and open-mouthed, horn-rim bespectacled and rather feeble-looking father were sitting with a couple of other relatives in the jury box, lending their moral support and family respectability to the defendant before the bar. The defense counsel explained that they had come down from Charlotte.

Altman's family were typical rednecks, deeply entrenched in the country for many generations. His uncle had been long the deputy sheriff of Pawley's Island, a summer beach colony on the ocean side of Waccamaw Neck. Gaede's family were proper middle-class folk; the brother had gone to a distinguished Ivy League school; Tom, the smuggler, had swung the other way, preferring a simple outdoor life. His family had bought him a shrimp boat, which he operated out of Georgetown and in the Gulf of Mexico. One local resident told me: "Tom's a good boy. He just made a mistake. He thought smuggling dope was like shooting ducks out of season."

Terri, twenty-two, looked like a typical Brooklyn hitter: squat, broad of back, with a bushy black Afro, dark olive skin, a visible grain of beard and a Roman face. He wore to court a green floral Hawaiian shirt tucked into his pants. His lawyer described him as "a deckhand hired to unload this stuff."

The trial consumed only one day. First, Altman pleaded guilty to the third count in the indictment: possession with intent to distribute. Neither he nor his partners had been charged with the fourth count: actual distribution. So by pleading guilty to one count, he reduced his maximum sentence from a possible fifteen years and $45,000 to five years and $5,000. Gaede and Terri copped the same plea. By mid-morning, it was obvious that the defendants were going down like a row of falling dominoes.

At this point a recess was requested by lawyers for Wendler and the Colombians. The courtroom emptied, and for the next few hours, intense negotiations went on behind the scenes.

Wendler and the Colombians were penned in a big cell on the floor above the courtroom. Their lawyers were all over the building. The government decided to press for prison terms only for the officers of the ship; the others could receive probation and be deported. The Colombians went for the deal, one by one.

Finally, the only man holding out was Wendler, a two-time loser, who was facing a very heavy rap. The judge told Wendler that if he pleaded guilty to one count, he would probably receive no more than four years, perhaps only three. If he went to trial and was found guilty, he would probably get eight to ten years. Wendler had the best dope lawyer in Miami: Marvin Swickle. He told his client that he had no choice. A jury would certainly find him guilty of more than one count and he would end up with twice the time than he would get if he took the court's recommendation. By four o'clock in the afternoon, the last of the twenty defendants was standing before the bench entering his plea.

The Colombians were now brought into court and given their sentences. Thirteen men were sentenced to two years probation and deportation. Three were singled out for heavier sentences. The captain of the *Kaki,* Ausberto S. Montenegro, who had threatened at one point that he would take his case to the U.N., was given twenty months and two years probation. The chief engineer, Cruz A. Arango-Marin, received sixteen months and two years probation. The navigator, Gustavo Hincapie-Parra, received an identical sentence. Sentencing was deferred on all the American defendants until a probation officer could prepare a report on them for the judge's advisement.

On August 5, the four American defendants appeared once more before Judge Blatt. The judge was in a somber mood. He reprimanded the defendants for attempting to smuggle in marijuana. He said that 95 percent of the hard-core drug addicts he had seen had started on marijuana. Then he proceeded to mete out admonishments and punishments. He told Altman that he had suffered sufficient punishment already through the humiliation he had undergone, but, the judge continued, he was going to impose punishment to deter others from similar crimes.

Altman was sentenced to two years with two years probation. Gaede received the same sentence and an admonishment. "People have got to realize we're just not going to have this. We're going to stop this, if we can," Blatt told Gaede, looking down at him owlishly from the bench. "And even people with the great, fine family that you have—you just did this. People have got to realize that no matter who you are, if you do this, you're going to jail."

The sternest treatment was meted out to Louis Gordon Wendler. Blatt listened to the lawyer's plea for clemency, which stressed the fact that the defendant had merely been an agent of the master smuggler. Judge Blatt listened impassively; then he leaned over and in his soft Southern low-country voice told the defendant, "You may not have been the leader of the plot, but certainly you were to be a major part in its success." He suggested that the unidentified mastermind of the dope ring had arranged for Wendler's $125,000 bond. He wound up his statement by sentencing the stiffener to four years in prison, a $5,000 fine and two years probation. The trial of the *Kaki* had ended.

What was the *Kaki*'s real story? Chances are it will never be known precisely beyond the narrow circle of big-time drug operators who loaded the boat and sent it north on its ill-fated mission. Putting together the scraps of evidence that have come to the surface subsequently plus a few educated guesses based on a general knowledge of the Colombian dope trade, one can sketch a hypothetical picture of the operation from the smuggler's angle.

The *Kaki* had recently been purchased from a Panamanian company by a Colombian cement manufacturer. At least one other boat was involved in the deal, and information gathered long after the bust suggests that the *Kaki* was just one of a fleet of five vessels operated by a large smuggling syndicate. A chance meeting between one member of the syndicate and a man whom I interviewed after the bust revealed that the *Kaki*'s original load was 80,000 pounds purchased for five dollars a pound in front. When seized, the vessel was carrying at the bottom of her hold 150 tons of gypsum, the bonding ingredient in cement. There are gypsum mines on the tip of the Guajira peninsula and a regular coastal trade in gypsum between the Guajira and Barranquilla. The *Kaki* was put to sea with papers testifying that it was bound for Savannah with a load of gypsum.

At the other end of the line, in the U.S., the ship was to make a series of drops. The first of these was made successfully. The syndicate that operated the *Kaki* is well known to law enforcement officers in Florida. Ralph Cunningham, chief investigator for the state attorney's office, one of America's most audacious and best-informed narcotics agents, put the bust of the *Kaki* into the wider context of big-time international drug trafficking:

"I am familiar with the *Kaki* operation. The freighter was

loaded at a dock. They don't have to load at sea in Colombia. The loading takes place right at the dock—just costs money, that's all. But we're not talking about much money. We're talking about $25,000; and though it's nothing to us, it's a great amount to them. Basically you are paying off the Customs officers, FA-2.

"The way it works is this: they set up these companies, corporations. They own two or three tankers. They pay $20,000 per tanker to get it out of a port. There is no way in the world you can take a tanker out of a port full of nothing but marijuana without the government knowing it. It's not like loading up a small boat, like a trawler or a shrimp boat off the coast. When you are talking about loading a freighter with *two or three hundred thousand pounds of pot!*—that's a big deal.

"Now, I am talking about American professional men as silent partners. And the Colombians have gotten so sophisticated, they have their own attorneys right here in Miami and in New York, too. They negotiate all these deals. You know who you're going to meet, when you're going to meet it. These freighters are in constant communication with simple side-band radios, and they talk about 2,500 miles with them. They just have everything down to a science. The freighter comes up the coast and makes about six stops. Each stop it meets about a fifty-to-sixty-foot cabin cruiser. The cruiser brings it in to about five miles offshore. There it meets smaller, twenty-to-twenty-five-foot boats. They bring it in to scattered points, unload it into campers and it is gone! That's one operation. The other is: we have here a lot of fishing houses. They buy them—they buy the whole goddamn company! It's not so big a thing. They have money, so they own the company. They have fish, too. They bring the stuff in at night, load it out, put it into refrigerated trucks and ship it out. You are talking about an eight-hour operation to load 100,000 pounds of grass.

"They're so damn sophisticated. What they will do is they have primary and secondary groups that they off-load to. Nobody knows what anybody is going to do till the last minute. They change things around from minute to minute.

"We had one guy that is a big man in this syndicate by the name of John David Steele. That lunatic, he got busted the other day. He got arrested in Orlando for carrying a .357 Magnum, a

.38 snubnose and a .38 automatic with an illegal silencer on it. He was a fugitive. He didn't show up for sentencing after that bust on the Pamlico River. Jumped $75,000 bond.

"I had Steele in a deal three weeks ago just prior to him getting arrested, and that's how recent he is into it. He is not the head man in the operation either, but he is really powerful with the South Americans. He has spent a lot of time down there; he knows all the people. He is an attorney, extremely intelligent man. He's got his shit together, to put it mildly. He's not the number-one man in the operation—who I can't divulge right at this moment—but he's probably number two or number three. The number one is an American. I am calling him number one, but we have had some rumors about an even bigger man, a *congressman.*

"When I started we were buying joints on the street, in '65. It has grown since then. We are talking now about attorneys, congressmen, just the super-biggest business firms—cops, lawyers, state attorneys, corrupt sheriffs. In Georgia they have two or more sheriffs they were paying off. I wouldn't be entirely surprised if their whole operation were out of South Carolina or Georgia."

When I relayed the gist of this conversation to Mr. Perkins, he said, "Damn! I'm gonna get me one of those tankers!"

OPERATION STOPGAP

By 1977, the flood of dope pouring into the United States from Colombia had grown so vast that Washington decided to take extraordinary measures to stem the tide. For years the drug enforcement officials had been pleading with each successive administration for permission to employ the reconnaissance facilities of the air force and the navy. The air force flies regular training missions off the coasts of South America, employing planes equipped with remarkable cameras that enable an observer to read a newspaper from five miles in the air. The navy operates surveillance satellites that monitor everything that moves across the Caribbean by day or night and that are capable of assessing the cargo carried by any given vessel. Up to this time, these resources had never been employed officially because the military were not supposed to meddle in matters of civilian law. It was not until Jimmy Carter—the first President who was supposed to be "soft" on dope—got into the White House that permission was given to use these national defense facilities to crack down on the Dope Game.

Operation Stopgap commenced in December 1977 and concluded four and a half months later in April 1978, the timing corresponding with the peak of the Colombian smuggling year. Every possible means was employed to identify and intercept the planes and ships leaving Colombia's Caribbean coasts. DEA agents with light planes were stationed in the area so that they could monitor the traffic at the strips every day. Paid informers were employed to provide information on ship loadings and departures. As so many vessels load by daylight in the Guajira, it proved a simple matter to identify most of the vessels and then track back to the States by satellite radar. The first thing the DEA realized when it began receiving round-the-clock sightings was that its estimates of the size of the Game were hopelessly inadequate. Pretty soon DEA agents were saying that the only two businesses bigger than marijuana were General Motors and Exxon. What's more, the DEA had to concede that for years it had been grossly overestimating its seizure rate. Instead of bagging 10 or 15 percent of the dope coming into the country, the new figure was reduced to 3 to 5 percent. Owing to the employment of the military technology, however, this old rate of seizures zoomed spectacularly during the first month of Stopgap, especially during the last ten days of 1977.

During these ten days that shook the smuggling world, in Southern Florida alone nine boats were seized, thirty-eight men arrested and 117 tons of marijuana seized—more than the entire catch in this area in the year 1976. In a massive five-part series titled "Drug Smuggling: Our Biggest Business," the *Miami Herald* catalogued the busts of this Christmas rush:

December 22: The 100-foot Venezuelan freighter *Isla de Aruba* is boarded by the Coast Guard. The vessel is carrying 64,240 pounds of dope.

December 25: Customs seizes a low-riding cabin cruiser a mile off Fort Lauderdale. The boat is stuffed with 5,000 pounds of weed.

December 25: Seven miles east of Key Biscayne, the Coast Guard seizes *Iris Marie*, a 40-foot fishing boat carrying 7,920 pounds of marijuana.

December 27: *Miss Connie,* a 125-foot trawler, is stopped near Orange Cay in the Bahamas. The vessel is crammed with 57,800 pounds of dope.

December 30: Again at Orange Cay, a hovering vessel, *Doña Petra,* is boarded by the Coast Guard, who discover in its hold bales of marijuana weighing 30,299 pounds.

December 31: The 55-foot motor yacht *Anjolin* is seized in Government Cut, Miami, carrying three tons of dope.

December 31: *Snippy V,* a 35-foot cabin cruiser, loaded with 7,000 pounds of weed, is interdicted near Baker's Haulover by the Florida Marine Patrol.

December 31: *Business Stinks,* a 32-foot sports fisherman, is captured with a two-ton cargo of dope.

December 31: Bales of marijuana, weighing 3,000 pounds, are found floating off Galt Ocean Mile in Fort Lauderdale.

When Stopgap concluded in April, it was acclaimed as one of the most successful drug enforcement operations in history. Peter B. Bensinger, the new head of the DEA, claimed that one-third of the marijuana coming into the U.S. had been intercepted, the final tally being 40 mother ships carrying 1,150,000 pounds of weed. Another million pounds of dope was seized in Colombia during the same period as a result of DEA-directed raids by the Colombian federal police. Did this all-out military operation seriously disrupt the flow of marijuana into America? The answer could be learned on the streets of any American city. The price of dope did begin to rise, but so did the quality. As in any war, the escalation of hostilities by one side begot an answering escalation by the enemy.

Once the smugglers realized that the long-anticipated crackdown on Colombia had occurred, they redoubled their efforts to beat the narcs. The two-engine planes were exchanged for huge four-engine transports, like the DC-6, which can haul at high speed 17,000 pounds of pot all the way from Colombia to the Southwest, Midwest or Northeast. Instead of sailing through the Windward Channel or the Mona Passage and ending up in the heavily patrolled waters around Florida, the smugglers boldly put out to sea and braved the storms of the Atlantic to land their cargoes on Long Island and the coast of New England, areas that had not seen any intensive smuggling activity since Prohibition. In the Pacific, the trade in Thai weed, interrupted by the end of the war in Vietnam, was resumed with heavily armed vessels sailing all the way from Southeast Asia to the Pacific Northwest.

At the same time, the cultivation of domestic weed was put on a scientific footing in Hawaii and California, with the result being an extraordinarily refined *sinsemilla* that sells for thousands of dollars a pound. Compelled to patrol the entire Atlantic Seaboard, the Gulf Coast and the endless shores of the Pacific, the Coast Guard was soon spread so thin that the rate of interceptions dropped as dramatically as it had risen.

Though the War on Drugs has finally become a military operation deploying the intimidating technology of the Defense establishment, no end of the War is in sight. In fact, it now appears that, as with Vietnam, the government's halfhearted and piecemeal commitment of its forces has allowed the "enemy" to build up his strength to the point where he is undefeatable by any measures that will be tolerated by American and foreign public opinion. Again, as with Vietnam, the prolongation of the War will serve only to make the struggle more bitter and evil, with each side abandoning the restraints that formerly curbed it and the consequent violence and corruption reaching unprecedented heights.

The most sinister and dismaying development in the War is the supplanting of the young men who were more adventurers than criminals by older men who are either securely placed white-collar operators or else hard-core gangsters. As the Game enters its next phase, its bosses will be middle-aged, middle-class business and professional men, who will be much more difficult to identify, prosecute and convict than were the hippies and college boys of the past; or the big players will be the Mob, which has been forced out of the heroin trade by the blacks and out of the cocaine trade by the Colombians. Four American Mafia families— the Lucchese, Colombo, Bonnano and Genovese Clans—have been identified recently in the Game. The grim logic of law enforcement is that the higher the stakes and the greater the penalties, the tougher and more ruthless are the players. Whereas in the past all the bloodshed was confined to Asia or South America, today the killing is going on in the heart of America, just as it did during the days of Al Capone. Dozens of drug-related murders have been recorded recently in Florida, New York and other major American cities. Marijuana Prohibition has become now a point-by-point replay of alcohol Prohibition. What was once an obscure and distant war has broken out close to home. End one war and start another—what a travesty of law and order!

8 Weed: Lethal or Legal?

MARIJUANA'S BILL OF HEALTH

While the War on Drugs is fought out on the high seas and in the coastal swamps and in the big cities, another war against drugs goes forward in the government-subsidized laboratories where countless scientists have labored for years to discover whether marijuana damages the brain or some other part of the human body. The number of these studies, experiments and projects has increased enormously over the years. Several hundred scientific papers are now published annually, detailing the latest findings of the dope labs. If the one war suggests Vietnam, this war suggests the battle against cancer or some other dread disease.

Very few of the scientists are truly impartial in their attitude toward grass. They undertake their experiments in the hope of being able to document some adverse effect of dope smoking. They do not rejoice when they discover that once again they must give marijuana a clean bill of health. On many occasions they have gone to the media with alarming conclusions based on very slight and debatable evidence. The tone of prejudice, of animus, is very strong in some of the leading authorities, like Professor Gabriel G. Nahas of Columbia University, a pharmacologist of distinction whose book, *Marihuana—Deceptive Weed,* is one of the best to date. Professor Nahas makes it perfectly clear that from childhood up he has been powerfully disposed against cannabis. Born in Egypt, he had pointed out to him as a child by his father, a physician, the derelicts of hashish eating in the streets of Cairo. His favorite ploy is imagining some far-fetched train of causations that commences with the slight biochemical alterations which marijuana induces in the body and then leads on like a chain reaction to some dreadful terminal effect. Professor Nahas is always eager to go anywhere and testify before any body concerning the sinister potentialities of what he calls, the "deceptive weed." Consequently, though he is a scientific observer, one cannot regard him as an impartial observer.

The medical literature on cannabis is for the most part of very recent origin, if one excepts the classic account of Moreau and a few old government-sponsored reports like the *Indian Hemp Drug Commission Report* of 1893–1894, the *Canal Zone Report* of 1925 (never published) and the *La Guardia Report* of 1940. In fact, one could say that the scientific literature on marijuana really does not commence until the year 1965, when Mechoulam synthesized delta-9 THC, thus opening the way for the precise measurement of the principal psychoactive ingredient. Until that breakthrough, experiments with marijuana were impossible to evaluate because there was no knowing the actual dosage employed. To say that the subjects received "small," "medium" or "large" doses, to record that they smoked one gram or swallowed thirty meant very little when one could not assay the potency of the preparations that were being administered. So, for all practical purposes, scientific research into marijuana is about fourteen years old.

During that fourteen years, scientists have learned more about marijuana than in all the preceding centuries. Though no great monies have been allotted to the work, though initially the number of researchers and institutions was small and the number of experiments very limited compared with other areas of scientific investigation, the strong white light of modern chemistry, pharmacology and medicine has been cast into this dusky and mysterious corner.

Sad to say, what characterizes most of this literature is the indecisiveness of the findings. Medically, marijuana is a Mexican standoff. You can't say it's good; you can't say it's bad. According to one study it does so-and-so, but according to the next study it really doesn't. Whatever the studies establish, there is always the possibility that everything will look different if the research is prolonged over a period of ten, twenty or thirty years. Everybody is always calling for long-term studies, but the problems of pot are today.

Basically, it is now agreed that all the terrible charges leveled traditionally against marijuana—murder, madness, heroin addiction—must be dropped forthwith. But a whole new bill of attainder has been drawn up from the experiments of modern geneticists and psychiatrists. Marijuana's principal antagonist in the U.S. Senate, James O. Eastland, has established the practice of holding annual hearings of his subcommittee to investigate the administration of the Internal Security Act (of the committee on the Judiciary) that are virtually tournaments of antidope champions. The procedure is to send a group of assistants to the medical library, where they compile a list of all the most terrifying accusations that have been levelled against marijuana in the recent scientific literature. Then the authors of these often arcane and highly technical papers, investigations that can only be understood and evaluated by a handful of specialists, are invited to Washington from Cairo, Athens, Bombay, Katmandu, Kabul or Rawalpindi to lay before the shocked minds and grim visages of the subcommittee the latest medical horror stories. It's the Harry Anslinger Show come back to earth, but with infinitely better material. Not only are the scientists internationally respected authorities instead of sleazy journalists, the stories they unfold are even more terrifying to our hypochondriacal age than were Anslinger's tabloid tales of killer weed.

In 1974, for instance, the senator printed in the minutes of his subcommittee hearings a scientific report that claimed that through a very difficult (and dangerous!) technique of brain X-ray (pumping air up the spinal column into the cranial cavity), it had been established that ten young men who had smoked marijuana daily for three to eleven years had suffered cerebral atrophy. Their brains had *shrunk!* They had brains like those of sixty-five-year-old men or boxers who had been punched out for years in the ring. Their complaints included "headaches, memory loss for recent events, changes in personality and temperament, decreased clarity of thought and decreased desires to work." Marijuana had reduced them to mushrooms.

Another scientist, deposing at the same hearing, testified that his researches showed that THC could pass the placental barrier in a pregnant woman. This meant that if a woman smoked pot while carrying, the mysterious chemical might seep through her womb and anesthetize the fetus. If the fetus were at some crucial phase in its development—the budding of the arms and legs, let us say—the growth process could stall and the baby could emerge a thalidomide freak!

The specter of the genetically malformed child was summoned up by yet another scientist who claimed that in his studies of the blood of pot smokers, he found an abnormally high proportion of broken or damaged chromosomes. As normal chromosomes are vital to the production of normal children, the image of a gene-scrambled hippie impregnating (without benefit of wedlock, of course) his dope-crazed doxy and begetting a monstrous birth were summoned up in the committee room.

Not content with these threats to the physical vitality and integrity of the human species, the subcommittee investigators put on the stand a couple of psychiatrists who testified that chronic smoking of dope produced an "amotivational syndrome." When whole populations get on the weed, it was argued, they go on the nod. Nobody wants to work or compete to make a living. It makes sense, too, because when you stop and think about it, who are the people that are deepest into dope? The Mexicans, the Egyptians, the Indians and the Africans. All the Third World Losers. The people we are always struggling to feed, clothe and delouse. No wonder Senator Eastland closed the hearings with a stern warning, à la Joe McCarthy, that we were spawning a "generation of zombies."

As nothing is more basic to the marijuana problem of the present day than an accurate appraisal of what dope will do to your physical and mental health, the compiler of this report (a lifelong hypochondriac who don't want *no* trouble!) has sifted through all the current medical literature trying to separate what is sound and beyond doubt from what is merely speculative or vaguely possible—or downright crazy and alarmist. The best way to understand the medical implications of pot is to start with the act of smoking and study the process of getting high step by step.

When you light up a joint, you initiate certain familiar physical and chemical processes. An analysis made a few years ago by the Federal Trade Commission details the whole process with scientific precision:

Cannabis cigarettes were prepared containing 1 gram of leaves with 1.4 THC content and 12% moisture; they were wrapped in 14-second paper 68 millimeters long. The cigarette was consumed on a smoking machine in a series of 35-millimeter puffs of two seconds duration every 60 seconds. All of the side-steam smoke [produced during static burning] and the mainstream smoke [from the puffing] were collected separately and passed through a fiberglass filter. Equal amounts (21%) of THC were received in the side-stream and mainstream smoke, while 52% was found in the 20 millimeters of cigarette end remaining unsmoked. Therefore it appears that about 10% of the THC is pyrolized [burnt up].

As this succinct analysis shows, roughly a third of the THC in a joint is wasted in combustion and uninhaled smoke; if the roach is not consumed, another 52 percent is lost. So an ordinary smoker is only getting one-fifth of the THC his joint contains. Now, let's take the next step.

When the smoke enters the smoker's lungs, it is transfused through the surface capillaries and enters the bloodstream. The THC circulates rapidly throughout the body and within a few minutes it lodges in a number of body organs. In experiments with rats (in which the drug must be administered orally or injected) the lodgment breaks down as follows: lung, 55 percent; liver, 12 percent; heart, 6.7 percent; kidney, 6.5 percent; fat, 5.5 percent; intestine, 3.5 percent; muscle, 3 percent; brain, 2.7 percent. As soon as the THC settles in these organs, it begins to break down into its metabolites or into waste products. After three days, the distribution of these metabolites is radically different: they are heavily concentrated in the bile, fat, kidneys, liver, lungs, uterus, intestine and even the spinal cord. Unlike alcohol, which is excreted from the body within eight to ten hours of its consumption, THC and its metabolites are not completely expelled from the body for *one whole week*. Like DDT, THC is highly soluble in fat. Instead of flushing out in the urine, part of it sticks in the various body organs. If the subject smokes within the week, the concentration in his tissues increases; if he smokes every day or many times a day, the concentration becomes even higher. The effects of this concentration of a relatively unknown chemical in the body tissues over a period of years is a question to which scientists are currently devoting a lot of thought.

THC hits the brain in exactly the same spot as does alcohol: the frontal cortex; the seat of all the higher mental activities. Likewise, there is the same concentration in the cerebellum, which may account for the loss of motor coordination under the influence of booze and pot. Unlike alcohol, high concentrations of THC are also found in the lateral and medial geniculate nuclei, which connect with the visual pathways and may promote hallucinations. Also there is a buildup of the chemical in the amygdala, which is where the antidepressants lodge in the brain; hence the euphoric effect of dope.

After the brain, the most important target of THC is the heart. Not until the *La Guardia Report* was compiled in 1940 did physicians discover the most consistent physiological symptom of marijuana: a marked increase in heart rate accompanied sometimes by tachycardia, or irregular heartbeat. If there is any anxiety on the part of the smoker this heart acceleration can be very marked; if the smoker is calm, it is only a moderate increase and is not accompanied by any significant alteration in blood pressure. It would appear, therefore, that smoking marijuana is not a good idea for people with heart disease.

Another familiar symptom of smoking pot is conjunctivitis, reddening of the eyes, which has nothing to do with the irritant effect of the smoke but is produced by dilation of the blood vessels of the eyes. Likewise familiar is the sensation of dryness in the mouth and the craving for food, especially sweets. Moderate levels of marijuana use generally have sedative effects; but consumption of large quantities have the paradoxical effect of overstimulating the user and destroying his ability to sleep.

None of the foregoing effects of pot would cost a pathologist a moment's worry. At the very most he would put marijuana down in his notebook as "mildly toxic." The only clear dangers in dope smoking are those that are analogous to the harmful effects of smoking tobacco, drinking alcohol and having anxiety attacks. Let's take them in that order.

After all we have learned about smoking in recent years, it is perfectly clear that repeated irritation of the delicate tissues of the mouth, throat, bronchial tubes and lungs is certain over a period of years—depending on the individual's degree of susceptibility—to produce effects that range from chronic coughs to lung cancer. Marijuana is no different from tobacco in this wise; in fact, the sort of marijuana that is generally available is much harsher and more punishing to the throat and lungs than is tobacco, a carefully cured, treated and filtered smoke.

Whether marijuana contains chemicals that make it even more carcinogenic than tobacco is an issue upon which it is much too soon to pronounce. A study at the University of Indiana in 1975—which employed a smoking machine to measure the difference between inhaling 2,000 joints of Mexican grass and 2,000 tobacco cigarettes—concluded that there was a greater concentration of cancer-causing agents in marijuana smoke than in cigarette smoke. The chemist in charge of the experiment suggested that "more potent marijuana containing larger amounts of the active ingredient [THC] might also produce more carcinogens when smoked." This would eliminate the possibility of protecting the smoker through the use of filters. He observed also that the marijuana smoker inhales more deeply than the tobacco smoker, drawing the smoke down into those portions of the lung that are least adapted to such irritation, that he holds the smoke within his respiratory system longer and that he smokes the cigarette farther down to the butt. Experiments on animals and long-term human studies like those which established the carcinogenic effect of tobacco smoking are needed to confirm the link between cannabis and cancer. The probability is extremely high that the correlation will be confirmed and marijuana will be found to offer an even greater threat of cancer than tobacco.

The one medical advantage that the grass smoker has had traditionally over the tobacco smoker is that he smokes so much less. Until recent times, most people who smoked dope did so only in the evenings or on weekends and they passed the joint around instead of smoking the whole stick themselves. This meant that even if the smoke were more irritating or the technique of smoking more damaging, the smoker did so little smoking that the effects on his health could not be really detrimental. As marijuana becomes more available, however, this traditional pattern of consumption changes. People smoke more and more. When you spend a lot of time with people who have virtually unlimited access to marijuana, you discover that they smoke all the time: when they get up in the morning, as they work through the day, as they drive, drink or play. Basically, their smoking pattern is no different from that of the heavy cigarette smoker. (Marijuana smokers are often tobacco smokers as well.)

One of the reasons for this increase in smoking is the phenomenon of tolerance. Back in the Sixties, when the hippies were selling America on dope, there was a lot of talk about "reverse tolerance" in marijuana smoking. It was observed that novice smokers frequently failed to get high after their first experiments with the drug, whereas experienced smokers could get off on just a couple of puffs. Subsequent scientific study of this phenomenon demonstrated that it had a physiological basis but that the effect of "reverse tolerance" was only temporary. If the smoker continued using marijuana regularly, he would develop true tolerance and require more and more dope to get the same effect.

One alternative to this steadily escalating irritation of the breathing apparatus is to ingest cannabis orally, as the Arabs have always done with their hashish confections. With modern technology, we could improve on Arab methods and produce pills of THC concentrate or even synthetic THC that could be consumed in exactly measured doses. The objection to this proposal is that for reasons that are not understood, cannabis is far more effective when smoked than when consumed orally. Smoking produces within a few minutes effects that may last for hours; oral doses of far greater potency do not manifest themselves for at least an hour, though the effects may last as long as six hours. As the oral dose is not felt at the time it is consumed, there is a strong tendency to take more dope than the subject can handle. Then, when the effects begin to manifest themselves, it is too late to stop; the trip is on and it may last until the dope eater is driven into extreme panic.

Another fallacy of the dope world that has been exploded by current scientific research is the idea that dope smokers, unlike drinkers, are no more prone to automobile accidents than sober folk. In fact, if you want the myth in its strongest form, the contention is that dope smokers are *safer* drivers than the average unstoned citizen because they bring such exacting concentration to bear upon every act they perform. (This concentration is so great with many doped-up drivers that I have often seen them miss turnpike exits.) Recent studies have shown that these claims are without foundation. Though the last word on smoking and driving cannot be pronounced until extensive studies have been made of actual road accidents and their correlation with dope smoking, the results of artificial tests performed under laboratory conditions suggest strongly that the pot-intoxicated driver is no less prone than the drunk driver to make errors in judgment and physical coordination. The only advantage that the doper has over the drunk is in the matter of aggressiveness in driving. The pot head is typically less eager to pass another car on the road than the drinker: he takes longer to assess the risks of passing and is less likely to accept these risks. On the other hand, the pot smoker is more likely than the drinker to get into his car and drive immediately after getting high.

The fact is that most people who smoke dope also drink alcohol; the idea that the two methods of intoxication are mutually exclusive is yet another example of the tendentious and erroneous rhetoric of the Sixties. When a person both dopes and drinks, the chances of his having an automobile accident are greatly increased. The pot impairs his motor responses, particularly his peripheral vision, and the booze spurs him on to aggressive passing and other bullish tactics on the highway. As the experiments have demonstrated, the greatest errors in tracking are those made by drivers who are both stoned and juiced.

A much more dangerous side effect of smoking pot is the possibility of the smoke habit escalating to more potent and dangerous drugs. We are witnessing currently an epidemic of cocaine usage, which would have been hard to imagine before the widespread experimentation with marijuana and other drugs in the Sixties. Cocaine can be rationalized like grass, as a "natural" substance, though the refining process required to extract the alkaloid from the coca leaf is just as unnatural as the refining of heroin from opium. It can be associated, like marijuana, with ancient folk usage, though the chewing of coca leaves is a totally different experience than the snorting of refined cocaine. There is also the cop-out that cocaine is not an addictive drug, though the whole notion of addiction as a compulsive bodily craving has eroded badly in modern times, and we now have come to understand that the basis for any addiction is primarily psychological. So the notion that marijuana leads to heavier drugs, which has been ridiculed and discounted for generations, is a contention that deserves very careful scrutiny.

The simple truth is that once one starts experimenting with drugs, he opens up a Pandora's box. The term "multiple-drug abuser," which is one of the most accurate if inelegant phrases for describing the current drug scene, suggests the true state of affairs. Once one has pleasured himself with one drug, he is naturally well disposed to the idea of drug usage in general. Smoking pot, for example, is like walking through the revolving barrel at the amusement park. You may stumble at first, but gradually you learn to keep your balance and enjoy the odd sensation. Eventually, you crave something more exciting; now you have the confidence to accept a new and greater challenge. Abstractly speaking, there is no reason why one should not taste every chemical pleasure. Millions of sophisticated dope users have judged the highest of all such pleasures to be heroin. Consequently, the cliché that smoking dope leads to mainlining horse (or sniffing it, to get around the needle phobia) is not that absurd when you view it from a more sophisticated perspective. What has to be stressed here is that the profound disposition in our society toward seeking pleasure through drugs is not something that can be checked by outlawing the mildest and most harmless of the popular euphoriants. Given the basic thrust, the process will continue whatever the legal status of marijuana. It is vain, however, given the present arrangement of taboos in our culture, to deny that the training ground for all illicit drug usage is marijuana.

The least-understood problem presented by cannabis is the occasional anxiety reaction. Here it would appear that we have a clear-cut case of the familiar panic in the face of a loss of self-control. Though marijuana is as much a soporific as a euphoriant, the dopey down stage following upon the initial high, some people become alarmed the moment they perceive the slightest alteration in their normal state of consciousness. Bad trips on marijuana occur generally when the smoker is inexperienced, emotionally perturbed, or in a strange or alarming social setting. They may also be triggered by very strong grass, which carries the smoker further than he is accustomed to going when high. Typically, a bad trip will produce symptoms of paranoia. The smoker will feel anxiety and disorientation. He may imagine that something dreadful is happening to him. He may feel a heart palpitation and think he is suffering a heart attack. He may suffer a delusion and think he is losing his mind. The panic induced by

these fears intensifies the emotional disturbance and may lead ultimately to some precipitous act designed to turn off the terror.

The remedy for marijuana-induced panic is precisely that for
any sort of panic. The frightened person must be assured by
someone he trusts, such as a doctor, that the anxiety will soon
end, that it is merely the effect of the drug and not some disastrous failure of his mind or body. Like any such experience, the
bad trip has one value: it teaches caution and moderation in the
future.

Though most of the medical research into marijuana has been
dedicated to turning up hidden dangers, there has been a small
but steadily growing body of work that has established the therapeutic values of cannabis. Marijuana has always been a specific in
folk medicine, a fact of which I received firsthand knowledge
when I lived in Jamaica. My landlord, a prosperous white elec-
trical contractor, told me that when his son was young, he had
suffered from asthma. When all the usual medical prescriptions
failed, the father became extremely distressed. Everywhere he
went, he discussed the boy's problem. One day he was talking to
the police chief of Montego Bay, a black. When the chief heard
that the boy was suffering from asthma, he reached into the
drawer of his desk and pulled out a bundle of *ganja*. "Take this
and brew it into tea and give it to the boy," he said. The contractor had never heard of this old folk remedy, but he was desperate
enough to try anything. He took the grass home, had the tea
brewed and fed it to his son, who was suffering shortness of
breath. Within an hour the boy began to breathe easier. The effect lasted for many hours. Next day, the father administered the
tea again. Within a couple of days the attack had passed.

When I heard this story, I assumed that the effects were psychological. Asthma is a notoriously psychosomatic disease; it could
be affected by a placebo. Recently, however, a whole series of scientific studies have confirmed the soundness of the Jamaican
household remedy. Cannabis does function as a dilator of air passages in the lungs. It is an excellent specific for asthma, especially
in forms that do not transmit the THC through puffs of irritating
smoke. Currently an aerosol spray with THC is being tested on
asthmatics with great success.

Another distressing condition for which marijuana has now
become the standard prescription is the nausea which accom-

panies chemotherapy for cancer. Not long after I published my first article on marijuana, I received a call from a doctor whose patient I have been for years. He told me that he had developed severe cancer and was receiving treatments that made him violently nauseous. Could I help him get some pot? I was astonished that a man with the whole world of drugs at his beck and call should want such a primitive remedy. Later, when I read the medical literature on the subject, I discovered that three federal agencies were investigating this valuable therapeutic effect.

Yet another therapeutic use of marijuana is in cases of glaucoma. Recently, Robert Randall, a twenty-nine-year-old speech teacher in Washington, D.C., made a formal application to the DEA for permission to smoke dope in order to save his vision. His appeal was backed by affidavits from his eye specialist and from a medical research group in California that had been treating him with marijuana. They discovered that when the young man smoked, the pressure within his eyeball was lowered sufficiently so that no further damage was caused to his visual nerves. Without this reduction in pressure, obtainable in no other way, he was certain to go blind. With permission to smoke dope, he had a chance of saving his vision. Permission was granted, and Randall also became the first subject in a federally sponsored program to test the efficacy of THC eye drops in cases of glaucoma.

When one examines the scientific literature on cannabis, the most conspicuous omission is in the area of the positive psychological benefits of dope smoking. Ours is a notoriously antihedonistic society. The notion of a serious scientist dedicating himself to finding new ways to give people pleasure is one that makes no sense to us latter-day Puritans. Even assuming, however, that the attainment of pleasure is not a proper goal for the "exact sciences," what is one to make of the familiar claims for marijuana as an aid to reflection, as an inspiration for art, as a tranquilizer and soporific, as an enhancer of erotic and other sensual experiences, as a promoter of that free flow of associations in which the psychoanalysts find such valuable revelations of the human psyche? We are easily alarmed at the prospect of a generation of ill-motivated, short-attentioned, memory-lacking dolts dozing over the assembly lines or nodding out in the missile silos. Anything that threatens our capacity to work can become matter for legislative concern. Yet one could argue just as persuasively, with an even greater showing of distinguished hands, that marijuana (and other drugs) have operated powerfully to effect many of the most valued mental achievements of modern civilization. The number of writers, musicians and painters, scientists, statesmen and businessmen who would step forward to testify on behalf of the inspirational qualities of marijuana is staggering. It would take a great many meetings of Senator Eastland's subcommittee to hear them all out. Likewise the number of ordinary citizens of all age groups who attribute to marijuana every sort of positive benefit from the improvement of their sex life to the lowering of their blood pressure to the soundness of their sleep to the enhancement of their appetite to the antidote to their incipient alcoholism to the solidifying of their ties to their dope-smoking children is something that no scientist—or politician—should lightly discount. The dope constituency in America is vast today. Unless one adopts the highly undemocratic attitude that the people never know what's good for them, the mounting tally of votes in favor of marijuana should inspire some sober thinkers to explore the possibility that this illicit substance is really socially beneficial.

SHOULD MARIJUANA BE LEGALIZED?

Though marijuana has proven to be a relatively harmless substance, there appears to be a profound reluctance on the part of the people who make our laws to recognize this obvious fact and make the necessary modifications in the criminal code. The most that is offered us by the Carter administration is the hope that one of these days the drug will be decriminalized—by the states. Decriminalization can be extolled as a step in the right direction; but as a rational policy it is preposterous, like being "a little bit pregnant." If marijuana poses no clear threat to its smokers, it is a violation of our civil liberties and the constitutionally endorsed right to the "pursuit of happiness" to bar the drug from consumption on the same terms as its natural counterparts, alcohol and tobacco. What is more, by compelling marijuana users to consume this product in the manner of bathtub gin, many real and present health hazards are created. By not subjecting the drug to the normal standards of control, anything can be marketed as marijuana. High-potency grades that can trigger dangerous anxiety attacks are offered with the same hand that passes stuff so weak that its sale is really a commercial racket. Plants that may carry dangerous germs or plant diseases (or defoliant chemicals that are pure poisons) are shipped into the country in vast quantities and dumped on unsuspecting users. Far from protecting the public health, the current laws expose millions of Americans to dangers that cannot even be measured.

Though the War on Drugs has failed completely to block the avalanche of dope that comes pouring into the country every year, the law does serve to put great numbers of Americans in jail or to compel them to engage in costly and damaging legal contests. In 1977, a record number of arrests (457,000) were made for simple possession. Though eleven states have decriminalized dope, thirty-nine other states have not done so, nor are most of them about to liberalize their laws. What's more, the cost of enforcing the current law is enormous. The federal government alone spends nearly $100 million a year prosecuting dope cases, to say nothing of the hundreds of millions it expends to maintain its huge drug enforcement apparatus. The only rationalization that hard-liners against liberalization of the law are able to muster is the oft-voiced fear that if the law is softened, the consumption of marijuana will be increased vastly. Marijuana consumption is increasing rapidly, but there is no correlation between this increase and the liberalization of the drug laws. In fact, in every case in which a study has been made of consumption rates before and after passage of a decriminalization statute, the finding has been the same: no discernible increase in marijuana consumption.

Were the government to lift the ban on marijuana instead of spending hundreds of millions of dollars every year to enforce an unenforceable statute, the position would be totally reversed. A study made for the purposes of this book estimated that by applying the same excises to marijuana that are applied to tobacco and alcohol, the federal government alone could realize about $5 billion annually. The states and local municipalities would profit in like manner. At the same time the farming, processing and marketing of marijuana would become major new industries.

The most important single benefit of the legalization of marijuana would be the wiping out of the marijuana underworld. The longer the present laws remain in effect, the more crime, violence, killing, social corruption and moral decay will be introduced into our society. The law has encouraged the growth of a vast criminal underworld which is not the old criminal underworld but a new gangland comprising for the most part young men and women who are not criminals by nature but who are compelled by the logic of their undertakings to engage in criminal acts that gradually escalate to an intolerable level. These young people are busy proving that crime does pay. Their example encourages the flouting of all laws. Eventually, they could spawn a generation of outlaws.

The bottom line of this balance sheet is the effect that continuing the current prohibition will have on the nations of South America. Here we encounter the most horrible examples of the perversion of law and order. A country like Colombia is literally being destroyed by dope smuggling. The government is corrupt, the people restive, the national economy staggering under conditions that could soon produce an explosion. In an age when America has become so conscious of the effects it produces on the rest of the world, particularly on the relatively undeveloped and highly vulnerable Third World nations, it behooves us to wake up to the deadly influences we are bringing to bear on our nearest good neighbors.

Marijuana should be a source of pleasure, not of pain and shame. We should be free to cultivate and sell and buy this harmless euphoriant. The only controls should be those that are imposed to protect the public from bogus or polluted merchandise. With the dreadful example of Prohibition before us, it seems nearly unthinkable that we should have done it again; taken some basic human craving and perverted it into a vast system of organized crime and social corruption. When will we learn that in a democracy it is for the people to tell the government, not for the government to tell the people, what makes them happy?

LETHAL WEED

The irrational and dangerous character of the American government's policy towards marijuana was snapped into frightening focus in March 1978. The Secretary of Health, Education and Welfare, Joseph A. Califano, Jr., announced that permanent lung damage could result from smoking Mexican weed that had been sprayed with a herbicide called Paraquat. A preliminary sampling of marijuana confiscated in the Southwest had shown that 21 percent of the grass was contaminated and that the average concentration of the chemical on the plant stuff was 450 parts per million, which drastically exceeded the maximum level allowable in American agriculture of 0.05 parts per million.

The panic that ensued after this announcement sent hundreds of thousands of people rushing to health clinics; it flooded testing facilities with thousands of specimens of marijuana; and it inspired a scramble in Washington, where officials of the government, lawyers for NORML (National Organization for the Reform of the Marihuana Laws), the Congress and the President all maneuvered confusingly to either clarify the problem and assign responsibility or to deny the danger and defuse the political issue. A fast program was launched to test the effects of inhaling Paraquat, and a couple of months after the first announcement the results were published. The findings were appalling.

A smoker who inhaled four or five joints a day for two months could develop fibrosis of the lungs: a condition that reduces the lungs' capacity to absorb oxygen and thereby lays the foundation for countless other organic ailments. Fibrosis is not only a serious disease; it is insidious, hard to diagnose and irreversible. Overnight a country that had become utterly blasé about smoking dope, a country with at least 16 million regular marijuana smokers, was put on notice that it had been poisoned by its own government.

In the confusion of statements and counter-statements that followed the initial reports, the medical findings were obscured by the rhetoric of the politicians and the dopers. When it was discovered that some of the testing had been inaccurate and no evidence was forthcoming of an epidemic of lung fibrosis, the panic subsided as quickly as it had begun. Congress ordered that the herbicide be mixed with a red dye—an order which the Mexicans refused to heed. Eventually, some people began to say that the whole issue had been a hoax engineered by the authorities to discourage the smoking of dope. When the National Institute of Drug Abuse confirmed the original warnings a year after they had been issued, the Paraquat scandal had been so completely forgotten that the media ignored the final word in the controversy.

By now it is clear that from the time the spraying program was instituted in 1975, certain officials in the government were aware of its dangers. They knew that some of the contaminated marijuana was being harvested immediately after it had been sprayed, and they knew that this poisonous leaf was indistinguishable by the consumer from pure marijuana. When pressure was brought to bear on the government by NORML and other interested parties, the officials of the government agencies involved in the program resisted the investigation and took the line that dope was illegal and therefore the dopers were not entitled to the protection extended to consumers of legitimate substances. Even when the scandal broke, President Carter continued to endorse the spraying, remarking: "I favor this program very strongly." Needless to say, without this wholehearted endorsement by the American government, the Mexicans could not have undertaken such a campaign. The $40 million allocated for the eradication, as well as the helicopters used for spraying and even the contract pilots had all come from the United States.

Whatever the final results of the Paraquat episode prove to be, no one should dismiss this scandal simply as a false alarm. What the incident really reveals is the enormous danger inherent in any policy that tolerates the use of a drug while seeking at the same time to cut off the supply of this drug by any and every means. As with virtually every other feature of marijuana prohibition, the Paraquat scandal reflects precisely the worst features of alcohol prohibition. Though the present generation cannot be expected to know such things, thousands of people were blinded, crippled or even killed during Prohibition by consuming liquor that was contaminated with deadly toxins.

The classic example was Jake Leg: a crippling affliction produced by drinking Jamaican ginger extract that had been stretched with triorthocresyl phosphate, an ingredient of varnish and lacquers. Like Paraquat, this chemical was tasteless and odorless. Like Paraquat, it was highly toxic. It paralyzed fifty thousand drinkers in the South and Midwest. The only important difference between the two cases is one of responsibility. Jake Leg was peddled by conscienceless criminals. Paraquat poisoning is the work of government officials whose sworn duty it is to protect your health.

The Paraquat scandal provides, therefore, the first and only confirmation of the alleged dangers of smoking marijuana. As Professor Nahas has long contended, marijuana *is* a "deceptive weed." The deceit, however, lies not in the drug but in the scientists who sanctioned the use of this poison without so much as troubling to ascertain its potential effects. The deceit lies in the government officials who have escalated the War on Drugs until it has become a war on millions of American citizens conducted with the same nefarious weapons that we were forced to abjure in Vietnam. The deceit lies in the Carter administration, with its hypocritical and now discredited drug adviser, Dr. Peter Bourne, who alternated during the height of the crisis between denying responsibility for what the Mexicans had done (as if they were not the creatures of our policy) and rejecting the protests of the potential victims on the grounds that they were consuming an illegal substance. Ultimately, the deceit lies just where it has always festered since the days of Harry Anslinger and Killer Weed: in the irrational and puritanical minds of the American majority, always eager to stamp out evil—like a weed.

Index